2nd EDITION
ALL NEW
SQUARE
FOOT
GARDENING

2nd EDITION

ALL NEW

SQUARE FOOT GARDENING

The Revolutionary Way to Grow More In Less Space

Mel Bartholomew

COOL SPRINGS PRESS
Growing Successful Gardeners™

MINNEAPOLIS, MINNESOTA

First published in 2013 by Cool Springs Press, an imprint of the Quayside Publishing Group, 400 First Avenue North, Suite 300, Minneapolis, MN 55401

Cool Springs Press titles are also available at discounts in bulk quantity for industrial or sales-promotional use. For details write to Special Sales Manager at Cool Springs Press, 400 North First Avenue, Suite 300, Minneapolis, MN 55401 USA.

To find out more about our books, visit us online at www.coolspringspress.com.

Library of Congress Cataloging-in-Publication Data

Bartholomew, Mel.
  All new square foot gardening : the revolutionary way to grow more in less space / Mel Bartholomew.
-- 2nd ed.
     p. cm.
  Includes index.
  ISBN 978-1-59186-548-3 (softcover)
 1. Vegetable gardening. 2. Square foot gardening. 3. Vertical gardening. 4. Gardening for children. I. Title.

  SB321.B275 2013
  635--dc23

                                2012042837

Printed in China

10 9 8 7 6 5 4 3 2

Layout: Danielle Smith

Cover photography: Paul Markert

Photo Credits:

Istock: 209

LDI: pages 13, 44, 54, 82, 92, 129, 180, 184, 211, 212, 215, 216, 218, 226, 235, 238, 241, 243, 250

Paul Markert: 84, 121, 122, 125, 126, 146 (top and lower right), 147 (both) 148, 149, 158

J. Paul More: pages 10, 20, 24, 30, 34, 38, 41, 61 (lower four), 62, 66 (all), 67, 71 (lower right), 73 (all), 74, 75 (top two and lower left), 89, 90, 97, 101 (both), 102 all, 103 (top), 108, 111 (all), 130 (all), 132 (both), 137, 142, 146 (lower left), 157, 162 (both), 163 (both), 166 (all), 169, 170 (left), 173, 192. 272

Shutterstock: pages 80, 145, 207, 208, 214, 219, 221, 222, 224, 227, 229, 230, 232, 233, 237, 240, 244, 247, 248, 249, 252, 255, 256, 259, 260

Neil Soderstrom: 118

Square Foot Gardening Foundation: page 154

DEDICATION
This book is dedicated to the loving memory of my
daughter, Gail Bartholomew (1954-2000). Gail was my
biggest supporter and was one of the original
members of the Board of Directors for the Square Foot
Gardening Foundation. She was most enthusiastic
about our school gardening program.

ACKNOWLEDGMENTS
I am most fortunate to be surrounded by a dedicated
staff who not only worked many late nights getting this
book ready, but who truly believe in and are dedicated
to the principles of Square Foot Gardening.

Chris Peterson
Editorial

and Victoria Boudman
My most able and devoted assistant

Contents

1

Introduction

Welcome to the newly revised *All New Square Foot Gardening*. In the years since the first edition was published, I've continued to refine the SFG method. That's why you'll find more information on things like how to include children (and grandchildren!) in your SFG, how to prevent pest and disease problems, and how to get the most of your SFG. New pictures show you SFG techniques in stunning detail and we've taken pains to make sure any and all questions you might have will be answered—even before you ask them!

Leaf lettuce is one of the most popular SFG crops—great tasting, easy to grow, and lots of varieties to choose from!

Introduction

The improvements to the Square Foot Gardening method that I've outlined in this book are going to save you time and effort, and ensure the success of anything you grow in your SFG box!

Mel Bartholomew

Why revise one of the best selling gardening books of all time? The old saying goes, "If it ain't broke, don't fix it." Well, Square Foot Gardening isn't broken, but I felt that we could improve many aspects of the method, explain the processes better with more detailed photography and illustrations, make the book more readable with a clean, updated design, and address issues that gardeners constantly ask me about such proper (and safe) pest control methods and getting children involved in SFG.

In this updated book on Square Foot Gardening, you can learn, as millions of others already have, how to become a successful gardener the simple and painless way. This easy-to-understand method will revolutionize the way you think about gardening; and the refinements I've included in this revised edition will inspire to get even more out of SFG.

FOR EXPERTS ONLY

A reporter once asked me if I thought I had invented "gardening for dummies," referring, of course, to the popular Square Foot Gardening method I developed in 1976. "No," I answered.

Actually, when I invented the Square Foot Gardening (SFG) method, I thought it would be for expert gardeners. My method was very precise and detailed, yet very simple and easy to understand, and it provided all the conditions necessary for successfully growing a broad variety of plants in a very different way. It also eliminated all of the wasteful, inefficient practices of traditional single-row gardening. I thought the experts would shout "Eureka!" and immediately bless all of the new ideas and advantages of this new home gardening method.

BEGINNERS UNDERSTOOD

As it turned out, the experts never understood this unique method. Apparently it was too simple and easy. But the beginning gardener, and those discouraged by previous failed attempts, understood it completely. They immediately saw the simplicity of SFG. The beginner's instant response was "I can do this!" while the experts continued to question every aspect of this revolutionary gardening method. They just couldn't admit that home gardening could be that easy.

TWO HOURS OR TWO WEEKS

In my lectures, I like to reassure audiences that if they are new at gardening, or perhaps afraid or overwhelmed by the idea of starting a garden, they will be able to learn this simple method of gardening in just an hour or two. However, if they are already "expert" gardeners, it will probably take them about two weeks! After the laughter dies down, I remind my audience that beginners readily accept the minimal amount of technical information needed to become successful gardeners because they want to know how to successfully garden.

The "experts," on the other hand, are so entrenched with the idea of single-row gardening as used in farming, with all of its wasteful methods, that they just can't see it any other way. You might say, "They are stuck in a rut." As a result, I've learned to leave the experts alone and concentrate on the beginner, or the tried-but-failed, gardener, and even the afraid-to-start person.

SFG appeals to other large groups of would-be gardeners. Years ago, I read some very interesting statistics (and I'm sure the percentages are similar today) about these gardeners.

75 Million vs. 10 Million

Every year there are about fifteen million people each who:

- would like to begin gardening.
- tried the traditional single-row gardening method, but failed.
- don't want to begin gardening because they have heard of all the hard work, time, and cost associated with gardening.
- are doing single-row gardening but are tired of the hard work, time, and cost associated with this impractical method.
- are unable to continue caring for their big single-row gardens.

Combined, that's an estimated seventy-five million people ready for a gardening revolution compared to about ten million single-row gardeners who are content with their method and don't want to change.

THREE DECADES AND THEN SOME

The first book I wrote on SFG in 1981 lasted twenty-five years and sold over one million copies, becoming the best selling gardening book in America. The *All New Square Foot Gardening* I wrote and that was published in 2007 has been a bestseller as well. Here is the story behind how I came to invent a better way to garden, and the ultimate success of SFG.

IT STARTED IN 1975

It all started in 1975 after my retirement from my consulting engineering business in New Jersey. In celebration, I moved my family to a waterfront home on the North Shore of Long Island. After a year of rebuilding the house and another year of landscaping and improving the grounds, I decided to take up gardening as a hobby. My first step was to attend a lecture on composting given by a local environmental group. It was a warm spring day in April—a great time to be out in the garden. A small group milled around at the advertised meeting point, but no instructor ever showed up. So, rather than disband, I suggested to the group that we each share our knowledge with each other and tell what little we knew about composting. We had a wonderful time and actually learned a little bit from each other. As we prepared to leave, someone asked me, "Can we do this again next week?" And I said, "Sure, why not?" Thus began my new career of teaching gardening while I was still a novice myself.

COMMUNITY GARDEN

The next step was organizing a community garden for this same environmental group. I found some land and convinced the town to cut down all the weeds and fence it in. A local farmer delivered two truckloads of well-rotted manure, and, after the ground was all fertilized and plowed up, we laid out plots and aisles and opened for business. All of the spaces were quickly taken by people in the community, and everyone started with great enthusiasm. Since most of the participants didn't have a garden at home and were novices, they were enthusiastic about obtaining instruction and insights on gardening.

So I initiated a Saturday morning gardening workshop and presented information on a different subject each week while everyone sat around on bales of hay listening. I was teaching basic single-row gardening because that's all anyone knew back then. I was busy studying and learning gardening myself, trying to keep ahead of everyone's questions! The local county agricultural agent helped out and everything went well until about midsummer. It was about then that our once-enthusiastic gardeners stopped coming out to the garden. However, the weeds kept coming—and growing! Pretty soon the place was overgrown and looked a mess.

FIRST RED FLAG

I was discouraged and thought I had better do some research to figure out why we had failed, so I visited many backyard gardens. What I found was a big space way out in the farthest corner of the yard, about as close to the neighbor's property line as possible. In most cases, these individual gardens were also filled with overgrown weeds. The first red flag went up in my mind, indicating that there was something wrong with traditional single-row gardening. I began to think about all the conventional gardening practices we'd been taught and began to question the efficiency of each.

THREE-FOOT AISLES

I questioned why fertilizer is spread over the entire garden area, but the plants are only placed in long, skinny rows with 3-foot wide aisles on both sides. I wondered why you were supposed to till up all the soil in an entire garden area when those 3-foot wide aisles consume over 80 percent of a garden area, although plants in rows require less than 20 percent of the garden space. Then I wondered why you would walk all over the rest of the garden area again, packing down all that newly tilled soil? And, why is an entire garden area watered when plants are only located in a 6-inch wide row in the center of a 6-foot wide strip?

TOO MANY, TOO MUCH

As I analyzed these traditional gardening methods, I realized that there is only one outcome you can expect when you fertilize and water a 3-foot wide aisle with nothing planted in it—weeds!

The following is a conversation I had with a friend of mine who was an agricultural agent.

"Why a 3-foot wide aisle on both sides of the planted row?" I asked.

"So you have room to get into the garden to hoe the weeds," he replied.

Row gardening is wasteful, inefficient, and a whole lot of backbreaking work. But don't tell the "experts" that; they've convinced themselves it's the only way to garden!

"But I don't want to hoe the weeds," I protested. "That's too much work."

"Well," he said, "let's face it. Gardening is a lot of hard work."

This triggered another red flag in my mind. Gardening shouldn't be a lot of hard work. Gardening should be fun! There's something wrong here.

This led to further questions. Why do the planting instructions on packages of seeds direct the gardener to pour out an entire packet along a row only to have you later go back and tear out 95 percent of the seeds you planted once they sprout? Why use up an entire packet of seeds for every row you plant? Isn't that rather wasteful? Why would they instruct us to plant that way? Who's in charge here, anyway?

THIRTY-FOOT ROWS

The next question I asked was why plant an entire row of everything? Just because my garden is 30 feet long, for example, do I really want or need a whole row of cabbages? That would be thirty cabbages spaced 12 inches apart. This brings me to another commonsense revelation that no one seems to have thought about. Why would I want thirty cabbages to ripen all at the same time? If everything is planted at one time, won't it also be ready to harvest all at once? It sounds like farming to me, but that's too much to enjoy at the same time for a homeowner. How many people go to the grocery store and buy thirty heads of cabbage once a year? Do you? So why grow it that way? There must be a better way to stagger the harvest, and the obvious solution is to stagger the time of planting whenever possible and to plant less.

BECAUSE THAT'S THE WAY

I soon realized that I had a lot of questions with very few answers, so I traveled all over the country seeking out the best experts: agricultural college professors, county agricultural agents, garden writers, radio and TV gardening personalities, gardening publishers, book writers, garden clubs—all those who were supposedly knowledgeable people in the field of gardening. I sought answers to all the gardening questions I had and, no matter where I traveled throughout the country from Maine to California, I kept receiving the same answer. Can you imagine what that answer was? It soon became apparent that the only reason traditional single-row gardening methods continued to exist was, "Because that's the way we've always done it!" Right then and there I said, "I'm going to invent a better way to garden."

FARMING

Part of the problem, I realized, was that single-row gardening was nothing but a hand-me-down technique from large-field crop farming.

Single rows make sense when you depend upon a mule or a tractor to plow up the soil and tend the crops because those big hooves or wheels take up a lot of room. But why had no one ever realized that in a home garden, there is no longer a need for all that wasted space? There only needs to be room for two feet—yours! Yet, every single direction for home gardening still instructs, "Space rows 3 feet apart." Perhaps that's really the gardening method for dummies!

EFFICIENCY

The next step I took was to list all of the ineffective, inefficient, and unnecessary steps that have been consistently taught for traditional single-row gardening and then find a better and more efficient way to accomplish the same task. I should mention here that besides being a civil engineer, I was also an efficiency expert. Before I sold my engineering company, my job was to travel to construction sites or manufacturing facilities to analyze current processes in order to identify and correct inefficiencies in facility operations. In other words, to find a better way. Thus, the challenge of inventing a new way to garden was right up my alley. The sequence of questions I asked and simple solutions I developed was actually very easy and straightforward, but it involved a little out-of-the-box thinking. Follow me along now.

ONE THOUSAND SEEDS

I have fun when teaching a class or seminar by asking, "How many seeds do you think are in a packet of leaf lettuce?" Some guess fifty, one hundred, two hundred, and some even venture a guess as high as five hundred seeds. I then astound them by saying that I once opened a packet and counted them, and there were well over one thousand seeds! Why plant hundreds of seeds in one long row, and then turn around when they sprout and thin them out to one plant for every 6 inches? It doesn't make sense, does it? It's a terrible waste of seeds and time and work—all useless, unnecessary work. My first solution was to lay down a yardstick and plant one seed every 6 inches. Then, I had nothing further to do and no wasted seeds. The next thought was, if you're growing, for example, lettuce, and the seed packet says to thin plants to 6 inches apart in the row, how far away does the next row really need to be? The answer, of course, is 6 inches—not 3 feet!

SINGLE ROW, DOUBLE ROW, TRIPLE ROW

Eager to test my reasoning, I planted two rows, 6 inches apart, to see how well the plants would do. It worked! The plants grew just as well in two rows as they did in a single row, as long as each plant had 6 inches all around. Next I tried a triple row—three rows where I

Plants spaced 12 inches apart, such as eggplant, are planted one per square.

Plants spaced 6 inches apart, such as lettuce, are spaced four per square.

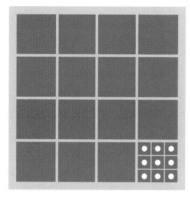

Plants spaced 4 inches apart, such as spinach, are planted nine per square.

Plants space 3 inches apart, like radishes, are planted sixteen per square.

placed all the plants 6 inches apart in all directions. Again, it worked! How wide could I make this, I asked? The answer is, as wide as you can reach in to maintain your garden; in other words, as long as your arms. But I still had a harvest too large to utilize.

SHORTEN THE ROWS

So what was the obvious solution? Shorten the rows! And they kept getting shorter and shorter, until they were only 12 inches long and 12 inches wide—a square foot planting area. How many plants could you grow in that square foot if each plant was 6 inches apart? The simple answer: four plants per square foot.

PLANT SPACING

So, in summary, if plants should be thinned to 12 inches apart, plant one per square foot. If plants should be thinned to 6 inches apart, plant four per square foot. If plants should be thinned to 4 inches apart then you can grow nine within the space of that 1 square foot.

If plants are thinned to 3 inches apart, you can grow sixteen in that same square foot. Doesn't it all make sense and seem easy enough?

NEVER WALK ON SOIL

I then wondered just how far someone could reach in to maintain a garden without compacting the soil by walking all over it. So, I got a little old lady and a big husky man and measured how far they could easily reach. I found that both could comfortably reach in 2 feet without losing balance. In order to reach in 2 feet and walk all the way around your garden, you end up having a 4 × 4-foot area. Now, the only soil that needs to be dug up, improved, watered, and fertilized is a 4 × 4-foot garden area and not all the aisles. That reduced the actual growing area in the garden by 80 percent. And, an added benefit is the growing soil in the 4 × 4-foot area is never packed down, so you don't have to hoe or dig up the ground to keep loosening the planting soil.

SOIL IMPROVEMENT

The next step was how to improve the soil. After listening to agricultural agents and reading books on soil improvement and conditioning, the only option seemed to require a great deal of work, time, and money. My research indicated that average soil conditions around the country were not well-suited for growing healthy vegetables and beautiful flowers. Thus, in most areas soils had to be greatly improved to obtain the best gardening results.

HORSE MANURE

Most soils only contain about 3 or 4 percent organic material. Thus, the traditional first step for improving soil in preparation for gardening was to dig or till up the soil in the entire garden as deep as you could and then add soil enhancers such as compost or well-rotted manure followed later by commercial fertilizers. This initial step rang a bell with me because, as a teenager, I was the one who had to turn over my mother's garden, digging the whole thing up every year. My father had to bring home bushel baskets full of horse manure in his brand new Chrysler. After we dumped it into the garden area, I had to do all of the spreading, mixing, and turning. As laborers in Mom's garden every spring, my dad and I were not happy campers, although she was thrilled with the results.

THE SEVEN-YEAR ITCH

I once conducted a survey, asking gardeners how long it took them to improve their soil until they got it just the way they wanted it. The average answer was about seven years—seven years of hard work to properly condition the soil for gardening! And do you know what statistics say the average homeowner does after seven years? They move! And guess who buys that home? Someone who doesn't even garden!

You can probably imagine the conversation between the new homeowners. "Henry, let's pave over that garden area; it would make a great place to park the trailer." Seven years worth of effort lost. There's something definitely wrong with this scenario.

START RIGHT IN A SINGLE DAY

I started thinking, "Why not have great soil during the first year of your garden, and every year thereafter, no matter where you live?" Of course, with traditional big garden areas, having the best soil conditions right away may be too costly and entail too much time and effort. Remember that after I did the math, I found that by switching from a traditional single-row garden to a 4 × 4-foot layout—which will produce the same harvest—80 percent of the garden area could be completely eliminated. This means that you can grow 100 percent of the harvest in only 20 percent of the space. That 80 percent of a single-row garden is wasted space—space that doesn't need to be fertilized, watered, or improved, but it does have to be weeded. Think of it. With the SFG method, seven years worth of work can suddenly be condensed into as little as a single day without all the effort!

THE 4 x 4-FOOT GARDEN

My first book showed how you could reduce the work by laying out a 4 × 4-foot area, then digging out 6 inches of existing soil and mixing in 2 inches of peat moss, 2 inches of vermiculite, and 2 inches of compost. These ingredients are available at any nursery. Many gardeners even make their own compost at home from kitchen scraps and other plant material. Mixing the ingredients together with the soil that you removed, you now have 12 inches of 50 percent improved soil. My thinking was that 12 inches of improved existing soil would be all that new plants would need to thrive with the plant roots staying within these 12 inches of improved soil. But the experts I consulted said that most vegetable plant roots need to keep growing downward, searching for water and nutrients many, many feet below the surface of the soil. "But," I thought, "if plants are provided a good growing soil composed of more than 15 percent organic matter, and if vermiculite and peat moss are mixed in, helping to retain water in the soil, plant roots would no longer need to continue growing downward in search of additional moisture and nutrients." Besides that, I wondered if they were right about the roots needing to grow deeper than 12 inches, how come most rototillers dig down less than 6 inches? Well, it turned out they were wrong. Our gardens thrived with less than 12 inches of improved soil and that was just the beginning! Wait until you read Chapter 2, which describes the latest advances in this "out of the box" type of thinking.

STAGGER THE HARVEST

I also realized that if each square foot could be planted with a different crop containing either one, four, nine, or sixteen plants, all properly spaced, it wouldn't be necessary to plant a whole row of just one crop. So, why not stagger your vegetable plantings, so that your harvest is also staggered? Makes sense, doesn't it? Yet we've been taught all our lives to plant everything all at once in long rows—another hand-me-down technique from large-field crop farming. If you're farming for commercial purposes, you want everything to ripen at once so it can be harvested together and taken to market. But with home gardening, you want to stagger your produce so you can use it throughout the season for daily consumption.

Of course, I'm not talking about canning, freezing, and other home-storage measures, although SFG is a practical gardening method for these purposes also. However, I've found that people are not storing homegrown produce to the extent they did in the past. Remember, I grew up in the days of the "victory garden," a result of World War II when Americans were encouraged by the government and by society to have a big garden that used the old single-row planting methods. Most people who grew up during those years hated gardening because of all the weeding and hard work it entailed. That carried over into a whole generation of people who stayed away from gardening just because of the negative memories associated with maintaining a large traditional garden. And, I might add, also from all the work of canning and freezing. So why does the government still teach the same old system more than sixty years later?

STOP PLANTING SO MUCH

I meet many mature couples where the husband proudly states, "I have a big single-row garden, and I grow a lot of produce." And the woman responds, "Oh, but I wish he'd stop. He grows all this produce that we really don't need anymore. Then I have to can and freeze it. I'm tired and don't want to do it anymore. We don't need it but he just keeps growing it!" With SFG, you don't have to grow so much at a time that it becomes overwhelming.

LOCATION

I began to realize another great advantage of SFG—by reducing the garden size by 80 percent, it increases the number of places where a garden will fit. A garden no longer has to be way out back, snugly put

Believe me, there are so many advantages to the SFG method, and the benefits and efficiencies only continue to increase.

up against your neighbor's property line. And since you don't have to fertilize, water, and weed the aisles, it can now be located near the house.

UP CLOSE AND PERSONAL

"Closer is better" is one SFG motto. When a garden is closer to the front or back door of your home, you pass by the garden more often. This means it is easier to take care of and can be more readily enjoyed, all of which results in a better garden and a happier gardener. The whole package fits together nicely. There are so many advantages to Square Foot Gardening, and the benefits and efficiencies of the concept only continue to increase.

THE SQUARE FOOT GARDENING STORY
Community Garden

Well, we tried all these new ideas in the community garden the next year, and, guess what? They worked! Everyone understood and grasped the Square Foot Gardening concepts quickly and easily, and since most of the participants were beginning gardeners who were well acquainted with the disastrous experience from the previous year—including the overgrown weeds and mounds of zucchini and rows of cabbage that ripened all at once—they were very willing to try another option. That next year, 1976, we were able to enjoy a very attractive and well-run community garden using the newly developed Square Foot method. The Bicentennial year of 1976 was a huge celebration across the country and we also celebrated my youngest son's July Fourth birthday. I decided to do three things: one for my country, one for my family, and one for myself. The official presentation of Square Foot Gardening was made at a hometown event that included a school project that I had organized. All the schools grew sunflowers, which were planted along Main Street as a beautification project. We had an all-day celebration of displays, talks, booths, and demonstrations on the new Square Foot Gardening method I had developed. I announced this was my gift to the country—a better way to garden.

Sharing Ideas, 1978 to 1980

Because of the overwhelming success of the project and the unique SFG method, many people encouraged me to write a book sharing my ideas. First, the local newspaper asked me to write a garden column. Then I began writing and producing pamphlets. Soon, magazine representatives started coming out to photograph my home garden and to write stories about my new ideas and the SFG method. The media attention grew and grew, so I thought, "Why not write a book?" I drafted an outline and sent it to two publishers, which both accepted the "how to" book on successful gardening using the new SFG method.

Garden Consulting, 1981 to 1984

At the same time, I also began doing gardening consulting work for several companies. You can imagine how "retired" I was now. One was a fence company, and, using their products, I began to develop vertical gardening methods, originally for tomatoes but later for all vine crops. Another company wanted to start a gardening tool catalog. So my job was to search the world for unique and unusual tools, test and evaluate them, make recommendations, and then arrange the writing of sample descriptions for the catalog. During this time, I wondered why we needed so much stuff just to garden. And, as you'll learn, I discovered that you don't.

PBS One Minute, 1981 to 1986

My publisher's predictions for my book were very modest, so they didn't promote my book the way I had hoped or even send me out for talks and appearances. Fortunately, some of the companies I was consulting for did send me on tours and allowed me to show the book and talk about Square Foot Gardening if I also explained and demonstrated their products. This proved to be a very valuable and rewarding period, and it wasn't long before a local PBS television station asked if they could send their camera crew out to my garden to shoot "A Minute in Mel's Garden" segment for the evening news. I was delighted to have the opportunity to share the SFG method. The response to that short segment was explosive. The television station received so much mail and so many telephone calls that they wanted to tape a show for broadcast every weeknight. So, once a week they came to my garden and taped five different segments. That again proved so popular that later they asked if I would be interested in a 30-minute national show. You bet I was!

Thirty-Minute PBS TV Series, 1982 to 1986

To make a long story short, my show aired the following year on PBS and was picked up by enough stations along the East Coast to pay for itself. The following year I started my own production company and distributed the 30-minute *Square Foot Gardening* show throughout the entire PBS system. Within three years it was picked up by every PBS station in the country and received the highest rating of any garden show. This involved a lot of travel, but it was all very exciting. My oldest son, Steve, became the show director, and we traveled around the country to different viewers' gardens that were particularly worthy of sharing with our audience. We were also invited to Disney World to shoot during the winter, an opportunity we couldn't pass up. All of this excitement and activity made it a very rewarding and exciting period of my life.

> *"Your method has given me the confidence to try veggies again after a few feeble attempts."*
> – Anne from Florida

More Television Opportunities

In addition to all the above activity and travel, many other opportunities occurred with TV networks like CNN out of Atlanta, Georgia, CBN in Virginia Beach, Virginia, and several appearances on ABC, *Good Morning Boston*, *Good Morning Philly*, and many other TV spots all around the country. All of that brought in a ton of mail (whoever had heard of e-mail back then?) and activities with companies interested in developing SFG products including some big companies such as Rubbermaid. This was exciting and eventful, yet at times stressful and exhausting. Since such a big part of gardening is in the harvest and food preparation, I convinced PBS to let us have the first cooking segment on a garden show. Now, of course, they all do that.

TV Book Tag

I originally offered the program to PBS free of charge if they would give me a one-minute book tag at the end of each show. At that time, PBS was commercial-free and had no corporate sponsors. But they were finally convinced that it would be worthwhile, allowing me to be the first person to have a book tag on a PBS show. As a result, a tremendous number of orders for the SFG book were received. We had to set up a toll-free number and a fulfillment company to process these orders. After six years, the operation became fairly routine and the challenge of creating something new was over. At the same time, some PBS stations started talking like they should share in the profits of the book sales, yet they still wanted the show free. Rather than compromise the initial agreement, I decided to take the show off the air and retire for the second time. This time, my retirement was "for sure."

Discovery Network 1989 to 1991

A few years later, an agent came to me and said that he could get the TV show back on the air. I didn't want anything to do with it; I was happily retired. But when he offered to do all the work and take care of all the details, I thought, "Well, what harm could there be?" (We never learn, do we?) I finally agreed, and he sold the show to the Discovery Network where it ran for two years and then on The Learning Channel for another year. I again took the show off the air. I decided that that was it—I really was retiring for good! (Yeah, sure!)

California Schools, 1996

Five years later, when I was traveling in northern California, someone invited me to come see a school garden. "It's a Square Foot Garden," they explained. I went and thought it was so impressive. The children were really enjoying the gardening experience, and the teachers loved it so much that I began to think that perhaps I really shouldn't be retired—I should be out teaching SFG to schoolchildren. So, again, I came out of retirement (you know the saying "fools rush in") and established a nonprofit foundation to design a program for teachers explaining how to teach Square Foot Gardening to students. We called the program "A Square Yard in the School Yard" since the children's gardens were 3 × 3 feet.

One of the great features of SFG is how easy it is for children (of all ages!) to participate.

Utah Schools, 1998

This phase of my life also involved a lot of travel. As I developed new staff members, we went from school to school donating gardens all the way from Maine to Florida and on to the California coast. When offering Square Foot Gardening to schools in Utah, we tried something new. Rather than going from teacher to teacher and school to school, we went straight to the state board of education. They liked our idea so much that they said, "We'll take a garden for every single grammar school in the state of Utah." We gulped and said, "Well, let's see what we can do."

Thanksgiving Point, 1999 to 2001

Over the next two years, we were able to do just that. Next, the school board asked if I would write a lesson plan for Utah teachers and students. I did, and it has now been modified for home schooling as well. We were then invited to put up a public display Square Foot Garden at Thanksgiving Point near Salt Lake City. Thousands visited the garden and, since Salt Lake City is home to the Church of Jesus Christ of Latter-day Saints (the LDS church or Mormons), SFG gained the attention of many LDS church leaders. They invited the foundation to teach SFG at the LDS Missionary Training Center in Provo, Utah. We showed missionaries how to instruct people living in Third World countries to use the Square Meter Gardening method, which we had converted from the Square Foot Gardening method.

Opportunities for the SFG foundation just kept on growing as we became involved with additional humanitarian organizations that sent aid overseas, many of which began including the Square Meter Gardening system in their programs. SMG was designed to appeal to families in Third World countries and improve nutrition by adding fresh vegetables to their diets. It is something that can be readily done, as the soil that is used in this program is pure compost since peat moss and vermiculite is either unavailable or too expensive to obtain overseas. An added advantage is that making compost cleans up the environment and gets all the family members involved.

SFG International Training Center in Homestead, Florida

Because gardening in Utah is at a standstill all winter, the logical direction to go that time of year is south. Through our work with several international organizations headquartered in Washington, D.C., the opportunity came to spend the winter in southern Florida where we set up an SFG International Training Center in Homestead. This proved very educational for us because the weather, plants, and techniques were much more like Central and South America. We provided a three-day training seminar for the people heading to those countries as representatives of various humanitarian organizations. This enabled Square Meter Gardening to be taken to quite a variety of people and places.

Overseas

When working with people overseas, the first step is to teach them composting. Since most Third World countries are located in tropical regions of the world, it's very easy to find materials that can be used to generate compost. One of the biggest successes in Square Meter Gardening is a project developed in India. It illustrates how easy it is to offer meaningful foreign aid to countries without spending millions of dollars. This success story began after a priest named Father Abraham received the Square Foot Gardening book. He read it and said, "We can do this!" As a result, he now operates a sizeable, well-organized 6-acre training center where hundreds—perhaps thousands— of people have come to learn the Square Meter Gardening method. The people are learning to successfully grow crops they can not only use at home but can take to market where they earn twenty times more than they did previously growing crops the traditional single-row way.

Single Rows Throughout the World

Believe it or not, many people around the world still garden and grow crops in single rows. When I was in the mountains of Nepal, I observed the farmers growing corn one spindly stalk spaced 1 meter (approximately 3 feet) apart from the next spindly stalk, with the next row 1 meter away. Through the interpreter I asked why they space and plant their crops this way. The answer, as you can probably guess, was "That's the way we've always done it. My father taught me, and that's the way his father taught him."

Just think of all the good that will be accomplished when SMG is adopted all over the world. It will allow families to improve their health through better nutrition. The woman of the family is our primary target for this project, as she is most concerned with the children's nutrition.

Certified SFG Instructors

We hold workshops to train SFG instructors and people who want to help others learn this simple, easy, inexpensive method that anyone, anywhere in the world can do. Just think—what if every woman in the world started just one SMG? Those nine crops could improve the nutrition of her children; many could even expand by planting more gardens for larger harvests and even to grow cash crops. One of our trainees who took our course for certification then went on a mission to teach schoolchildren music at orphanages in an African country. At the same time, she started many SFG projects; her stories of success were heartwarming and inspiring.

Garden of Eden

After enjoying three very productive years with our SFG Display Gardens at Thanksgiving Point, Utah, we had to make a decision because developers were going to build a new building where our gardens were located. Rather than move the gardens to another location, I decided it was time to get away for a sabbatical to do some planning and writing and discovered the beautiful, small mountain community of Eden, Utah. I intended to only stay and write for a few months. Knowing I would need some clerical help, I placed an ad in the local newspaper and received an overwhelming response from people wanting to help with SFG. Those initial few months stretched into years, and Eden became an appropriately named home base for spreading SFG throughout the world.

SFG, Improved

By 2005, I had made enough changes to the SFG method that it merited a whole new book. I subsequently collected those improvements to the method in the *All New Square Foot Gardening* book, published in 2007. This meant training a whole new crop of teacher/instructors in the new methods, and getting the word out about the changes. I developed ways for the disabled and elderly to have their own Square Foot Gardens, to make your SFG even easier to tend, and other substantial improvements.

I've traveled far and wide, both in America and abroad, to spread the word of the new and improved Square Foot Gardening. And there's a lot left to do.

Most recently, we've expanded the line of readymade SFG products we're offering through the Square Foot Foundation's website and retailers nationwide. These products—such as pre-fabricated boxes and premixed Mel's Mix—make it easier than ever to start your SFG.

Now it's come time to refine SFG. We've introduced a whole new look to the book with pictures that better illustrate the fine points of building and working with your Square Foot Garden. I've added information on Square Foot Gardening with children, and some great pointers on how to deal with pests and diseases in your SFG. This fine-tuning makes sure that the SFG method just keeps getting better and better.

A Square Meter Garden such as this can be a way for Third World families to climb out of poverty, improve their nutrition, and live better lives.

A Message from The Square Foot Gardening Foundation CEO

Victoria Boudman

Hi, my name is Victoria and I am a Square Foot Gardening addict! First, I have to tell you that I worked for Mel and the SFG Foundation for almost two years before I had my first garden. I do mean first! I had never gardened before. One day Mel asked the staff, "Do you all have a SFG at home?"

Was I worried? You bet I was, but I couldn't show it. I finally gave into peer pressure and jumped in with both feet. I planted two 4 × 4 boxes, one 2 × 4, a smaller 3 × 3 and finally a 4 × 4 pyramid. Enough for my whole family. I went hog wild, and laid down a weed mat and placed the boxes down. I filled them all with the prebagged Mel's Mix and added my grids. It was that simple and I was now hooked. It was so easy. Of course I had no idea what I was doing. I was nervous. Would I be able to grow anything? What would people say if they found out that Mel's righthand gal could not grow anything?

Oh the horror of it all! It kept me awake that first spring season.

Not to worry—everything produced. The tomatoes and green peppers, the strawberries and radishes, the chiles and flowers. I even grew heads of lettuce, not just the leaf varieties. That fall I was able to show off my SFG to a class of our Certified Instructors in training. The thrill and rush of the success was astonishing. It just about grew itself. It was then that I realized that anyone could grow a Square Foot Garden. If you have any doubts whatsoever, read this book and you will join millions of others who say, "I can do this." After all, this is the largest selling garden book in America.

Victoria Boudman

CEO

The Square Foot Gardening Foundation

SFG Foundation

THE SFG FOUNDATION AND MEL'S MISSION

Mel Bartholomew founded the Square Foot Gardening Foundation, a 501(c)3 nonprofit in 1996 to pursue the mission of solving world hunger by teaching people around the globe how grow enough food for themselves and their families, with limited resources, expertise, time and effort. Mel and the Foundation have executed that mission with zeal since the opening of this century. They began by developing the school-based program "A Square Yard in the School Yard," and the Foundation continues to promote and spread Square Foot Gardening in schools across the country. The method serves as an excellent way for students and young people everywhere to learn about math, science, botany, nutrition, and other academic subjects, as well as discovering how to become independent.

But Mel and Foundation didn't stop there. They have traveled to Africa, South America, India, and beyond. The idea has been to teach and spread the "Square Metre Gardening" method, an international adaptation of the Square Foot Gardening method.

This has involved a twofold approach, including teaching and training individuals as instructors who can spread the SMG method throughout the world, and working directly with non-governmental organizations and other nonprofits to go right to where we're needed most. Mel himself has taught large groups in El Salvador, India, and Europe among many other international locations.

SMG instructors have made their way to Mexico, where they put in a kitchen garden for an orphanage teaching the children there how to be self-sufficient and eat well despite having few resources. One instructor went with her daughter to Kenya, where they launched the SMG method with a church garden. Others traveled to Peru to work with government officials in spreading the method among villages there. The stories go on and on, and many of these instructors travel on their own dime, without much in the way of acknowledgment or reward other than knowing that they are changing the world.

The Square Foot Foundation's programs aren't focused just overseas. As effective and helpful as SMG has been in foreign countries, the foundation also spreads the word of Square Foot Gardening throughout America, in communities where the poor can learn to help themselves, feed their families nutritious and delicious meals, and possibly even earn money from their own SFGs. Mel and the Foundation have worked with communities across America to launch community gardens and teach individuals from the homeless to the impoverished the benefits of Square Foot Gardening.

And it's not just the people the Foundation is helping. The Square Metre and Square Foot Gardening methods save precious resources and help in the fight against climate change. These are low-cost, low-effort, space-saving methods of gardening that can be instituted just about anywhere, with a bare modicum of resources.

Because of its rapid expansion and extensive humanitarian programs, SFGF now reaches out to partnerships, individual and corporate donors, and grants as sources of additional funding to help sustain its global and local initiatives. Although the Foundation has many achievements to its credit already, it looks to a future full of opportunities to fulfill its ultimate goal of ending—not just reducing— World Hunger. You can learn more about the Foundation, its work and programs on the website http://www.squarefootgardening.org/.

this can make a difference

SFG, Newer and More Improved

Ten major improvements from the original method make Square Foot Gardening more productive, the work much easier, and the cost of gardening lower. At the same time, these changes make it easier for the beginner.

I can tell you from firsthand experience, you're going to be amazed at all the things you can grow in the Square Foot Garden!

All New Square Foot Gardening offers ten new major improvements to the original SFG method. Now, with these improvements, anyone can be a successful gardener.

TEN MAJOR IMPROVEMENTS TO THE ORIGINAL SQUARE FOOT GARDEN METHOD

1. Location—Close to the House
2. Direction—Up, Not Down
3. Soil—Mel's Mix
4. Box Depth—Only 6 Inches Deep
5. No Fertilizer—You Don't Need It
6. Easy Access—Above the Ground
7. The Aisles—Comfortable Width
8. The Grids—Prominent and Permanent
9. Novel Idea—Don't Waste Seeds
10. Expanded Opportunities—Tabletop Gardens

Yes, it's true; this improved gardening method makes gardening even easier than before. You're going to love every one of these improvements.

You will now be able to reduce the size of your SFG so much that you can locate it close to your house for better care and more enjoyment. You'll never have to dig up your existing soil anymore as you now build your new garden on top of it. No more hard work or heavy-duty tools needed. All you'll need is 6 inches of a perfect soil mix from three common ingredients available everywhere. This mix never needs changing and no fertilizer is ever needed using this natural, organic method.

You'll use bottomless boxes made from common lumber, have aisles that are wide enough to comfortably move about in, and each box will have a permanent grid for that unique SFG look and use. You'll use a minimum of seeds, so you won't have to buy new packets every year. Best of all, some of your boxes can have bottoms so you can move them or place them at tabletop or railing heights for easier care and unique locations.

1 LOCATION–CLOSE TO THE HOUSE
Single-Row Gardens Are Too Big

One of the biggest problems of single-row and bed gardens is their size. They're big! They take up so much room that they are usually located way out back. That usually meant it was out of sight, resulting in out of mind. It became less and less tended as the year went on. But, guess what still grew? Weeds! And these pesky plants can quickly inundate and choke out your crops. Without your attention they'll take over the garden.

No More

All that has been changed for the better. SFG takes only 20 percent of the space of a single-row garden. That means it can be located much closer to the house where it will get more attention and care, resulting in a better-looking garden and a more usable harvest.

Split It Up for Best Location

In addition, your garden doesn't have to be all in one place. You no longer have to rototill or water one big garden area all at once. You can split up your SFG so that a box or two are located next to the kitchen door, while more boxes can be located elsewhere in the yard. Small, individual garden boxes allow you much more flexibility in determining location. Now your garden can be located near where you walk and sit, or where you can view it from the house. It can even be located in a patio or pool setting, where you relax. Your SFG becomes a companion rather than a burden.

2 DIRECTION–UP, NOT DOWN!
Build Up, Don't Dig Down

The second improvement involves locating your garden on top of your existing soil rather than digging down. Most of our readers complain about the terrible soil in their areas. In fact, as I lecture around the country and the world, the question I hear most is, "What can we do about our local soil? It is so hard to work and garden in." The first *Square Foot Gardening* book I ever wrote directed gardeners to dig down 6 inches and improve their existing soil by adding equal amounts of really good ingredients. Even though you had to do that only the first year and it produced a fairly good soil, people complained that it was still a lot of work involving heavy tools and a great deal of effort. Everyone wants a simple, easy way to garden. So, back to the drawing board.

This got me to thinking. Could I find a better way? So, I asked myself, why do we really need to improve our existing soil if it's so bad? Couldn't we just start with a perfect soil mix aboveground and eliminate the need to ever dig up or improve our existing backyard soil? You probably could if your garden wasn't so big . . . but hey, SFG isn't big. In fact, it's one-fifth the size of conventional gardens. So, if we could find a perfect soil mix, there would be no more digging and no more tilling. Doesn't that make a lot of sense? It became possible with All New Square Foot Gardening to have a very condensed no-work gardening method and never have to be concerned again about what kind of soil you have in your yard. Wow!

No Sweat

Just think of the implications if you forget about trying to improve your existing soil. It no longer matters what kind of soil you have! Use the time you save to start a compost pile instead. If you start with a perfect soil mix, it will save a lot of time and money. You don't have to have your soil analyzed anymore, and you don't have to have a pH test made . . . you don't even have to know what pH is! You don't have to buy any heavy tools or go to the expense of having someone rototill your garden every single year. You don't have to buy special ingredients to loosen your clay soil or solidify your sandy soil. And most importantly, you no longer have to do any hard work. You'll have to find another way to get some exercise—so go mow the lawn. This major advance in home gardening changes all of the rules of gardening and eliminates all of the hard work and undesirable parts of single-row gardens. Hey, gardening can be fun now!

So, if you are not going to use your existing soil but instead use a perfect soil mix, what is it and how and where do you get it?

> The key to success of the All New Square Foot Gardening method is to avoid the poor qualities of local soil by building up rather than digging down.

3 SOIL—MEL'S MIX
What's In It?

There are three characteristics of a perfect growing mix. First of all, it's lightweight, so it is easy to work with and easy for plants to grow in. Next, it is nutrient-rich and has all the minerals and trace elements that plants need without adding fertilizers. Finally, it holds moisture, yet drains well.

After many experiments, I found that three of my favorite ingredients made the perfect mix when combined in equal portions:

■ ⅓ Peat Moss—Available at any garden center or supermarket.
■ ⅓ Vermiculite—Buy the coarse grade in large 4-cubic-foot bags at any garden center or home improvement store. Phone ahead to be sure it's available in that size.
■ ⅓ Blended Compost—If you don't have your own compost operation, then buy bags of compost at the garden center to get started. Then, start your own compost pile as soon as possible. I'll explain some simple steps for foolproof composting later in the book. However, one word of caution here: You must have a blended compost, so don't buy all the same kind. Pick out one bag of this and one bag of that. But, more about that in Chapter 5.

What Do These Ingredients Do?

All three of these ingredients are natural—not manufactured. They all drain well, so there are no puddles to waterlog the plant roots; but they also hold large amounts of moisture so the plants will grow well. This mix is a pleasure to work with, has a light fluffy texture, and smells good.

The first two ingredients have no nutrients, but the last—compost—is loaded with all the nutrients and minerals that you could imagine. Compost is the most important ingredient of the three, and making your own is good for both the environment and the garden. This is about as organic as you can get.

If you don't think this perfect soil mix will work in the garden, ask yourself, "What do professional greenhouse growers use for growing crops on their benches? Do they go out and dig up the fields for soil?" Of course not. Professional growers mix up a perfect potting soil from several other ingredients and never use local outside soil.

When you buy a windowbox at the store, what do you fill it with—your yard soil? Of course not. You buy a bag of perfect potting soil. So why can't we do the same for our vegetable garden? Well, there are two reasons:

One, no one ever thought of it—and two, it would be prohibitively expensive for the typical single-row garden that everyone has been using all of these years.

So, how can we do it now? Because SFG reduces the garden size down to only 20 percent (that's one-fifth as large), so it is now possible to consider using a perfect soil from the very start. An additional reason is found in the next major improvement to Square Foot Gardening.

4 BOX DEPTH–ONLY 6 INCHES DEEP

"Go deep," they said. "Don't bother," I said.

For years, experts said your garden soil had to be improved at least 12 inches deep; some even said 18 inches. But my experiments were proving otherwise, especially when I used good homemade compost as one-third of the mix. I asked myself, "If six inches of perfect soil is good enough for windowboxes and commercial greenhouse benches, why not in backyard gardens?" And why dilute it by adding the mix to poor existing soil? Why not use this perfect soil mix in your garden and forget all about the soil underneath? Well, the experts still pooh-poohed the idea. But guess what? It works! Of course, everyone realizes that you couldn't do that in a huge, old-fashioned, single-row garden or even in raised bed gardening, but it can easily be done in a small-space Square Foot Garden!

> "We owe much of our love of gardening to the simplicity of SFG."
> – Manja from Oregon

Can you really grow vegetables and flowers in only 6 inches of soil regardless of how good it is? I've been doing it for the last ten years in my display and home garden, and it really works. Of course in my lectures when I mention the 6 inches, I can see the audience squirming in their seats, heads shaking and hands rising with the usual question, "How can you grow long carrots or potatoes in just 6 inches of soil?" It's a good question, so we developed a special feature of SFG where you build a 1-foot × 1-foot box one foot tall for long root crops.

Why only 6 inches deep? Why not be safer and go 12 inches deep? The main reason is there is no need to do so. In addition, it is much cheaper, easier, and less work. Just think—it is one-half of the cost and one-half of the work, so why double the depth? But if you're still skeptical go ahead and use your time and money to go 12 inches deep, but it's really not necessary.

The next question is, "How come all of the experts have been so wrong for so long?" It is not that they were wrong, it is just everyone in the garden industry had trouble thinking outside the box or even questioning all the traditional methods. Stuck in a rut they were, and in a single-row rut at that!

Here's another startling revelation I am going to make. It is going to shock and dismay the gardening world, but you are going to love it.

5 NO FERTILIZER–YOU DON'T NEED IT

Square Foot Gardening needs no fertilizer ever! How can that be? After all, the gardening industry is built on using fertilizer. When I first developed SFG, I dealt with all the information about fertilizer—organic and chemical types—how to measure and rate it; all about NPK and what that means; and the list goes on and on. That was necessary because at that time we were just improving our existing soils, and they still needed fertilizer. All the experts agreed. But my own experiments and thoughts about an all new out-of-the-box idea of not improving your existing soil but rather of starting with a perfect soil mix was working so well that I began to consider another new idea—that you don't need to add fertilizer. The compost was providing all of the nutrients and trace elements the plants needed. Besides, compost was all-natural and couldn't burn or harm the plants. The proof of the pudding was to just look at my garden. It was one of the best gardens I have ever had and has remained so ever since.

This was when I was able to simplify my original book's formula for the perfect soil mix to only three ingredients: one-third each of peat moss, vermiculite, and blended compost, and completely eliminate the use and expense of fertilizer. So much simpler!

Well, again, all the experts pooh-poohed the idea and still do, but guess what? It works! I haven't used any kind of fertilizer in my home, display, or demonstration gardens for more than a decade. If you go to our website at www.squarefootgardening.com, you'll see how bountiful and beautiful the gardens look. And this is not just gardening the first year but year after year after year. Just think—no more tilling, no more digging, and no more fertilizer! The only thing we ever add to our soil is a little more compost. Is this great or what?

Now all we need is some way to hold or contain our aboveground 6 inches of perfect soil mix. So, how about a box?

6 EASY ACCESS–ABOVE THE GROUND

I think having your garden contained in a box adds uniformity and structure, not only to your garden but to your life. Once limits are placed on almost anything, you will find it much easier to take care of and therefore you will be more comfortable with it and enjoy it more.

The basic 4 × 4-foot bottomless boxes are easy to build out of common lumber, bricks, blocks, or even stone. These small boxes, filled with the perfect soil mix, will grow five times as much as the same space in a single-row garden. So, you don't need many of the boxes. There are no weeds to hoe. No existing soil to till. Why, once your boxes are built and your perfect soil is added, there is virtually no work at all.

Once you build the basic 4 x 4 SFG box with rotated corners, add six inches of Mel's Mix, and add the square foot grid. Now, you're ready to plant.

If you place the box on top of the existing ground, you eliminate all of the usual gardening concerns and work of improving your existing soil. It also eliminates the great deal of gardening knowledge that you would need if you were going to be concerned with using your existing soil. You'll see as we go along that there are so many advantages of not using your existing soil. You'll wonder why no one ever thought of it before. The 4 × 4-foot boxes have been chosen because it's a size you can walk around and easily reach into to tend your plants; this eliminates the need for stepping on the growing soil and packing it down, which then eliminates the need to dig or loosen it. See how everything in SFG is interrelated and works so well together?

For bigger gardens, you can always put some of the boxes end to end to create a 4 × 8-foot or a 4 × 12-foot garden box that you will still be able to walk around, yet reach in. If your box is located next to a wall, fence, or building, keep the boxes only two feet wide so you can reach all the way to the back. They can be any length. Boxes can be made from any type of wood. The best is free wood that is found at a construction site. Just ask the foreman of the project if you can have the scrap 2 × 6-inch boards. If you are going to buy your lumber, boxes can be made from pine or fir for the least cost, or cedar or redwood for longer lasting use. If you decide to treat or paint the wood, be careful not to paint inside the boxes where the Mel's Mix comes into contact with the wood; you don't want anything harmful to leach into the soil. I do not recommend using pretreated wood for the same reason.

7 THE AISLES—COMFORTABLE WIDTH

The width of your aisles is another improvement I have made for the All New Square Foot Gardening method. This is more important for comfort, safety, and looks, than for efficiency. If you notice the garden on the cover of the original *Square Foot Gardening* book, there were no boxes and the aisles were 1 × 12-inch boards separating the 4 × 4-foot areas. I designed it that way to be the most space-efficient but, as someone once said, "This is one time when Mel was too efficient!" But the wood was free, so hey, can you blame me?

Straight and Narrow

The 12-inch wide board was difficult to maneuver on, and you had to keep a pretty good balance to stay upright. I found that the average gardener needs to have more room to move about on than those 12 inches. In addition, you couldn't get close to each 4 × 4-foot planting area if you wanted to use a wheelbarrow, garden cart, or harvest basket. Can you just picture two people working in that garden with 12-inch wide paths, and one says to the other, "Excuse me, I need to get through." Can you imagine the answer to that?

The Ideal Width

So what is the ideal aisle width? Two feet is still a little tight, so I recommend a minimum of three feet between your boxes. It turned out that for accessibility, kneeling, working, and harvesting, the ideal distance was 3 or even 4 feet between boxes. In fact, if your garden has several boxes, you can vary the aisles. Play around with some ideas on paper—then, once your boxes are built (and before you fill them with soil, I should add), you can move them about until you get them just right. Think of it as arranging furniture in your yard.

If you've placed your SFG boxes on top of lawn, you can leave the grass but you'll need to mow.

Shredded bark placed over landscaping fabric eliminates the need for any maintenance or dealing with weeds in your aisles.

Paving your aisles takes more work and expense, but it's a way to match the area around the SFG to nearby patios or walkways.

DRESS IT UP

The aisle space between your boxes can be left in grass or covered with any type of ground cover. In our TV show, we tried all sorts of things to create some very interesting looking aisles. At other times, we just removed any weeds or grass, then laid down weed cloth and covered it with materials that were comfortable for walking on such as crushed stone, compost, or ground bark.

8 THE GRIDS—PROMINENT AND PERMANENT

When I first developed the Square Foot Gardening method, I advocated laying out a 12 × 12-inch grid for the garden. Then, in my travels around the country, I heard a lot of people say, "Oh, I do Square Foot Gardening," or "I have a Square Foot Garden." But when I went to see them, the size was right but they had no grid!

In our introductory film, we show the people in our class how a 4 × 4-foot garden looks without a grid and ask them, "How many plants could you plant there? How many different crops?" They draw a blank because it looks like a small area that isn't going to contain very much. As soon as we lay down the grid, they suddenly light up and say, "Aha! I see! Sixteen spaces, so it'll take sixteen different crops! Later, as soon as one square is harvested, I can add a trowel full of compost and replant that square foot with a different crop without disturbing anything else around it." Bingo! They see the light.

There are many, many interrelated reasons for the "different crop in every Square Foot" rule, and you will see and understand these as we go along. They deal with nutrients used, limiting over-ambitious planting, staggered harvests, weed and pest control, beauty of the garden, companion planting, simplification of crop rotation, cutting planting time in half, and many more factors that result in a very unusual and innovative gardening system. When you have no grid, your garden has no character. If you're having visitors over, they may not even notice your garden if it's laid out in plain beds. But if it's a Square Foot Garden with very prominent and visible grids, they will say, "Hey, what's that in your yard? It looks great!"

Grid Materials

In the past, whenever I used string or twine as a grid, it eventually got dirty, rotted, and finally broke. In addition, you had to drive in nails to tie the string to, and it just never looked good. I talked with many others who had the same bad experience so I experimented with all kinds of different materials for making grids. If I could condense thirty years of experience into my current advice, it would be—don't use string or any other floppy material. A firm, rigid, prominent, and visual grid permanently laid on every one of your boxes will make all the

See how the grid defines a Square Foot Garden? Without a grid, it's hard to visualize the harvest.

difference in the world as others see it but mostly in how you use and enjoy your garden.

With a very visible grid, your garden takes on a unique character. It will not only look spectacular, but you'll be able to immediately visualize your planting squares. Without a grid, your garden is not a Square Foot Garden.

9 NOVEL IDEA—DON'T WASTE SEEDS
New Seed Planting Idea

When I first started gardening, I found the traditional method of pouring out an entire packet of seeds along a single row was so wasteful that I couldn't believe that's the way we've always done it. Why would anyone tell us to waste a whole packet of seeds along a long, lonely, single row, especially knowing that we would have to go back and thin out 95 percent of the sprouted plants in order to leave only one plant every few inches.

Did no one ever think, "Let's just plant a few seeds every 3, 4, or 6 inches?" I guess it took someone outside of the garden industry to think of it.

At first, I advocated single seed planting at the proper spacing for that particular plant, but many people found it tedious and even difficult, especially with small, unusually shaped seeds. Besides, as someone once teased me and said, "If a packet of leaf lettuce contains one thousand seeds and I only plant four in each square foot, how old will I be before it is time to buy another packet?" She'll have to leave her seeds in her will!

So back to the drawing board I went. How about just a few seeds in each hole—just a pinch of seeds? After testing this idea with many people and checking their dexterity and ability to pick up just a pinch (two or three seeds), this seemed to be the answer.

A Snip, Not a Tug

But I was against thinning—that's when you pull out all the seedlings except the one plant you want to grow to maturity. Thinning is a lot of work and also seems to disturb the roots of the remaining plant, and that's not good. But then I thought of an absolutely perfect solution. If you plant just a few seeds—a pinch—in each hole and two or three seedlings come up, you just take a pair of scissors and snip off all but the strongest one. That eliminates any disturbance of the plant you want to keep, and you're not tempted to replant the others. The only thing you need to do is just muster the courage to make that initial snip and it's all over.

So now we've been able to improve the single-seed planting and, at the same time, end up with one strong plant in each location, which is just what we wanted. At the same time we're not wasting a lot of seeds. After planting that square foot, put the packet in safe storage, and if stored properly that packet will be good next year, and the year after, and the year after. Many seeds last up to five years if stored properly. (So, how come no one ever told us that before?)

 ## 10 EXPANDED OPPORTUNITIES– TABLETOP GARDENS

Make Them Portable

Now that we no longer need to improve our existing soil—and SFG takes up only 20 percent of the space for 100 percent of the harvest—and we need only 6 inches of lightweight soil mix, we can build a 4 × 4-foot box, and add a plywood bottom drilled with drainage holes. This means you can carry it to any location you want, even moving it to suit weather, climate, an event, a situation, or even a person's needs, abilities, or disabilities. If the size or weight seems too much for you to handle, think about using a 3 × 3-foot, a 2 × 2-foot, or even a 2 × 4-foot box for ease in moving.

James, Bring Out the Good Boxes

Smaller sized SFG boxes can become wonderful patio boxes, and it's even possible to plant several so there is always one or two with flowers in full bloom or salad crops ready for harvest. The rest can be kept somewhere less visible. With a system of rotation, there will always be a few garden boxes ready to bring out to show off. There's nothing like the visual impact of a beautifully planted box filled with vegetables, flowers, and/or herbs. If you're giving a talk or doing a presentation on gardening, the "seeing is believing" technique will cinch your talk.

And just think, you won't have to answer the usual question about SFG, like "How on earth can you grow a garden in only 6 inches of soil?" Or, "How can you grow without fertilizer?" Now, you just point and smile!

BEST OF ALL

I think Square Foot Gardening's best feature is that it now makes gardening available to just about anyone you can think of, regardless of their age, circumstance, location, ability, or disability—anyone, anywhere, can now garden using the All New Square Foot Gardening method.

REASONS TO MOVE YOUR PORTABLE SFG BOX

WEATHER–To protect it from:

- Frost

- Thundershowers

- Hurricanes

- Hail

- Snow

- Wind

- Heavy rain

- Intense sun

CLIMATE–Move your SFG box for:

- More shade for a spring crop as the weather gets hotter

- More sun in early spring

- More shade in summertime in desert areas

EVENTS–Move it to:

- Enhance or decorate for a poolside party or barbeque

- Behind the garage for a start-up nursery

SITUATIONS–Place the box:

- On a tabletop for a sit-down gardener

- In the garage if you're expecting extreme weather

- On the deck to clear the yard for a football game

PERSONS–You can:

- Take it to Grandma's for a birthday gift

- Take it to school for show-and-tell

- Take it to class for teaching SFG

- Take it to school for the science fair

Plan Your Garden

Getting the most out of your
Square Foot Garden starts with deciding
on the number of boxes you—and your
family—need and picking the perfect
location to grow the crops you want.

With a little planning,
your SFG will provide
you with food from
spring through fall.

The big dilemma is, should you first design the layout for your garden, then try to find a spot where it will fit? Or, should you first find the best spot for a garden, then design a layout that will fit into that spot?

This chapter solves that dilemma by addressing the three components of Square Foot Gardening.

■　Size　　　　■　Location　　　　■　Design

SIZE

Your garden will be laid out in square or rectangular boxes separated by walking aisles. Build your boxes from materials like wood, bricks, or blocks. If you don't like the idea of common wood, which will eventually rot or be eaten by termites, use a more expensive wood like cedar or redwood. You can even use some of the manmade composite "wood" or recycled plastic or vinyl. The wood I like best is free wood. You can usually get it from any construction site, but always ask the foreman first.

If you decide to use lumber, you'll be happy to know the advantage of 4 × 4 gardens is that all lumber comes in 8-foot lengths. Most home improvement centers will cut it in half for you at little or no cost. Your boxes can be made from just about any material except treated wood because the chemicals used to treat the wood are not something you want leaching into your garden.

How Much Is Enough?

If you're figuring a SFG for an adult, remember that:

1. One 4 × 4 Square Foot Garden box (equal to 16 square feet) will supply enough produce to make a salad for one person every day of the growing season.

Salad　　　　　　　　Daily Vegetables　　　　　　　　Preserving

2. One more 4 × 4 box will supply the daily supper vegetables for that person.

3. Just one more 4 × 4 box will supply that person with extra of everything for preserving, special crops, showing off, or giving away.

So, each adult needs one, two, or three large boxes of 4 × 4, depending on how much they want. In square feet, that is 16, 32, or 48 square feet.

If you're figuring a SFG for a child, remember that:

1. One 3 × 3 Square Foot Garden box (equal to 9 square feet) will supply enough produce to make a salad for one child every day of the growing season.

2. One more 3 × 3 box will supply supper vegetables for that child every day.

3. Just one more 3 × 3 box will supply the child with extra of everything for show-and-tell or science projects at school, special crops, showing off, or giving away. So, each child needs one, two, or three small boxes of 3 × 3, depending on how much they will eat. In square feet, that's 9, 18, or 27 square feet.

Suggestion: Since the kids will grow into teenagers, you may just want to make everyone's box a 4 × 4. On the other hand, different sizes make the garden look interesting and more personable. The 3 × 3 can later on be stacked on top of a 4 × 4 to start a pyramid garden—but more about designing your garden later.

YOUR FAMILY–YOUR GARDEN

According to surveys of homeowners, the average conventional single-row garden measures 20 feet wide by 35 feet long, which equals 700 square feet. To grow the same amount, a Square Foot Garden will need only 20 percent or one-fifth of that growing space to equal 140 square feet. That's quite a difference isn't it?

DOWN TO SIZE

Whenever I'm giving a lecture I like to illustrate the difference between a conventional garden and a Square Foot Garden. I'll walk down the middle of whatever room we're in and, standing in the center, stretch out my arms sideways, as I say, "If this whole room were our garden, when you switch to Square Foot Gardening, you'll no longer need everything on this side." That cuts the room in half.

HOW MANY SQUARES?

Number of Boxes or Square Feet	Salad	Supper	Extra	Total
Mom				
Dad				
Grandpa or Grandma				
Brother				
Sister				
Pets*				
Other				
			Total squares	

*Well, some dogs eat veggies and cats love catnip.

You can enter the number of boxes—big for adults, small for kids—or square feet.

Then I turn to the side that remains, cut it in half with my arms again, and say, "Everything on that side we don't need." That cuts that half in half again. And then I add, "That's still too much room. We can still cut down this remaining corner even more so we end up with only 20 percent of the total room. We can grow as much in this size of a Square Foot Garden as we previously could in this entire room." You suddenly begin to think of the reduced amount of work, equipment, supplies, and fencing. Then you begin to see many of the advantages of being able to locate the garden where you wish and all the possibilities in your yard. Visualizing the great difference of space needed for a Square Foot Garden is really the first step in learning and appreciating the entire system. Then you can begin to take advantage of all the other attributes you will discover with SFG.

All That in One Box

How much salad could you pick every day from this little garden? More than you can imagine. So as an illustration, I've listed some examples of what you can harvest from just one 4 × 4 box in one spring season.

SFG FOR A TYPICAL FAMILY

For easy multiplying, round off the adults' measurements of 16, 32, and 48 to 15, 30, and 50 square feet per person. For children, you can w30 square feet. To figure the area in square feet compared to boxes, try this. A family of two adults plus one teenager plus one child needs:

(2 + 1) x 50 = 150 square feet
+ 1 x 20 = 20 square feet
Total: 170 square feet

FIRST HARVEST FROM EACH SQUARE

BOX SQUARE NUMBER

1	2	3	4
5	6	7	8
9	10	11	12
13	14	15	16

1 one head of cabbage

2 one head of broccoli

3 one head of broccoli

4 one head of cauliflower

5 four heads of romaine lettuce

6 four heads of red lettuce

7 four heads leaf lettuce, then sixteen scallions

8 four heads of salad lettuce

9 five pounds sugar peas

10 eight bunches of Swiss chard

11 nine bunches of spinach, then nine turnips

12 sixteen small, ball carrots

13 sixteen beets, plus four bunches beet greens

14 sixteen long carrots

15 sixteen radishes

16 sixteen radishes

START SMALL

Once you decide on the final size and layout of your garden, keep in mind you don't have to build the entire garden right at the start. Try a three-phase plan instead.

If you build and plant just one-third of your ultimate garden boxes and grow for one season—for example, the spring season—you can then see how much you'll harvest and see if you've correctly judged the amount you really need. Then you can go into phase two, or the summer crop, and build more boxes according to your layout or master plan. At the end of the summer crop, move on to phase three, building more boxes if you still need them, to prepare for planting a fall crop.

Yes, it's okay to lay out the whole area and to design it for the ultimate use, depending on how big your family is and how much you think you want to harvest. Just don't do everything the first season. I've seen so many people start out too ambitiously, and they become overwhelmed because they underestimate how much they can actually grow in such a small area. Their gardens are actually larger than they need so there is more to take care of—and all while they're learning a new system. Take it easy and start small.

If you have a single-row garden and don't really want to give it up yet, I suggest taking one small corner of your old-fashioned garden and planting it in just one or two 4 × 4 boxes, mix the correct soil (don't just shovel your existing soil into the boxes no matter how good you think it is), put down the grid, and try planting this way. Next year, I'll bet you'll probably be ready to convert your entire garden into a SFG.

Overall Size of the Boxes

Once you decide on the overall size and number of boxes, the next step is to determine the dimension of the aisles. We'll cover this in more detail later, but for now you can figure on a 3-foot aisle between all 4-foot boxes. You could also decide now if you want to join several boxes together end to end to create a rectangular box of 4 × 8, or 4 × 12. This will save a lot of yard space but you may not like the look or you may find walking around a long box inconvenient. I would never make a box longer than 16 feet or you'll end up trying to cross it in the middle and then—whoops!—there you are, stepping in your garden. I hope no one saw you! If you are going to be putting some boxes against a fence or wall and can't walk all around to reach in, those boxes should be only 2 feet wide. Everyone wants to make them 3 feet wide (I will never know why) but then they always come back and complain it was too wide because they couldn't reach in that far.

Don't Forget the Aisles

The whole idea of Square Foot Gardening is to walk around your garden boxes and reach in to tend your plants. This way, the soil never gets packed down and you eliminate digging it up to loosen it again. In fact, the only tool you really need once you fill your boxes with Mel's Mix is a small hand trowel. (It doesn't have to be the strong, expensive kind from Sweden. The one dollar variety works just fine and can last a lifetime.)

So how wide should your aisles be? It depends a lot on how much room you have and what kind of a look you want for your garden. If you're going to have many boxes—remember, we suggest you begin using only a small number because you can always add more later— you may want to have, for example, a center aisle that is 4 feet wide so you can easily get in with a garden cart or wheelbarrow, or so several people can walk down the aisle at once. (Hey, how about a garden party or a wedding?)

I would suggest you make aisles no narrower than 3 feet; 2-foot wide aisles will seem crowded once plants grow and some cascade over the sides of the boxes. A 2-foot aisle can shrink down to 18 or even 12 inches. Since SFG takes up so little room, why crowd all your boxes together? The more spacious your all-new SFG is, the more time you are likely to spend there enjoying it.

Draw It Up

Once you get a rough idea of how much space you'll need, make a quick sketch more or less to scale. You don't need graph paper (unless you're a designer or want to use it); just draw the 3-foot aisles slightly smaller than the 4-foot boxes. Now you're ready to tour your property looking for nice open areas near the house. Later in this chapter we'll discuss design in more detail.

> *"Gardening has always seemed too overwhelming. Now with your method, I can't wait to start."*
> *– Alejiendra from Venezuela*

LOCATION

There are five major things to look for when touring your property for a SFG location. Use these as a test for the area you're considering for your All New Square Foot Garden. (Remember, convenience is king so make sure you follow Rule 1.)

1. Place it close to the house for convenience.
2. Pick an area that gets six to eight hours of sunshine daily.
3. Stay clear of trees and shrubs where roots and shade may interfere.
4. The area should not puddle after a heavy rain.
5. The existing soil is not really important, since you won't be using it.

1 **CLOSE TO THE HOUSE**

With the All New Square Foot Gardening Method, you have so many more places to put your garden than ever before. Keep in mind foot traffic and sites where you will often notice and enjoy your garden. If your SFG is near traffic paths, you'll walk past the garden more often, hence take better care of it (remember—no need to change into gardening clothes, or run and get some tools). This means it will always look nice and the end result will be that you'll enjoy it more, as will every other member of the family. (Chapter 10 covers different locations like hillsides or heavily wooded areas.)

I Can See Clearly Now

When you think about observing your garden, consider where you can frequently see it—especially from inside the house. What room are you in the most? Can you see the garden from there? The reason is not only for your pleasure but for protection. If it is close, you will see problems (like deer, wilting plants, a neighbor's dog or cat) when they begin rather than hours later after all the damage is done.

Remember the Square Foot Garden way is to treat your plants just like you treat your children or grandchildren, and you know you would be glancing out the window at them. I believe that every plant out there is constantly seeking your attention by saying, "Look at me, look at my new blossom, look how big I'm getting." Isn't that just like children?

Placement of your Square Foot Garden opens up so many doors to the way you care for, enjoy, appreciate, and harvest it. Plus you'll show it off more often and get the whole family involved. It's even possible to split up your garden and place some of your boxes in different locations for perhaps a different visual effect or a different purpose.

HOW MUCH SUN WILL YOUR BOXES GET?
The numbered boxes represent potential locations around a garden. As the sun rises in the east and sets in the west, the boxes are shaded to various degrees by the house and tree. So box 7 is in the sun all day, while box 2 is in shade for much of the day.

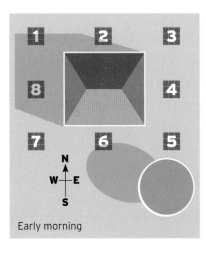

Early morning

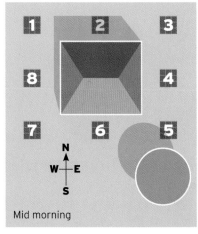

Mid morning

2 SUNLIGHT

The next thing to consider in selecting a location is sunlight. Growing plants need sunlight. How much they need depends on the type of plant. In general, large-flowering or fruiting plants need a lot— at least eight hours a day. These types of plants are referred to as a "summer crop" or "warm-weather plants" and include most of the favorite things that people grow, such as tomatoes, peppers, squash, beans, and sunflowers.

In determining the amount of sunlight an area receives, keep in mind that it changes throughout the year with the seasons. In early spring and again in late fall the sun is lower in the sky than in the summertime. And of course, there are not as many hours of light in the day in the spring and fall as there are in the summer.

If You Only Have Shade

If you have shady conditions and no other place to locate your garden, you can still have a thriving garden but you'll have a limited selection of crops to grow. So, obviously, you'd stay away from the tomatoes, peppers, and squash and plant the root and leaf crops like radishes, spinach, and lettuce. Of course, there are many flowers and herbs that love shade, so check with your local nursery if you are in this situation.

Too Much Sun

Sometimes you might have a location that gets full sun all day long, from sunup to sundown. That would actually be too much for some of the cool weather and leafy crops, as well as many flowers. Of course, with a big, huge garden there's not much you can do. But with a Square Foot Garden, it's very easy to provide shade by building a simple support and covering the 4 × 4 box with some shade cloth. That's all covered in Chapter 4.

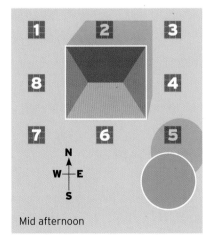

Mid afternoon

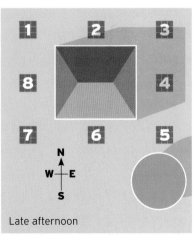

Late afternoon

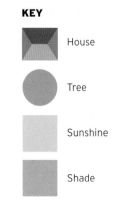

KEY

House

Tree

Sunshine

Shade

3 AVOID TREES AND SHRUBS

When choosing your SFG location, stay clear of trees and shrubs for two reasons. The first is shade as we just discussed. Second, if they sense a well-watered perfect soil nearby, these roots will come straight as an arrow into your soil. If that's the only location you have, then there is a way to counteract that situation. Put a plywood bottom on your boxes and raise them up off the ground. You can raise them up by just putting a brick under each corner and one in the center. Or you can use a cement block, or even two blocks and build little piers and have it as a garden you sit down beside to harvest. Then, of course, the tree's roots won't even know that the garden is there. This is a nice way to have a shade garden right under a tree along with a bench or a few lawn chairs. Keep in mind that shrubs are just as bad as trees as far as providing shade and root interference. Most shrubs are more shallow-rooted than trees. Keep in mind, too, that as trees and shrubs grow, their shade will increasingly cover a larger area.

4 NO PUDDLES, PLEASE

Roots will drown in accumulated and stagnant water, so you don't want to locate your SFG in an area that holds water after a rain. The materials in Mel's Mix, though they drain well and hold a lot of moisture, will soak up all the water in a standing puddle and your plant roots will be harmed. Areas that puddle also promise mud in the aisles, which makes gardening less fun.

If you have no other place and can't drain the area, then of course you could fill in the low area with sand to raise your box slightly and/or you could again put a bottom on it and raise it up with stones, bricks, cinder blocks, or something similar.

5 EXISTING SOIL— WHO CARES?

When you're choosing a location, it doesn't really matter about the condition of your existing soil. Many of the other gardening books tell you how to go around the yard and dig test holes and see what kind of soil you have. Or, how about all the unnecessary advice on how to take a soil test and what the results mean? Forget about all that now. You don't have to know about it because we're not going to use your existing soil. We're going to build bottomless boxes above

Where a box will sit on hard landscaping or on wet ground, you can raise each side of the box up slightly to allow for better drainage before lining the box.

the ground. You can even put your boxes on the pavement or a patio and it won't make any difference.

THE ENVELOPE, PLEASE

The best location is where you can see your garden more often from more directions. Things like sunlight and avoiding trees and shrubs are merely precautions to help make your garden more successful. So walk around your yard and think about the best place to locate and enjoy your garden.

DESIGN

Now that you've determined how many boxes you'll have and strolled around your yard to find the best spot(s), it's time to think about design. You can lay out your boxes so they turn corners, even intersect each other, but keep in mind traffic and walking around. Don't make dead ends or narrow places. Keep 3- or 4-foot aisles, and leave bigger areas for chairs, benches, and entranceways. Here is a fun idea: explain to the entire family the basic size and layout then let each member draw up ideas and plans. Maybe everyone could have an area to design, build, and plant. Wouldn't that be a great family project? Then, take a picture and send it to me so we can share all kinds of designs with others.

Line Them Up

You can probably guess that, being a former army officer, I am going to want all the boxes lined up neatly and precisely, even perhaps having them in a row (oh, what an unfortunate word)—excuse me—in a line. I might want the entire area to be a square or at the very least a rectangle . . . but that's just me. How about you—do you want a U-shape or an L-shape? Do whatever appeals to you.

Gardens Aren't Just for Yards Anymore

Here's another idea—no matter the season, you can build a SFG box with a plywood bottom and place it on your patio or picnic tabletop near your back door. You may want to use smaller SFG boxes on the patio or deck such as 2 × 2 or 2 × 4.

BE CREATIVE

You don't have to be a landscape architect to measure and draw up what you imagine. The design is just as important as the size. You're going to be spending a lot of your time in your SFG—not working or weeding, but just enjoying and relaxing. Be sure to make room for some chairs, a bench, a water fountain, or a birdbath. One of the advantages of a Square Foot Garden is that you have options in how you put it together so that it's perfect for you.

4

Building Boxes and Structures

If you like to build things, you are going to love this chapter. A Square Foot Garden can be a lot like working with Erector® sets, Lincoln Logs®, or Legos®. Since SFG grows so much in so little space and is made with readily available materials, the basic box projects outlined in this chapter won't take all your time, space, or money.

Building the basic SFG box takes very little skill, effort, materials, time, or expense. And the return on investment is amazing.

Why Boxes?

Contain your garden plants in raised boxes and you control just about everything that happens to those plants. Keeping your plants happy and growing their best starts with building their new SFG home.

Just as a reminder, there are several reasons we build boxes for our Square Foot Gardens.

1. Looks neat and tidy.
2. Organizes and simplifies your gardening chores.
3. Holds a special soil mix aboveground.
4. It's easy to add protective features.

If your garden is boxed in, it has already-established limits for you. And if you make sure to add a grid, it establishes not only a pattern but a formula for success.

Boxes also hold your perfect soil mix so that it doesn't spill out or wash away in a heavy rainstorm. When garden beds have no borders between plant-growing soil and walkways, there's a greater chance that someone will step into the growing soil—a big no-no for this SFG method.

"SFG is more than a hobby, it's a movement."
– Ross from South Carolina

Let's start with the basic 4 × 4 SFG box. Examples of box materials that can be used include:

- Natural wood
- Manmade wood
- Recycled plastic
- Vinyl
- Or any other manmade material available in lumber sizes

Recommended Material Size
- 1 × 6-inch lumber for the most economical, low traffic garden; or
- 2 × 6-inch lumber for sturdier boxes or heavy traffic garden areas.

ROTATE CORNERS
When constructing your SFG box, cut all four pieces of your wood sides to the same length, and then rotate the corners to ensure you end up with a square box. If you want a different look than the rotated corners, measure the thickness of the lumber and subtract that from two of the sides and add it to the other two sides so you still end up

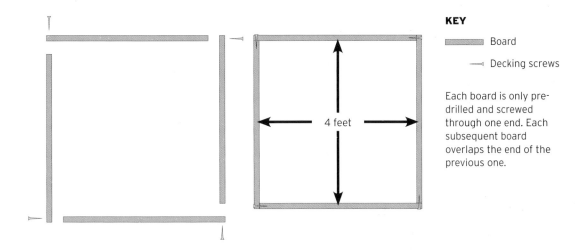

KEY

━━━ Board

⊸ Decking screws

Each board is only pre-drilled and screwed through one end. Each subsequent board overlaps the end of the previous one.

4 feet

with a square box. It is not critical that your garden box be exactly 48 inches either inside or outside, but it should be square so each square foot planting area is the same size.

Attach your box with coarse-thread deck screws that are twice as long as the thickness of the lumber. Use three screws per corner. Pre-drill your holes in the first piece of the two pieces you're connecting; the threads will embed themselves into the second.

CONSTRUCTION DETAILS

Work on a hard surface—like a driveway, pavement, or sidewalk—and keep your frame flat so it won't end up crooked or twisted. When your frame is all screwed together, carry it to the garden area, lay it down, and see how it looks. If you want to preserve the wood, you could use linseed oil. It's also possible to paint or stain the bottom, outside, and top. Lèave the inside unpainted so there's no possible contamination to the growing mix.

OTHER BOX MATERIALS

SFG boxes can also be constructed with brick, cement blocks, prefabricated stone, or large rocks. Stone for your SFG box can be manmade preformed sizes or natural slate, round, riverbed, or any other type of decorative stone that is easy to place and forms an interesting border.

PENNY PINCHER

My idea of the best kind of wood is free wood. Go to any construction site, tell the foreman you are building a Square Foot Garden, and ask if they have any scrap lumber. Chances are they will be throwing out just what you need. They may even cut it for you if you ask nicely. Then your box is free.

How To Build an SFG Box

Make sure you've collected everything you'll need for the box before beginning the project: Four 4-foot, 1 x 6 or 2 x 6-inch boards; six 4-foot wood laths; weed cloth; Mel's Mix; decking screws and a power drill.

Stack the four boards for the box sides in the stepped design shown at left; drill 3 holes in one end of each board, by sliding each board back as you're finished drilling the holes.

ASSEMBLY & FILLING

Screw three large, coarse-thread deck screws through the pre-drilled holes, overlapping board ends until you have a complete frame.

Move the frame to its final location, remove grass and weeds, and cut weed cloth to the outside dimensions of the frame.

Add Mel's Mix until it covers the bottom and then water. (Do this three times until your box is full.) Then, add the grid and plant!

To ensure proper drainage, drill holes in the plywood bottom of your tabletop garden—one per square foot and one extra in each corner.

Plywood Bottom

If you decide to create a bottom for your SFG, use plywood sheeting and drill ¼-inch drainage holes, one per square foot plus an extra hole in each corner. You attach this bottom by putting it on top of the assembled box sides, screwing it down, then flipping it over so the box sides are sitting on top of the plywood bottom.

Plywood thickness depends on the size of the box. A 2 × 2 or 2 × 3 box—anything spanning less than 3 feet—needs ½-inch plywood. Your 4 × 4-foot boxes need ⅝- or even ¾-inch plywood bottoms. Use the ¾-inch plywood if you are going to move it often. If the box is going to rest on sawhorses or cement blocks and span a large, unsupported distance, it requires thicker plywood. I use regular plywood although some like to spend extra for the longer lasting, but much more expensive, marine or waterproof plywood.

SPECIAL STRUCTURES

For out-of-season gardening, you can create spring, summer, fall, and/or winter boxes. These are just 4 × 4 foot standard garden boxes or smaller 2 × 4 size that can be modified for special uses; we'll explain that in Chapter 9. Depending on the time of year, boxes can be equipped with double decks, extensions, covers, or special modifications to allow a longer growing season. Usually these modifications are weather-related items like covers to shade tender seedlings in the summer or a frost protector either in spring or fall. You will determine the best modifications, depending on your particular weather and environmental conditions.

RAILING BOXES

If you have flat railings, it is very easy to set a box right on top of it. For stability, it should be bolted to the wood railing. If you can't bolt your boxes down and you're higher than the first floor, I would place the boxes on the floor. Consider the strength and size of your railing and the surrounding environment, and make sure your railing boxes aren't too big.

Railing boxes make a decorative and excellent garden, particularly if you add trailing types of plants that add some color and character. There are various holders sold at home improvement stores that snap onto your railings to accommodate standard-sized boxes. Hang the box over the outside edge, and it won't take up any of your valuable deck space, and, should it drip when you're watering, the water will bypass the deck below. However, if your box is on the inside of the railing, it would be much safer.

PYRAMID BOXES

Be creative and make your SFG uniquely yours. Why not get fancy and stack one on top of another to create pyramids? Why would you do that? Because they're spectacular, and they will be the highlight and focal point of your entire garden. Construction is very simple with just a few braces for stability.

Step Up, Young Lady

The next fancy garden layout would be to make a standard 4-foot wide by any length box but every 2 or 4 feet step up by one level. There are many arrangements you could design, and they would be limited only by your imagination. Build them the same way as the corner pyramid with an inside brace for every 4-foot section.

Make Boxes Extra Deep

Making boxes that are extra deep mean they are extra dramatic. I know I've told you that 6 inches of Mel's Mix is enough for all plants, but your garden becomes more dramatic when the container is extra tall. If you decide to build your box taller, just use 8-, 10-, or 12-inch lumber instead of the normal 6 inches. The only drawback is cost. But no matter— you're after a dramatic, spectacular look now. Since the plants don't need more than 6 inches of Mel's Mix, don't spend your money on filling the entire depth with Mel's Mix. Use sand (cheap and available at any home improvement center) on the bottom layer. "I'll just use my existing yard soil," someone says "and save even more money." Don't! Most soils don't drain well and have weed seeds. Remember weeds? We don't have them anymore in SFG, so if you're going to multiple layers for your garden boxes, fill any space below 6 inches with just ordinary sand.

One-square-foot boxes are the perfect size for the steps leading to your front door.

A Special Box for Carrots, Leeks, and Potatoes

There is one last item that you might want to construct—your high-rise boxes for carrots, leeks, and potatoes. These root crops need deep soil so instead of digging down as in most gardening methods, we take the easy way and build up. Build a 1 × 1-foot box either 6, 9, or 12 inches tall out of plywood or any thin type of lumber. See Chapter 6 for details on planting and growing.

GRIDS AND MATERIALS

Grids are a must. Every box should have its own permanent and prominent grid. I'm so adamant about having a grid on every box I tell people that if your SFG doesn't have a grid, it is not a Square Foot Garden. But with a grid, it's an attractive, unusual, and unique garden. It tells the story of SFG in one glance. In addition it has many unseen benefits, so stick with me on this one and build a grid for all of your boxes.

SAFETY FIRST

If you're starting with used lumber and it already has paint on it, you must make sure that it's not old paint, especially if it's peeling or crumbling; some older paints contain lead, which is toxic. You don't want that in your garden. I also don't recommend using pretreated timbers or lumber because it also can leach chemicals.

Blinds

The first Penny Pincher tip is slat-type or Venetian blinds. They come in many widths and lengths, and if you visit a local thrift shop you can usually find a used set at a great price. Find one that's at least 4 feet wide. Cut off the strings and lay out the strips. Trim the ends with a pair of scissors so they fit your box, drill holes at the half and quarter points, and attach them together with some sort of screw, nail, or snap-fastener. The one problem I've found with blinds is their weight. When you first start your garden in the spring, it's usually windy. Sometimes the blinds blow around a little just because the garden is empty and they have no protection from the wind. One solution is to attach them to the soil with a long galvanized nail at every 12-inch intersection. This helps hold them down so they don't blow away.

Wood Lath

The second inexpensive material is wood lath, which is sold in home improvement centers. Believe it or not, they already come 4 feet long with square ends. Sometimes they're a little crooked, filled with knots, or break easily, so sort through them. But they're very, very inexpensive—less than a quarter each. Once you lay them out and drill holes at the 12-inch intersections, they're very easy to connect together with a nut and bolt or some other type of fastener. Because the wood lath is rigid, it can span from one side of the box to the other side in case your Mel's Mix is not level with the top of the box.

Attach Your SFG Grid

JOINING

Drill holes at the intersections of all the grid lath pieces.

Next, insert a pin or bolt to hold the grid together.

SECURING

Drill holes at ends of each lath piece, into the sides of the box.

Secure the lath strips to the box with screws driven through the holes.

Once the grid is attached, your SFG is ready for planting.

Otherwise, it can just lie on top of the soil. If your grid spans across the box sides, keep the grid from moving about by drilling a hole in the ends of the two center slats and screwing them to your wooden box. Some people like to take the wood lath grid up for the winter so it doesn't get wet and rot as easily. Unscrew the four screws, fold the grid, and hang it on the garage wall. Put the screws in a plastic bag and hang it up with the grid to keep the screws safe and dry over the winter.

Fun Ideas

You may be able to find other scrap wood strips around. Carpenters often have strips left over. You just have to keep your eyes open. "Quick, Henry, stop the car. I saw something back there." Or, if you have a table saw, it's easy enough to cut strips of wood yourself.

The wood or blind grids can be painted, which kids love to do, creating fancy combinations of colors. For the best visual effect, I think plain white is best. (Kids will say, "Blah!") You can also write on them. (Kids will say, "Cool!") Some people like to record what they've planted. It's fun to have visitors sign your grid,

> **Grids need to remain in place during the entire growing season. Remember you're harvesting and replanting each square throughout the season. Besides that, you want to make sure everyone notices you have an authentic SFG.**

especially children and grandchildren. Let them pick out which square they like best, and tell them it can be theirs. When they call, you can tell them how their plants are doing. I bet they'll call more often.

PROTECTING YOUR SFG

To protect one or more squares next to each other from weather or pests, the first step is to make a wire U-frame cage to fit over those squares. You may want to make several U-frames of different sizes that can be used for 1, 2, or 4 square feet and another for an entire 4 × 4 block of 16 square feet. Basically, you want to make a wire cage that will fit over the top of each of these areas. Later you can attach a covering made from any number of materials to protect those squares from a variety of hazards. I've found that the easiest cage is made from plastic-coated wire fencing. This can be cut with wire pliers and easily bent over a straight edge to almost any shape. You can make a four-sided wire box from two U-frames or just a two-sided one. There is quite a variety of fencing wire to choose from so check out what is available. It comes in rolls of different widths and lengths as well as different openings and wire thicknesses. You may want to call ahead to several places to find the best choice.

Chicken Wire

Another common material I like to use is chicken wire. It comes in smaller 1-inch openings or larger 2-inch openings. The 1-inch size is much stronger but will cost a little more. The 1-inch size also takes a little longer to bend into shape but will keep out more critters than the 2-inch size. Chicken wire can be cut with pliers or cutting shears. It's sharp, so be sure to wear gloves. You can buy a whole roll of it, 3 or 4 feet wide. In many hardware stores you can buy whatever length you want from their roll, and they will cut it for you!

Full Cage

A chicken wire cage over the entire 4 × 4 makes it fairly easy to protect your garden against unwanted rabbits, birds that dig up and eat newly planted seeds, cats that like to dig in the soil, too much sun on newly planted and delicate seedlings, or strong wind gusts during the windy season. Build your wire cage to fit the plants' mature sizes. (Once plants start growing through the wire, it is very difficult to take the cage off.) Grab the cage wire with your fingers and lift the whole thing off, tend to the plants, and then put it back down. A full cage needs a wooden-frame bottom for support, but it then fits nicely on your wooden garden box frame. See how everything in SFG fits together so nicely, just like Legos.

Construction

To make a wooden bottom for a wire cage, attach four pieces of 1 × 2 inch pine lumber 4 feet long in a box shape with two deck screws at each corner. Then cut and shape your chicken wire or fencing wire to the 4 × 4 box to create any height you want. Staple the wire to the wood frame using ⅜-inch staples, and then wire or tie the vertical corners together or wherever the wire forms a corner. If you are using chicken wire or any wire that has sharp edges, you may want to cover the sharp points—including where the wire is stapled to the wood—with something like duct tape (choose a nice color) to prevent getting scratched while you're moving your cover. Another way is to attach the wire to the inside of the 1 × 2 frame. It's a little more work to staple the wire to the inside, but there won't be any sharp points to scratch you. If you have a couple of these cages made up ahead of time—one or two that are 6 inches tall, another couple 12 inches tall, and a few at 18 inches tall—they will be available at the right time they're needed for your garden. Don't forget you can use them as a framework for spring protection from cold, cats, or crows. They can be summer protection from sun, wind, and rain, and fall protection from deer, frosts, and snow. They can be stacked on the ground in a pile or hung on the garage or fence wall.

> "Square Foot Gardening is great for the family. Each person has his or her own plot."
> – Gary from Michigan

COVERS

Materials used for covering the wire cages can be anything from clear plastic to protect plants from wind or cold weather and snow, sleet, or rain—to some sort of cloth like cheesecloth or floating cover to protect plants from insects getting in to lay their eggs.

Clothespins

A cover can be easily held in place with clothespins. The cover can be open on some sides to allow air to circulate or it can be completely enclosed. One consideration, of course, is whether too much heat will build up inside the cage, and that depends on the season and the amount of sunlight your garden receives in your area. When there is too much sunlight for newly planted transplants, just put a shade cloth over the top of your cage. If you have several newly planted squares among other well-established plant squares, you can attach shade patches over just those plants that need a little shade.

Building a Wire Cage for Your SFG

MATERIALS

To build a protective cage for your 4 x 4 garden, you'll need: four 1 x 2-inch boards, 4 feet long; chicken wire; plastic ties; cutting shears; and a power drill.

PREPARATION

Arrange your boards as shown in the photo, and drill two holes in the end of each board.

ASSEMBLY

Screw the frame together using coarse-thread deck screws.

Roll out the chicken wire and cut to length, for sides high enough to cover your mature plants.

Place your frame in the center of the long piece of chicken wire. Brace the frame with your foot and band the chicken wire up, and then do this on the other side. Remember to wear gloves!

Set your wire frame over the wood frame and secure it to the frame with plastic cable ties or heavy-duty staples. Take care not leave any sharp wire edges.

Once the chicken wire has been bent on all sides, remove the frame and connect the four corners at three locations using plastic ties.

The frame is lightweight and easy to lift off your SFG box. Remove it to water, plant, prune or harvest.

Protective Dome Supports

A dome support is so easy to make. Just bend a 10-foot length of ½-inch PVC pipe from corner to corner of your box, and then another from the opposite corners; then tie or bolt it at the intersection at the top to make a dome that can support any type of cover. Think of it as the structural framework for a greenhouse—in the early spring it can be covered with clear plastic, in the late spring with cheesecloth to keep out egg-laying insects, and in the summer with shade cloth to provide a little shade for tender young plants. You can provide protection the same way for the fall crop.

Covered Wagon

Another neat looking PVC frame is one in the shape of a covered wagon. This takes a little longer to make and requires just a bit more material, but it gives a lot more room and is much easier to use when you have a cover over the frame. It requires the same two 10-foot long PVC pipes, but they're arched over each end of your box. Then, you need an extra 4-foot-long piece of pipe that becomes the strut holding the two arches from collapsing. Tying the intersection will not work in this design, so you have to drill holes in the center of the arches and in each end of the strut, so that a bolt will connect the central strut to the top center of each arch. Use a bolt and nut that won't tear the plastic or net covering. Now you can see the shape is much more conducive to lifting one side to work inside, and it makes it easier to throw a blanket over the entire 4 × 4 frame on a cold night.

For those who don't want such a high frame, just cut the 10-foot PCV pipes down to 6 or 8 feet and you'll have a much lower wagon top. For those of you thinking, "I'll just buy one 10-footer and cut it in half," that won't work. The arch over a 4-foot span has to be more than 5 feet long.

PLANT SUPPORTS

What do you do with heavy fruiting plants such as peppers, eggplants, and giant marigolds? The easiest way to support the branches of these plants without doing a lot of staking and tying is to make a permanent cage that the plants can grow through. The cage's height depends on the height of the mature plants. This could be for 1 square foot, 2, 4, or for the whole 16 square feet in a 4 × 4 garden; it all depends on what is planted in each square. The cage can be self-supporting with sides that stick into the soil just like the wire U-frame previously mentioned, or, if you are making a support for the entire 4 × 4, it is very easy to put a stake of some sort in each corner—either wood or metal—and then suspend the wire horizontally between these four corners.

Building a Dome Support

Bend two 10-foot, ½-inch diameter PVC pipes from corner to corner.

The bent PVC pipes should form a dome as shown here.

Secure the dome at the intersection of the bent pipes using a plastic cable tie.

This simple PVC frame, covered in thick, durable plastic sheeting, can protect your plants from many things, including harmful weather and unwanted nibblers. (I'm not talking about you!)

Building a Covered Wagon Support

PREPARATION

Locate the centers of your two PVC pipes, and mark those points.

Drill holes in the centers of the pipes, at the marked points.

Place each pipe in a corner and bend as shown to the adjacent corner, so that the supports are parallel.

Drill holes in the ends of a 4-foot PVC pipe that will be the supporting strut. Attach it to the arched supports with a cable tie.

CORN PROTECTION

Everyone loves corn—especially chipmunks, squirrels, and raccoons!

To keep them out and your harvest in, try this foolproof secret. Put one steel fence post in each corner of your 4 x 4 foot garden. Use tall metal 5- or 6-foot fence posts, and then, when corn reaches 4 feet, run chicken wire with 1-inch openings around the outside, forming four walls. Next, add one more piece across the top at a height of about 4 feet.

This will keep the critters out of the corn and prevent the crows from eating the seeds and seedlings when first planted. Then, as the corn grows, it will grow right through the top of the wire, which will support the tall corn stalks when the wind blows—at the same time, keeping the raccoons and chipmunks out before the corn can be harvested. You can easily tie the horizontal top wire with temporary bows so that you can undo a few and still reach in. Since it is chicken wire, make sure you wear a long-sleeved shirt when you reach in so you don't get scratched. You'll be able to water easily either by hand or using a long-handled wand and shut-off valve on the end of your hose.

Even better, if you are supporting the entire 4 × 4-foot area, put in the four corner stakes and then horizontally tie on some nylon tomato trellis netting. This netting is available at most garden stores and is particularly good because it is soft and cushiony and won't cut the plants when they rub against it in the wind. It also has large openings you can reach into and the plants can grow through. It won't bother any of the shorter plants either. It is very easy material to work with and well-suited for gardening. Corner posts must be very strong and firmly held so the horizontal wire or netting won't sag. Posts can be constructed of wood and driven into the ground or attached with deck screws to the inside or outside corner of the wood frame. You can also use PVC pipe or even metal pipe or fence posts. The many options available show how flexible Square Foot Gardening can be.

Hold Me Up

Tall lanky plants such as dahlias, gladiolas, and sunflowers may also need extra support as they mature and grow in height. Sunflower seeds will need temporary protection when first planted to prevent birds or rabbits from digging up the seeds and to prevent other birds from eating the young sprouts. Temporarily covering your garden with chicken wire 6 inches over the box will provide this protection until the plants get that tall. Then, after the plants reach a height of about 3 feet, it is time to put in four corner posts—strong steel fence posts and nylon netting horizontally at several different levels. Start the first at 3 feet and the last should be as high as the fence posts. This will support plants through to maturity and keep them from falling over in heavy wind and rainstorms.

VERTICAL FRAMES FOR VINE CROPS

When I first invented the Square Foot Gardening method, I knew one of the real challenges was going to be some of the big sprawling vine crops like tomatoes. Without a doubt, tomatoes are America's most-loved garden vegetable. However, they can take up a lot of room and can become unsightly by season's end if they are allowed to grow without proper care. Also, if left to sprawl over the ground, tomatoes can attract additional pests, and many get damaged or ruined from foot traffic. The whole idea of growing tomatoes this way seemed very non-productive.

I was determined to find a better way to grow tomatoes and what I devised turned out to be not only good for tomatoes, but for all other vine crops too. Every plant that has a vine that sprawls all over the ground—even pumpkins and watermelons—can be grown vertically as long as you have a strong enough support; the result is a spectacular sight with very little wasted ground space.

Air Rights

Being an engineer, I thought of buildings in a city. Buildings aren't constructed as one-story structures that sprawl outward over the landscape; space is too valuable to do this. Instead, designers and contractors use what is called air rights, building straight up into the air, floor after floor after floor. Why can't plants be grown the same way? Well, I discovered they can! All you need is a strong framework and something to hold the vine onto the framework. Did you know that vines grow better vertically than horizontally? Growing plants vertically prevents ground rot and discourages pest infestation. I know slugs aren't happy about my way of vertical gardening; I hear they get dizzy up high, but that's their problem!

Nature Supports

Through the years I experimented with all different types of materials and frames. Finally, I settled upon one that was so simple, easy, and inexpensive to use that it was almost ridiculous. Then I began growing all different types of plants vertically. I originally thought I would need to design some special way to hold up and accommodate heavier fruits such as winter squash and pumpkins, but as it turned out,

Pea and bean netting can be stretched taut across a box frame and held in place by four metal posts. Plants will then grow up through the netting and be supported.

these plant vines seemed to understand the situation; the stem supporting the heavy fruit grows thicker and heavier as the fruit becomes larger. If you have a framework and support that will hold the plant, the plant will hold the fruit; it is as simple as that! Mother Nature always seems to know best.

Best Material

I use the strongest material I can find, which is steel. Fortunately, steel comes in tubular pipe used for electrical conduit. It is very strong and turns out to be very inexpensive. Couplings are also available so you can connect two pieces together. I designed an attractive frame that fits right onto the 4 × 4 box, and it can be attached to the wooden box with clamps that can be bought at any store. Or, steel reinforcing rods driven into the existing ground outside your box provide a very steady and strong base; then the electrical conduit slips snugly over the bars. It's very simple and inexpensive to assemble. Anyone can do it—even you! To prevent vertically grown plants from shading other parts of the garden, I recommend that tall, vertical frames be constructed on the north side of the garden. To fit it into a 4 × 4 box, I designed a frame that measured 4 feet wide and almost 6 feet tall.

Tie It Tight

Vertically growing plants need to be tied to their supports. Nylon netting won't rot in the sun and weather, and I use it exclusively now for both vertical frames and horizontal plant supports. It is very strong—almost unbreakable—and guaranteed for twenty years. It is a wonderful material available at garden stores and in catalogs. The nylon netting is also durable enough to grow the heavier vine crops on vertical frames, including watermelons, pumpkins, cantaloupes, winter and summer squashes, and tomatoes. You will see in Chapter 8 how easy it is to train plants to grow vertically. To hold the plants to the frame, I have found that nylon netting with 7-inch square openings made especially for tomato growing works well because you can reach your hand through. Make sure it is this type so it won't cut the stem of the plant when it blows against it in the wind. This comes in 4-foot widths and can easily be tied to the metal frame. It's sometimes hard to find, so call around.

Winter Storage

Because the netting is loose, it can flop around unless you tie it very tightly to the frame; this is the first step. At the end of the season the frames can be left up or they can be slipped off the steel rebar and hung on a garage wall. Although the conduit is galvanized and endures many years of service, it eventually will rust—especially at the bottom where it comes in contact with the ground. If you do hang up your metal frames in the winter, for safety reasons make sure you cover or clearly mark the steel rebar that is left sticking out of the ground. You can flag it with brightly covered tape, paint it, or find caps that can be screwed on to prevent someone from tripping.

COMPOSTERS

A composting operation can be as simple as a pile of leaves, weeds, and kitchen scraps. Mother Nature does it all the time. Go to any forest or field and you'll see she gets the job done without any structures. But people are different. We like to conserve space, keep things in their place; and we usually want to build a container or enclosure for our compost materials, which speeds up the operation by creating bulk, which then allows the pile to heat up and decompose faster.

What can we buy or build? There are many compost containers on the market mostly made from plastic. All work well, are attractive, and reasonably priced. There are composters that tumble or turn, speeding up the process, but they cost more and worst of all—you still have to turn them. It's fun at first but it gets old very fast.

Make Your Own

We need a structure that will hold a pile of material in either a round or square shape. Wire fencing works well for round and even square structures if you use four fence posts. Make wire cylinders at least 3 to 4 feet in diameter. The exact length of fencing you'll need isn't critical. Instead I am just going to tell everyone to buy 10 or 15 feet of fencing and shape it in a cylinder by attaching the ends together by bending the cut wire ends.

So, if you want a 3-foot diameter composter, buy 10 feet of fencing. If you want a 4-foot diameter, buy 15 feet of fencing and have enough for a door. And, if you don't like round composters, buy four 6-foot long steel fence posts, drive them in each corner of your composter location, bend the wire around those, and you'll have a square composter, much more suited to SFG. Find the best location for your composter and fill as explained in Chapter 5. When full or ready to

---

PENNY PINCHER

Here's a no-cost easy way to make your composter out of wood. Women tell me they love this because it requires no tools, wire cutting, equipment, or familiarity with construction. Find four wood pallets of similar size and appearance. The place to find them is behind the stores and shops where the dumpsters are. Ask first, just to make sure they are being thrown out. If you can find four of about the same size and look, your finished composter will look like it's custom made just for you. A brick or stone under each corner helps keep the wood off the ground to keep it from rotting; corners are tied with rope, cord, or chain. It doesn't have to be nailed or screwed together, and it doesn't have to be real tight. You may want to have the pallet boards face outside to look nice, and you can make them all run either horizontally or vertically—whatever looks best.

If you don't have a compost pile yet, start one now. It's essential to the Square Foot Gardening method.

turn, just lift up the wire cylinder, place it next to the pile, and use a garden fork to fill the cylinder in its new location—you've just turned the pile!

With a Gate

Another idea is to have an enclosure that's easier to get into to mix and water or even turn. Make an entrance opening with or without a gate. Start by driving two steel fence posts in the ground at your selected location; make them about 3 or 4 feet apart. Then attach your wire fencing to these posts. Two options are available for you— with and without a gate. If you want a gate it will cost you an extra 3 or 4 feet of fencing. No big deal, and it will look nicer and be neater when the enclosure starts filling up. You still tie or wire the fencing to both fence posts; one becomes the hinge, the other the door latch.

Make the latch S-hook from wire, or you can buy this type of hook at the store. You can have one compost bin or two together or even three depending on how large your operation is.

Weekly Bins

Just like the wire enclosures, you can have one, two, or up to six bins all together for Monday through Saturday. (Don't forget we rest on Sunday!) When and why would you need more than one? When you get serious about composting, you may be able to get enough material to fill up one every week. Then, for mixing (as explained in Chapter 5), you just move material from a full bin into an empty one right next to it. The nice thing about a series is you only need three pallets for each additional bin.

I could include directions for other materials to use like bricks or cement blocks, landscape timbers, or logs, but no one is going to build a composter out of those materials. They would be too expensive and inefficient. They may look good in books but not in our system because they are just not practical.

Of course, no one says you have to have an enclosure, but if you're a Square Foot Gardener and you have nice square boxes for all of your garden, why would you want just a pile for your composter?

AISLES

"Put your best foot forward" is the saying, but what are you going to put it on? Grass, brick, boards, gravel, or just plain dirt? Most people put their Square Foot boxes in their yard and leave the grass for their aisles. This helps keep a natural look. And don't worry, the grass won't get a lot of hard use because there's not that much to do in an SFG. If you want to leave natural soil in your aisles use an action hoe once a week to rid your aisle of pesky weeds.

If you don't want grass in your aisles, lay down a mulch. Here again, you want to first dig out any weeds or grass; then to prevent weeds from growing back without using chemicals, you can put down a landscape fabric or weed cloth. There are many on the market today. They come in 3- or 4-foot wide rolls and do quite a good job. (Don't use regular black plastic—it won't drain and it's slippery.) Then just cover the cloth with at least 1 or 2 inches of mulch.

You can also use gravel, which comes in all different kinds and sizes, colors and shapes, or you can use other types of ground cover like ground up bark or pine needles; I've even seen people use straw, hay, salt hay, or even leaves collected and saved from last fall. As you walk, these materials break up and gradually decompose, creating something you can add later to your compost pile.

You can also build walkways out of brick, wood planks, or paving stones. Again, take out any weeds and put down a weed cloth first. You can create some very interesting patterns with bricks and paving blocks. Keep the joints fairly tight so the surface doesn't shift.

PENNY PINCHER

Some gardeners use indoor or outdoor carpeting either face up, or if you don't like the color or texture, face down. This is a good way to smother and kill grass or weeds in the aisles without any digging. However, once it rains, indoor carpet gets soggy and smelly, so out it goes. Where do you get old carpet? Go to your local carpet store; they have tons of it out by the dumpster. Don't ask them to deliver it though. If it's new stuff you are going to buy, they may deliver that free once you buy it. They'll even cut it for you to the width of your aisles.

Brick Paths

In my PBS TV garden, we had a small 15 × 15 area with several boxes and plain dirt aisles. I spent five minutes every week running an action hoe over the soil to cut off any new weeds, and it looked pretty nice. But then in one of the classes I was giving, some of the ladies wanted to know how to lay brick so I thought this would be fun to teach as well as improving the garden. So without moving the boxes, we laid down many layers of newspaper. Next we added a 1-inch layer of sand and then started laying bricks right on that sand base. No mortar or cement is needed—just fill in the tight joints with loose sand. When we got to the existing 4 × 4 garden boxes, we just went right around them. It went well and in one afternoon it was all done. What an improvement—wow! We added some patio furniture, and this area became a favorite spot to sit and enjoy the yard and gardens. We also began to notice more of a different kind of visitor to the garden—the

Frost-resistant bricks or pavers make smart paths. Bed them down on a sand bed and take time to tap each brick down as shown so it is even and level with the other bricks.

birds and bees and butterflies and so many more insects. And all for the price of a few bricks (well, a small truckload actually) and a little sand.

One Last Idea

How would you like to carpet your garden . . . wall to wall? Well, you can. Buy new or used indoor/outdoor patio carpeting. It even comes in a grass style but, don't worry, you won't have to mow it!

LET'S REVIEW

When building a SFG, start with the basic building block—a 4 × 4 bottomless wood box. Then, depending on the situation, add special features to solve any gardening problem or to protect your garden from any hazard. Some of the simple additions you can add to your SFG boxes:

- A wire bottom to keep out moles, voles, and gophers
- A weed cloth bottom to keep out weeds or grass
- A chicken wire top to keep out cats, dogs, and rabbits
- A PVC top frame then:
- Clear plastic to create a miniature greenhouse
- Bird or deer netting
- A blanket to protect plants from frosts
- Floating covers to protect from insects
- The possibilities are endless for everyone, from apartment dwellers to the elderly, and even people with special needs.

After all this talk about building all these different things for protecting your garden, I don't want you to become worried, thinking that you have to spend a lot of time creating complex structures for your SFG. It's not so! We've just learned how easy it is to adjust a SFG to improve its flexibility and to accommodate unique gardening situations. This is readily done since a SFG is so small and manageable. For the most part, your plants will just sit there quietly growing, looking better and better every day. So relax and enjoy!

Family

But remember, protecting your garden is a lot like protecting your children—if it's cold, add a blanket (a sweater); if sleet and hail are predicted, add clear plastic (a raincoat); and if it's windy, add an extra shield against the wind (a windbreaker). Since you wouldn't let your kids play out in the cold winter without a snowsuit for protection, do the same for your plants. Keeping this in mind, you'll be able to come up with easy and practical solutions for protecting your garden from the worst of conditions. That makes it very rewarding because then you can enjoy your garden much longer every year.

Mel's Mix, Essential for Square Foot Gardening Success

Mel's Mix is the most important, productive, essential, necessary, critical, major subject and is the backbone of the entire book and the Square Foot Gardening method!

Mix up a batch of Mel's Mix once and you're done with the soil for your SFG!

The Perfect Soil

Mel's Mix is the reason all the other improvements are possible. So, please, pay attention, study, and learn everything in this chapter so you can make your Mel's Mix the best you can. This will allow you to automatically have all the other benefits and improvements that come so naturally to (the all new) SFG.

Don't Skimp On This

Now, with All New Square Foot Gardening you'll never have to do all the hard work, expense, and time-consuming, back-breaking labor of improving your garden soil every spring like we used to do. Your Mel's Mix is ready to go whenever you are. It never has to be replaced and you don't have to do a thing except plant your seeds.

Mel's Mix may be the most costly part of SFG, yet at the same time it is the most cost effective. How can it be both? The answer: if you try to skimp on this item, you'll be disappointed in all the rest. But, if you do it right, all the other advantages of SFG will fall into place and you will be the richest gardener on the block. Sorry to be so adamant, but this is really what makes SFG so different and successful. We have never had a failure of SFG except when someone decided to skimp on the ingredients to save a few bucks.

Let's review what this perfect soil will do for your garden, then the why and how so you fully understand the nature of the mix.

We'll go through each of the three ingredients indicated—compost, peat moss, and vermiculite—and what each one is, why you need it, and where to obtain it all. Then I'll discuss how to mix, moisten, and place it in your boxes. If you do it right, you'll have the most enjoyable gardening experience of your life. That wonderful feeling will be repeated every time you plant and replant every single square foot. Your hand will just slip through the loose, easily worked, earthy-smelling soil, and you will sigh with happiness and smile every time. It is truly an emotional experience that very few gardeners have ever encountered. But enough talk and teasing—let's get started!

No More

The list at right is just some of the knowledge you had to learn about backyard soils in the past. But not now! Forget about every one of them. Why? Because Square Foot Gardening is now so simple you don't have to learn all the intricate details of soil structure, texture, and drainage. You don't even have to know what pH means, how to pronounce it, or which letter is a capital and which is lower case (or why people are always getting that mixed up). Why, you may ask? Because I've designed our perfect soil mix with the correct pH level (acid or alkaline) for just about all plants.

For those of you who crave more information, a good, blended, balanced compost—one of the ingredients in Mel's Mix and what you will add to your boxes after each harvest—made from at least five different ingredients will not only have a pH close to neutral, but it also balances the acidity in peat moss. In addition, since we don't use your existing soil (remember we only need 6 inches of pure Mel's Mix), you won't be concerned with what type of soil it is or what the pH is. You won't have to buy a pH soil test kit or take samples to your county extension agent. You won't have to learn that eastern U.S. soils are slightly acidic while western soils are more alkaline, and you won't have to learn what to add, how much, and when. You won't have to buy a spreader or any of that stuff.

No Fertilizer, No Mess

Mel's Mix has all the nutrients, minerals, and trace elements that plants need. So forget all about fertilizer. Isn't that amazing? Not only do you not have to buy it, you don't even have to learn about it. SFG is an all-organic, all-natural method.

Come spring you'll find there is no work to do; there is no going to the store, reading labels, lugging big bags or bales of soil additives home, no spreading them out, working in lime, getting a rototiller running and working—then trying to turn over that wet, mucky soil, getting it all over your shoes and tools—oh, what a mess that was. But that is all a thing of the past. Why, you don't even have to do the soilball test in the palm of your hand only to find out you have to wait

THINGS YOU HAVE TO KNOW TO ACHIEVE . . .	
. . . Backyard Soil for Single Row Gardening	**. . . Mel's Mix for SFG**
■ Structure	■ The Formula
■ Drainage	
■ Texture	
■ Organic content	
■ pH	
■ Fertilizer	
■ Blending	

another week because your soil is too wet or still frozen. (What's the soilball test, you ask? I'm not going to tell you because you don't need to know it any longer.)

Your Mel's Mix is always ready to plant no matter what the weather. It's always loose, friable (which the experts define as that which is easily worked—good and crumbly), and ready for the right time of year to plant. It drains and becomes unfrozen so much quicker than regular garden soil.

MY SIMPLE FORMULA

1/3 **Garden Compost**
1/3 **Peat Moss**
1/3 **Vermiculite**

Mix equal parts of each, measured by volume not by weight.

WHERE HAVE YOU BEEN?

Planting a garden will no longer depend on when the soil is ready but only on the right date to plant seeds and transplants. This is just one more simplification of gardening the Square Foot way. How does that all sound? Simple and easy—no work, no muss, no fuss. I have had people ask me, "Why weren't you born one hundred years ago so I could have started with Square Foot Gardening instead of having to do all the work of single-row gardening all my life?" Good question!

NO DIGGING

Using Mel's Mix completely eliminates all the hard work of digging and moving existing soil. A 4 × 4 × 12-inch-deep area contains 16 cubic feet of soil that weighs well over 400 pounds. That's a lot of soil to dig up and move around. All gardening in the past has been based upon improving your existing soil. Don't even be concerned about it. You don't have to know anything about soils. Just start with a perfect growing soil—Mel's Mix of one-third compost, one-third peat moss, and one-third vermiculite measured by volume.

LIKE A SPONGE

Through many experiments, I came up with the very best ingredients for that perfect growing soil. Of course, I made sure they were all inexpensive, readily available, and able to hold just the right amount of moisture for plants while not becoming too soggy for roots, which might drown your plants. I created a formula that holds moisture yet drains well.

At first this seemed like an impossible task, but then I thought about sponges. When you take a dry sponge and slowly add water to it, it just keeps soaking up water until it's finally saturated. At that point, any extra water just drains out the bottom. Well, it turns out that two of our ingredients—peat moss and vermiculite—do exactly that same thing. It takes a while to wet them and keep them moist so you have to keep adding water, but finally, when they become saturated, any excess water just drains right out the bottom. Peat moss and vermiculite are sold at garden nurseries, home improvement centers, and even some grocery stores.

MATH 101

The biggest problem turns out to be arithmetic, not the materials. All three ingredients in Mel's Mix are sold in different-sized bags or bales, and this may make it harder to figure out how much of each you need. But, don't worry, I'm going to give you some examples so you won't even have to think about the math.

Three ingredients make up Mel's Mix: Peat moss, vermiculite, and blended compost. Combined properly, Mel's Mix retains moisture, drains perfectly, and has all the nutrients and trace minerals a plant could ever want. Note: If the volume is not marked on the bags, compare them to similarly sized bags on which the volume is marked.

Make a neat cut in the top of your bags. This way, when you've finished making your own Mel's Mix, you can reuse the bags to store any leftover mix.

1 COMPOST

Let's take a minute to describe compost. It is one-third of the Mel's Mix, and it is also what you add to your All New Square Foot Garden after you harvest each square foot. So what is it, how do you make it, and why bother?

Compost is absolutely the best material in which to grow your plants. Good compost has all the nutrients needed for plant growth. It's loose and friable and easily worked. It holds lots of moisture yet drains well. It's easy to make yet hard to find. The best kind is homemade compost that you make in your own backyard. The worst kind is the single ingredient byproduct some company has produced and bagged.

Good and Bad

So, let's simplify garden composting and garden compost. First off, it's a very confusing subject because the word "compost" is both a noun and a verb. As a noun, compost is described as a rich, crumbly, soil-like material used in gardening. As a verb, it is the process of breaking down plant material that is no longer growing through a decomposition process.

To complicate the understanding of the garden-related, breaking-down process (compost as a verb), there are actually two types of processes—aerobic, with air; and anaerobic, without air. Both are a natural, Mother Earth process. But the first, or aerobic, has no odor, heats up, and does its job with little microbes wearing white hats (the good guys). The second, or anaerobic process, smells, is messy, and is very objectionable. The more common name for this is rotting. I don't have to tell you that all these microbe bugs wear black hats (the bad guys). It's true all those bad-guy, black-hat items will eventually decompose, but you don't want to be around while they do.

What to Use

Any plant material is perfect for adding to your compost pile as long as it's not hosting a plant disease or pest. When the ingredients are all piled together and if they have enough bulk, they will decompose organically by the aerobic process all by themselves. But it takes time; Mother Nature can't be hurried. Some people say, "I can't wait for a year or two. How can I speed this process?" The answer—mix, mash, moisten, and move.

Needs Mass

Using the right ingredients and mixing, mashing, moistening, and moving them will help speed the composting. But there is one more ideal condition, and that is mass. The more bulk you have in your pile (up to a certain point), the faster it will compost or decompose. If your pile is taller than 4 feet, you'll have a hard time adding new ingredients. If the area is larger than 4 × 4, the air will have trouble getting into the center where all the action is and the white-hat, good-guy microbes will turn into the black-hat, bad-guy microbes and the pile will start to decompose anaerobically (without air) and start to smell. If you don't have enough bulk—smaller than 3 × 3, your pile will just sit there and do nothing except cry out, "I'm going to wait for Mother Nature."

We keep calling it a pile, and you may wonder if it will be ugly and messy. But the pile can be contained very nicely with a homemade or store-bought container called a composter. (Oh no! Another name!) So now, I'm going to be composting my compost in my composter. You've got it! See, that wasn't so bad.

MEL'S MIX IS MADE FROM . . .

One-third by volume garden compost

On-third by volume peat moss

One-third by volume vermiculite

Garden compost that is dark, crumbly and ready to use. If there are a few large bits that have not broken down, simply add them back into the compost bin.

QUICK COMPOST

Keep everything moist, make a big pile, and keep turning it. How often? Every day if you want the finished compost in two weeks; every week for results in three months; or every month for it to be ready in a year. The ideal conditions for the fastest results are:

1. Mix—add as many different, plant-based ingredients as you can find.

2. Mash—chop everything up into small pieces.

3. Moisten—not dry or wet, just moist.

4. Move—keep turning the pile towards the center where all the action is.

The results will be the most amazing material you could hope for in your garden. It's often called black gold because of the color of the finished product called compost.

Still Confused?

I had no idea people would be so confused about composting until I realized that only 10 percent of gardeners actually compost, another 10 percent don't ever want to compost, and the middle 80 percent say they would like to but are confused and scared by the process. Of course, much of that confusion is from not knowing how to compost aerobically.

Let's summarize.

Compost Ingredients

What you need to remember about the ingredients is that animal byproducts are not good for your compost. Eggshells are okay; just crush and sprinkle around. Manure is okay from plant-eating animals, but no manure from meat-eating animals.

TURN THE HANDLES OR CHOP, CHOP, CHOP

If you are in a real hurry, there are expensive, but effective, rotating drum composters you can buy. You just turn a handle, flip a container, or push a barrel around, and the contents are mixed and moved. Great idea, and they work if you do it regularly.

TIPS FOR SUCCESSFUL COMPOSTING

	Do	Don't
Ingredients	Add plant material such as top growth, prunings, roots, and kitchen scraps	Do not add any animal parts such as bones or synthetic materials
Bin Size	About 3 x 3 feet	Smaller than 3 x 3 feet or larger than 4 x 4 feet
Moisture	Moist	Too dry or too wet
Mixing	As often as you can	Never

I've also heard of, but never tried, the closed, black-plastic-bag-of-ingredients-left-in-the-garage-over-the-winter method. Be careful when you open the bag because, as you can guess, that method uses the black-hat, no air, anaerobic process that smells.

Some gardeners have tried using plastic or molded garbage cans or even larger trash containers. You have to drill or poke holes in them so the air can get in, but if the lid is tight-fitting, you could roll it around every day.

On my PBS TV program, I showed how to make a rolling composter out of an old, cleaned oil drum. You could push it with your foot to roll it around. It was great.

I've found from my own experimenting that, no matter what method you use, the sooner you mix and move and the more you mash (cut or chop), the sooner and faster you'll start the composting action going. Just add compost ingredients by mixing it in with the top of the existing pile. Each time you add a lot or just a little, stir it into the top of the pile and mix it in well. But, don't just add it in layers.

PRACTICAL COMPOSTING TIPS

Mow Those Leaves

Save some of your leaves from fall to add to the compost pile next year rather than all at once. After you rake them up, run the lawnmower over them to chop them up and then stuff into plastic bags (make sure they are dry) or, if you are a "neatnik," store them in gray garbage bins stored along the wall of your compost operation.

Dry That Grass

Others like to save their grass clippings the same way, but you have to be very careful. If piled up, fresh green grass will quickly turn into a black-hat, anaerobic operation that's a stinking, slimy, gooey mess. Grass clippings have to be dried before adding them to the pile or

DETAILED LIST OF INGREDIENTS

Yes	Caution - Limited Amounts	No
Each item should be under 20 percent of total by volume	*Each item should be under 10 percent of total by volume*	*These items should not be added to a compost bin*
Straw	Corn cobs	Diseased or pest-laden materials
Hay (including salt hay)	Shredded twigs	Meat or bones
Leaves	Shredded bark	Grease
Grass clippings (dried)	Pine needles	Whole eggs
Old sod	Hedge trimmings	Cheese
Reject or spoiled garden produce	Wood shavings	Seeds and fruit pits
Vegetable and fruit peels	Sawdust	Cat or dog manure
Newspaper (shredded)	Coffee grounds	Bakery products
Eggshells (crushed)	Peanut shells	Dairy products
Stable or poultry manure		Kitchen scraps
Tea bags		

stored for later addition. It does seem like an oxymoron to dry the grass clippings only to moisten them in the compost pile, but now I'm sure you can see why we do it that way.

I compare it to my mother's meatloaf. She would dry bread and then crumble it to make bread crumbs. She would then add milk to moisten everything. If she had just added moist, fresh bread, it would have gotten clumpy and gooey. The compost is similar. If material is put in wet, it packs down in clumps preventing air from entering the pile, and then it rots and smells.

So spread your grass clippings out on a tarp or the driveway, turn them a few times with a rake or flip your tarp before storing them or adding them to your compost pile. How long? Until the grass is brownish and dry to the touch. It depends on the sun, humidity, and rain, as well as the climate of your location.

> "My square foot garden has been the most productive, lowest maintenance garden I've ever had."
> – Pat from Utah

Mix and Turn

This is a good time to remind you that the center of the pile is where most of the action is. It will be the hottest (up to 150°F or 65°C), the moistest, and with the most white-hats running around decomposing the ingredients. Knowing all that when you turn the contents of one compost bin into another, you will be putting the top of A into the bottom of B—assuming you have two bins or piles side-by-side—then you make sure you put the outside material of A into the inside of B. Get it? It's just like the theory that opposites attract. Mix in (at the same time) opposite colors, wetness, size—everything opposite for the fastest operation. In other words, brown with green, wet with dry, coarse with fine. That's all easy to remember—just think of opposites attracting and you'll have a great operation.

IF YOU DECIDE TO BUY COMPOST

Don't buy all of one kind of compost if you decide to not make it yourself. Don't let the clerk sell you the "best and most popular," especially if it's loose and not bagged. Here's why. All commercial compost is a byproduct from one industry. It might be the wood, cattle, mushroom, cannery, cotton, or soybean industry that has a waste product and they have to get rid of it. They said, "What if we take our waste product (sawdust, manure, vines, pulp, or husks) and compost it, people will pay us and take it away." Everyone laughed but, by golly, it happened just that way. Now every industry with a waste product is finding ways to get rid of it at a profit all the while protecting the environment. What a good deal. The only setback for gardeners is most bags of compost come from a single product and have only one ingredient.

What's the solution? Buy a variety of composts and mix them together. Now, you are more likely to get a better mixture.

GO BIG TIME

If you are really into this, you can brainstorm to think of places that throw out organic or plant material. Like a bird shop and all those bird droppings that go on the bottom of the cage. And, how about the annual fire department community breakfast—fresh fruit, banana and orange peels maybe, but also how about eggshells? Just ask ahead—take boxes or bags and ask them to separate the trash. Or, how about the annual 4th of July watermelon picnic in town? There are all kinds of places where you can collect ingredients for your compost pile. And, you know, the nice thing is that you'll find the same situation the world over.

When I'm visiting foreign countries, my hosts say, "We are poor here, and we have nothing to compost." I take them on a tour and find all of these places that have things that could be composted. It's always things people are throwing out. I've done that in India, Haiti, Argentina, Nepal, Thailand,

PENNY PINCHER

Your home operation should include every different thing you can think of. Go to the grocery store and ask for the produce manager. Many stores throw out tons of spoiled vegetables and fruits they can't sell. These are from all over the world, so just think of the different soils and climates all that has grown in and what different vitamins, minerals, and trace elements they contain. If they're not diseased, chop them up and mix them in the compost pile. Anyplace people gather, there will be waste thrown out. Check out farmer's markets, local fairs or street carnivals, flea markets, even places like Starbucks (guess what they would have for you there?). In addition to compost material, many of these restaurant-type places have big buckets used for pickles, mayonnaise, or oil that make great water buckets—all free for the asking.

Ghana, and even in London, Paris, Amsterdam, and New York City, so don't be afraid to go, look, and ask—it's out there.

2 PEAT MOSS

The second ingredient in Mel's Mix is peat moss. It's a natural material occurring on the earth that has been made after millions of years from decomposing plant material. You can usually determine how old peat moss is by measuring how deeply it's buried. It is commonly used in agriculture to improve existing soils because it makes them lighter, more friable, and water retentive.

There are plenty of debates about the use of peat moss because it's a nonrenewable resource. Because there is a limit to this valuable material I'd like to guide you in using it responsibly while maximizing its benefits.

Only a Little

The SFG method uses only 20 percent of the space of traditional single-row gardens. Therefore, you automatically use only 20 percent—one-fifth—as much peat moss, an 80 percent reduction. In addition, with Square Foot Gardening, you add peat moss once and only once when you first create your Mel's Mix. Thereafter, you'll never need to add peat moss to the garden. (What you will add is compost, which is renewable.)

In the United States, most peat moss comes from the northern states and Canada where it is still readily available. Because it's such a valuable resource, SFG says let's not waste it. Instead let's get rid of all single-row gardens that require five times as much nonrenewable materials to improve the soil year after year. Let's be conservative and sensible and use what we have, a beneficial, natural material, but make it longer lasting.

3 VERMICULITE

Vermiculite, the third and final ingredient in Mel's Mix, is also a natural material and is obtainable all over the world. It's mica rock mined out of the ground. Once the rock is collected, it is then ground up into small particles and heated until it explodes just like popcorn, forming small pieces from as large as the tip of your little finger down to almost a powder. However, this material is filled with nooks and crannies, just like an English muffin. These nooks and crannies hold a tremendous amount of water and yet can breathe, making the soil extremely friable and loose. The moisture is always there for the roots to absorb. Remember that roots don't grow through soil; they grow around soil particles. That's why plants do better in a loose, friable soil because the roots have an easy time growing.

Certified

Vermiculite is graded into several sizes—fine, medium, and coarse—and is also tested and qualified for different types of uses. The coarse agricultural grade holds the most moisture while at the same time giving the most friability to the soil mix. You may find that some stores do not carry vermiculite. If you ask them why, you might hear a story that started many years ago when one mine in Montana was shut down because part of the mine was found to contain asbestos. Now, shutting down a mine because it contains asbestos makes sense.

However, some newspaper stories associated the problem with all of the products coming from the mine. Although the mine was shut down and the industry has produced a great deal of evidence that the contamination was not in the vermiculite, the story surfaces every few years as if it was new, thereby getting everyone upset all over again. It was a serious situation, but as a result, the good news is that all the vermiculite mines around the world and products sold are now meticulously inspected by everyone; the bags we buy now even come with a "Certified Asbestos Free" sticker.

Locating it can be difficult. Let your fingers do the walking and call around. Call all the major nurseries, garden supply centers, and major home improvement stores and try to get the garden manager on the phone and ask them if they carry the large 4-cubic-foot bags of coarse

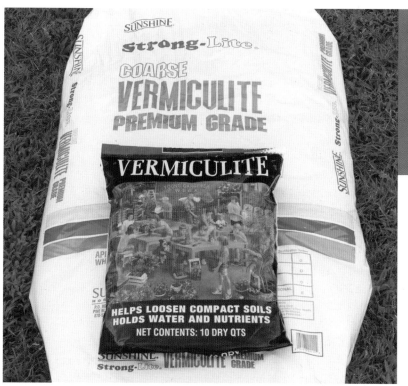

Smaller bags, such as the black bag of vermiculite shown here, are much more expensive than larger quantities. Look for vermiculite in 4.0 cubic foot sizes. Don't settle for smaller bags measured in quarts.

vermiculite because you're building a Square Foot Garden. If that fails, look under "greenhouse supplies or suppliers" in the yellow pages for wholesale distributors. Some people have found it at farm feed stores or even on the Internet.

There is one caution when you mix it, and it is the same caution with peat moss. Both materials are dusty when dry right out of the bag so wear gloves and a painting mask. Mix only outdoors on a calm day.

Perlite Instead of Vermiculite?

Perlite is another natural material mined out of the earth and used in agriculture for the same purpose as vermiculite—to break up and loosen poor soils and to retain moisture. I personally don't like or use perlite, and here's why. It is hard as a rock, rather coarse and gritty, and I don't like the feel of it in the soil mix. It doesn't hold moisture like vermiculite. In addition, it floats to the top of the soil mix as you water your garden and because it's white, it looks rather unsightly and unnatural. And it makes me sneeze! Many people do use perlite instead of vermiculite and, in fact, most of the commercial mixes are made with perlite because it's cheaper. It's a matter of preference and availability, but I know which one I'm buying.

BUYING WHAT YOU NEED

If you found the math about area difficult in previous chapters, don't even bother with volume. Get the kids to do the math for you.

Why concern yourself with volume? Because you need to know the quantity of the three ingredients for Mel's Mix necessary to fill your boxes, and the packages for the different ingredients come in different sizes. But the good news is they usually use cubic feet as their measurement. If not, disregard weight and estimate by volume.

So, let's review how to figure volume. Volume is merely: area × depth = cubic feet. In other words, square feet (the area) times the depth equals cubic feet.

Our 4 × 4-foot box is 16 square feet in area (that's 4 feet times 4 feet). If it were 1 foot deep, the volume would be: 16 (the area) times 1 (the depth) equals 16 cubic feet. But it's not 1 foot deep, it's only 6 inches deep so we need only one-half or just 8 cubic feet for our 4 × 4 box. The math looks like this: 4 times 4 divided by one-half foot equals 8. Or to show it mathematically, $(4 \times 4)/2 = 8$. (Now don't laugh, kids, some of the parents will be thankful for this kind of help).

Peat Moss (Compressed bale)

Full bale: 3.9 cubic feet compressed = 8 cubic feet loose
Half bale: 2.2 cubic feet compressed = 4 cubic feet loose
(These measurements aren't exact, but we're not mixing a cake here.)

Vermiculite (coarse)

Don't buy the small 4-quart sized or similar bag—insist on the 4-cubic-feet big bag. Call ahead to locate.

MEL'S MIX VOLUME

Now here's the tricky part. Since all the products for Mel's Mix come in different volumes, you'll have to purchase them already knowing how much you'll need to mix correctly and fill your boxes completely. Let's use a hypothetical example. If we had 4 × 4 boxes, they would each have a volume of 8 cubic feet, as we determined already. So, if we had six boxes to fill, we would need 6 × 8 = 48 cubic feet of mix. (Six boxes times 8 cubic feet for each box equals 48 cubic feet of mix.) One-third of the total for each ingredient = 48/3 = 16 cubic feet of each. (A total of 48 cubic feet divided by three different ingredients equals 16 cubic feet of each ingredient.)

> ### AREA x DEPTH EQUALS CUBIC FEET
>
> Multiply the width of your box, and divide it by 2 to figure out how much volume your six-inch-deep box will hold.
>
> (4 x 4) / 2 = 8 cubic feet
>
> (4 x 8) / 2 = 16 cubic feet
>
> (4 x 12) / 2 = 24 cubic feet
>
> (4 x 16) / 2 = 32 cubic feet

Shopping list

- Peat Moss: 16/8 = two full bales
- Vermiculite: 16/4 = four big bags
- Compost: Whatever it takes to get 16 cubic feet of five different kinds. Forget weight, measure by volume.

More Shopping Lists for Different Sized Batches

If you had three 4 × 4 boxes (24 cubic feet total), you would need:

- two 4-cubic-foot bags of coarse vermiculite to equal 8 cubic feet.
- one 3.9-cubic-foot bale of peat moss (expands to 8 cubic feet).
- and 8 cubic feet from at least five different types of compost bags.

If the bags are sold by weight only, estimate volume by comparing to similar sized bags that note volume.

If you had one 4 × 4 box and one 2 × 4 or one 3 × 3 box (12 cubic feet), and you wanted to mix up half of a batch to start with, you would add together just one 4-cubic-foot bag of vermiculite, half of a 3.9-cubic-foot bale of peat moss (or if you can find the 2.2-cubic-foot bales that expand to equal about 4 cubic feet loose), and two of the 2-cubic-foot bags of compost. If the compost comes in other sized bags, you may have to do a little arithmetic. That's enough Mel's Mix to fill one 4 × 4 box that needs 8 cubic feet

> *"Your book, website and method are just fantastic."*
> *– Annie from New Jersey*

plus one 2 × 4 box that needs four cubic feet, or one 3 × 3 box that needs 4½ cubic feet.

HOW TO MIX

This is where making your Mel's Mix and filling your boxes starts to get fun. Mix it all at once if possible (storing any excess in recycled bags). But if it's too big a batch to handle, split it into smaller batches.

Here's a suggestion: Use a pair of scissors to cut open your bags carefully along the top so you can reuse them. At the same time explain to the kids the environmental three R's—reduce, reuse, and recycle. Our Square Foot Gardening system is a great example of:

1. reduce, by 80 percent,
2. reuse, save the bags, and
3. recycle plants in your compost.

Get a large tarp, at least 16 × 16-feet, and open it near your garden where you have all your boxes built and located. Make sure you have them in their final resting place—check with the boss one more time and ask, "Are you sure this is where you want all the boxes, dear?"

All of the three ingredients are dusty when dry, so do this when there is no wind. Don't do it in the garage, or you'll get dust all over your nice new car or workshop. Wear a painter's mask and have a hose ready with a very fine spray. Don't forget to have a few mixing tools ready like a snow shovel, a hoe, or a steel rake.

Count out the bags and boxes, do the math one more time and start opening the bags and pouring the contents out on the tarp without walking on the ingredients. Roughly mix the three ingredients as best you can as you pour it.

Then drag two corners of the tarp to the opposite two corners. You'll see the material roll over, mixing itself. When you've pulled the tarp so that the mixture is almost to the edge, move 90 degrees and pull those two corners over. You just work your way around the tarp and repeat pulling corners together until your Mel's Mix is uniformly mixed. It's finished when you don't see any single material or one color.

Use the hose with a fine mist or spray to wet down any dust, but don't spray so much you make puddles or wet the ingredients so the mixture becomes too heavy to move easily. Don't let the kids play in the mixture, or they will crush the large particles of vermiculite. (By the way, I'd save a small plastic bag of vermiculite for seed starting. We'll get to seed starting in the next chapter.)

The next step is to fill the boxes, wetting down the mixed-in layers only as you fill it. Once the box is full and the top leveled off, don't pack it down. It will settle just right by itself.

How to Make Mel's Mix

Empty the five bags of different kinds of compost in the center of a large tarp. You'll wind up with a large pile of blended compost.

To mix the composts, take two corners of the tarp and drag the tarp over itself until the pile rolls to the edge of the tarp. It helps to have two people to do this.

(continued on next page)

How to Make Mel's Mix (continued)

Once the compost is well mixed, add the vermiculite.

Next add in the peat moss, dumping it on top of the other ingredients.

These ingredients can be dusty, so mist them lightly before mixing. You may also want to wear a dust mask.

The finished Mel's Mix should look similar to this, with all the ingredients well distributed throughout the mix.

Using a Wheelbarrow

You can mix your Mel's Mix in a large-capacity wheelbarrow. Add equal quantities of garden compost, vermiculite and peat moss, each in a third of the wheelbarrow.

Use a garden spade or shovel to carefully mix all the ingredients thoroughly. The ingredients may create dust; you can mist the mix lightly, but don't soak it. When mixed, simply tip directly into your SFG box.

Working with Mel's Mix—especially when using your hands—it's easy to see the difference between this perfect soil and yard soil. The structure and quality is unequalled.

If you have any leftover Mel's Mix, put it back in the empty bags you set aside for reuse. That extra Mel's Mix will come in handy to fill four-packs and use for transplants as well as extra to top off the boxes when the soil level settles. Turn the bags inside out if you want a plain look, label with a marker, and put them aside. Since you don't really water the mix until it's in the box, your stored mix will be fairly dry and lightweight to carry.

To fill other boxes, work with someone else to drag the tarp close to the new boxes. Don't try to carry shovelfuls of mix to the box as it will spill and be wasted. This is precious stuff. (Remember what Grandma always said, "Waste not, want not.")

That's also why we don't water the Mel's Mix in the tarp, but as you are adding it to the box—that way the remaining material in the tarp doesn't get so heavy that it is hard to drag. As soon as you add your grid to each box, you are ready to plant.

> **Don't wet the soil any more than is absolutely necessary; use a fine spray to reduce any dust. Soil becomes very heavy when wet, and it would be difficult to drag the tarp around your yard.**

You have now completed the most important and rewarding step in SFG. If you followed the formula correctly, and didn't add any of your existing soil, it will stay loose and friable as long as you live and you will be so excited and happy. You may have to keep one square just for show; visitors to your garden will watch as you say, "Just look at this soil as you run your hands through it." Many of you will then add, "Here, you try it. Just feel this soil." (But don't become a pest.)

AN AFTERTHOUGHT

I want to make doubly sure you got the message of this chapter, so I'd like to summarize the critical facts about compost. You need blended compost made from at least five different ingredients. Mix several different types of compost together if you buy your compost. Most commercial composts have only one or two ingredients because they are merely leftover waste materials or byproducts from an industrial or commercial operation. By themselves, they do not make a good ingredient in Mel's Mix.

However, the good news is, if you can find at least five of these individual composted materials you can mix them together to make a well-rounded blended compost ingredient for your Mel's Mix.

And if you did your job and got a blended compost made from at least five major ingredients, you will be blessed with the most wonderful garden you could ever imagine. And no more work ever.

6

How to Plant Your All New Square Foot Garden

Now we're getting to the interesting and fun part of Square Foot Gardening. You've learned all of the basics. You've picked the size, shape, and location of your garden. You've built the frames, put in the Mel's Mix, and added the grids. Now it's time to plant.

Planting Square by Square

This chapter is going to instruct you on your plant choices, how to put your seeds in the garden with the proper spacing (it's as easy as Zip-Zap, Bing-Bing-Bing—you'll see), and growing your own transplants for the quickest, most dependable growth.

VISUALIZE THE HARVEST

In SFG, begin by visualizing what you want to harvest. This simple step prevents you from planting too much. Picture a large plant like a head of cabbage. That single cabbage will take up a whole square foot so you can only plant one per square foot. It's the same with broccoli and cauliflower. Let's go to the opposite end of the spectrum and think of the small plants like radishes. Sixteen can fit into a single square foot. It's the same for onions and carrots—sixteen per square foot. (Yet that's a 3-inch spacing between plants, which is exactly the same spacing the seed packet recommends as it says "thin to 3 inches apart.")

Mel's got the proof! With your grid in place, it's easy to have a stunning garden by planting a different crop in every square.

PLANT SPACING

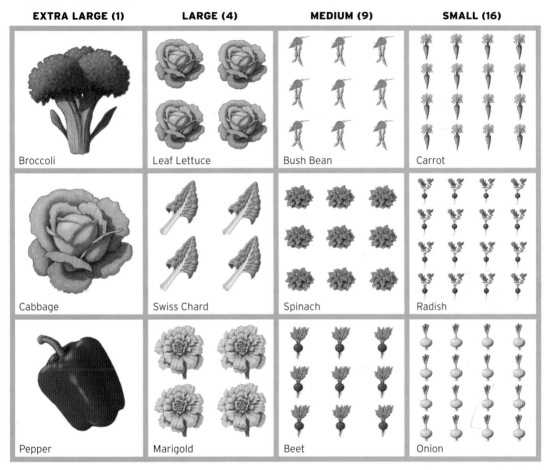

EXTRA LARGE (1) — Broccoli, Cabbage, Pepper

LARGE (4) — Leaf Lettuce, Swiss Chard, Marigold

MEDIUM (9) — Bush Bean, Spinach, Beet

SMALL (16) — Carrot, Radish, Onion

Small, Medium, Large, Extra Large

Think of these plants as if they were shirt sizes. Shirts come in all four sizes: small, medium, large, and extra large, and so do our plants. It's that simple.

The extra large, of course, are those that take up the entire square foot—plants like cabbages, peppers, broccoli, cauliflower, and geraniums. Next are the large plants—those that can be planted four to a square foot, which equals 6 inches apart. Large plants include leaf lettuce, dwarf marigolds, Swiss chard, and parsley.

Several crops could be one per square foot if you let it grow to its full size or it can be planted four per square foot if you harvest the outer leaves throughout the season. This category includes parsley, basil, and even the larger heads of leaf lettuce and Swiss chard. Using the SFG method, you snip and constantly harvest the outer leaves of edible greens, so they don't take up as much space as in a conventional garden.

Medium plants come next. They fit nine to every square foot, which equals 4 inches apart. Medium plants include bush beans, beets, and large turnips.

Another way to get the proper spacing and number per square foot is to be a little more scientific and do a little arithmetic as shown below.

You can see that one, four, nine, or sixteen plants should be spaced an equivalent number of inches apart. This is the same distance the seed packet will say "thin to." Of course we don't have to "thin to" because we don't plant a whole packet of seeds anymore. So if you're planting seeds, or even putting in transplants that you purchased or grew from seed, just find the seed packet or planting directions to see what the distance is for thinning. This distance then determines whether you're going to plant one, four, nine, or sixteen plants.

Just because we're talking about measuring in inches doesn't mean you have to get out your ruler or yardstick, and you don't have to do any complicated measuring or figuring either. This is when the grid becomes handy. When your square foot is bordered by a grid, it's much easier to think one, four, nine, or sixteen plants in each square foot.

All you do is draw lines in the soil with your fingers! For one plant per square foot just poke a hole in the middle of the square with your finger. For four per square foot, draw a vertical and horizontal line dividing the square in half each way. The plants go right in the center of these four smaller squares.

HOW MUCH TO PLANT

I recommend, especially at the beginning, that you plant only what you want to eat. Occasionally try something new, of course, but especially at first only grow those vegetables and herbs that you normally eat.

Remember, plant each adjoining square foot with a different crop. Why? Here are several reasons:

1. It prevents you from overplanting any one particular item.
2. It allows you to stagger your harvest by planting one square foot this week and another of the same crop in two weeks or so.
3. It promotes conservation, companion planting, crop rotation, and allows better plant hygiene and reduced pest problems.
4. It automatically helps to improve your growing soil three times a year in very easy, small steps. Remember the saying, "Square by square, you'll soon be there."
5. Besides all of the above, it looks pretty.

Dividing Your Squares

Each square foot in your SFG can grow one, four, nine or sixteen plants. Here's how to mark out the spacing for planting.

Extra large plants are sown right in the middle of the square. This ensures that the plant doesn't grow into neighboring squares.

For large crops that are grown four to a square, divide the square into four equal sections and poke a hole in the middle of each smaller square.

Sow nine medium plants in a square by dividing the square into nine sections using two fingers spread apart to draw two lines horizontally and vertically.

To sow smaller plants sixteen to a square, divide the square into quarters and then make four holes in each quarter, using two fingers as shown.

Planting Your Squares

SOWING SEEDS

Use your fingers to divide each square into the appropriate number of smaller squares (here into quarters for large plants), and poke a hole in the center of each.

Tip out seeds into the palm of your hand and pinch two to three between your finger and thumb.

Drop the seeds into the hole, taking into account the sowing depth recommended on the seed packet. Cover the seed with Mel's Mix.

Water the square. Use a watering can or your cup and bucket of sunwarmed water, with your hand over the mouth of the cup, fingers spread slightly to sprinkle the water.

PLANTING YOUNG PLANTS

Mark the square for planting as you would with seed. Make a hole with a pencil, moving it around to widen the hole enough for the seedling's or transplant's root ball.

Remove the seedling or transplant from its container, being careful not to damage the young plant. Make sure the root ball is slightly loose.

Settle the transplant or seedling into the hole. Gently firm the soil around the base of the plants, creating a depression around the base to hold water.

Asparagus is a perennial plant that will crop again and again over many years so I suggest you plant a whole box just with asparagus, using these bare roots.

Divide the square into quarters, in the center of each quarter make a little mound 3 inches high to take each bare root plant.

Position the plant at the top of the mound and let the roots hang down, spread them out, and then push in place.

Add more Mel's Mix to cover the roots to an extra depth of 2 inches or so. It can take a couple of years before you can harvest.

Just like a patchwork quilt, the different colors, leaf textures, plant densities, shapes, and heights, plus the visible grid will give you a very distinctive, photo-opportunity garden. You'll just love and admire it every time you see it.

Some people ask, "Why can't we plant all sixteen squares with leaf lettuce or spinach or Swiss chard or whatever we want to plant?" Oh, that's going right back to the single-row mentality. Square Foot Gardening begins with visualizing the harvest. It's very difficult to put in four tiny plants of Swiss chard and think that's going to be enough for the whole family, but one square of red and one square of green chard usually is more than most families eat. Proof of the pudding . . . how many bunches of Swiss chard did you buy last week or even last month? The stores have it, it's fresh, and it looks good, so why didn't you buy any more than you did? Well, it's the same answer as to why you shouldn't plant too much of one thing.

It's worth repeating here that the biggest problem for single-row gardeners has always been "I planted too much. I can't take care of it. It's too much work and I'm sorry now." All that has changed with SFG and you now have boundaries (the grid) and the opportunity to ask yourself, "For every single square foot I plant, is that enough? Do I really want more? Would it be better to plant another square foot of the same thing in a week or two or three?"

TIME OF YEAR

Keep in mind that you can build a Square Foot Garden anytime of the year—spring, summer, fall, and even winter. For most of the country, you could start planting in any season other than winter. What time of the year is it right now for you and where are you in the sequence of a yearly gardening cycle? Think of it like the movie theater before the main feature. You're all settled in with your popcorn, ready to devote your full attention to the movie. In the gardening year, this is usually the equivalent of springtime. What if you came in the middle of the picture? For gardening that would be summertime. You can still plant a warm-weather crop even if you missed the spring crop. If it's now fall, you can still start your SFG with a great cool-weather crop and get some valuable experience before next spring. Start whenever you get the urge to plant.

For convenience, we'll start with the beginning of the garden year for most of the country, springtime. (Some parts of the country, like Texas and Florida, can grow all year long. You lucky people.)

Seasonal Plants

You can get at least three crops a year in every square foot of your SFG. Every choice is going to be fun, exciting, and tasty. Of course, your selection depends on the time of year, and what you and your family need and want. There are two types of crops when you consider weather. The first are called cool-weather crops that do best in the spring and fall, but won't survive in the hot summer. The second group is the warm- or hot-weather crops that, you guessed it, don't do well in the cool weather of spring and fall, but thrive in the hot weather of summer.

HARDINESS AND PROTECTION WITH SFG

SFG's size makes it very easy to protect your new plantings from an extra early or late frost. There's a lot more information about frosts and freezes in Chapter 9, especially if you are interested in extending the season, as well as ways to protect your plants so you can get more from your garden.

Plants aren't all the same, of course. They are just like people. Some can stand the heat, cold, or humidity better than others. We classify these as hardy, and those that can't handle it as non-hardy. Each of the four seasons has three time periods—the early season, midseason, and late season. If you're thinking about a spring crop, for example, there may be some vegetables that can only grow in the mid-part of the spring while others can tolerate a little more cold in the beginning of the season, but can't stand any heat at all near the late part of the season. It takes a little while to get used to which is which, and how best they fit in with your planting schedule.

Though the weather is never exactly the same every year, it helps to know a plant's hardiness. Don't worry—you'll learn it in time. This is not an exact science so relax if you're a beginner and just enjoy the ride. Don't expect to find a perfect list because how well plants thrive differs in different parts of the country and of course, different years, sometimes for no explainable reason. If you lose a few squares of something one year it's no big deal. It doesn't mean you're not going to be a great gardener.

Frost Dates

Although people like to celebrate the first day of spring (March 20th) according to the calendar, plants don't give a hoot about our calendar—they respond to weather. In the spring we need to know the date of the last frost in our area. That will help us determine when to plant. Each different crop—whether cool-season or warm-season—will need to be planted so many weeks before or after that last day of frost.

HOW NOT TO SELECT PLANTS

Looking through a seed catalog is not the best way to decide what to grow. They make it all look so good and sound so exciting that you can easily get carried away. I recommend you review your shopping list from last week and last month. That eliminates the "Oh, I'd like to grow that!" or "Wouldn't it be fun to grow peanuts?" Start simple and easy with the foods you already eat regularly. Expand and experiment later on.

So often I hear "But I'm so anxious to start my SFG. I've always wanted a garden. I want to grow everything." Well, if you've been wishing and wanting to grow for twenty years, spending the first year getting experience and confidence with the SFG method won't make any difference. Then spend the next forty years enjoying your garden. Don't ruin a lifetime hobby by starting off too big.

For plants, the fall growing season begins not with the first calendar day of fall (September 23rd), but with the first frost and continues until the first freeze of the fall. The average dates of your first and last frost depend on where you live in the country and the regional and local variations of weather. All we can do is go by the past and hope it will be similar this year. To help, the government collects dates for your area and calculates the average date from the past one hundred years. Of course, the average is only a guide.

> "You have got me so excited about gardening again; I love teaching SFG. It is so much more successful than other methods. I don't know why all gardeners and farmers aren't using it."
> – Mike from Utah

How do you find your local frost dates? The Internet is the best resource for detailed information. You can also call your local county extension agent or most area nurseries. To find your local extension agent, look in the government blue pages for your county in your telephone book, then look for the heading "Extension of [your state] University."

Frost Date Websites

You can access your frost dates on any number of websites, by entering "frost dates" in the search engine. The best one I've found is www.victoryseeds.com/frost. This Internet site has the frost dates and hardiness zone maps for the entire United States as well as Canada, and links for hardiness zones for Australia, Europe, the Ukraine (in English), and China (also in English). The hardiness zone map for the United States is interactive, you just point to where you live and click, and you get the information. This site also links to your local university extension service. Let the experts advise you on the varieties that will do best in your local area.

SEQUENCE OF GROWTH

Did you know that plants grow and bloom everywhere in the same sequence? In other words, throughout the country, daffodils bloom in the springtime, then a little later tulips bloom, then it's time for the lilacs to bloom. (Did I leave out dandelions?) Start noticing the sequence in your location. It would include trees, shrubs, flowers, even weeds.

I read a book once about following spring north. It's theoretically possible that if you drive fast enough (and eat and sleep quickly), you could see nothing but tulips in bloom all the way from Georgia to Maine.

If you know what kinds of plants are summer crops (the most popular and well-known vegetables), it's easy to remember that everything else is a spring or fall crop. Summer crops include beans, peppers, eggplants, tomatoes, and squash. If you plant these when it's too early or cool, they'll either die or their growth will most likely be stunted for that year.

CHARTS

I've designed charts for All New Square Foot Gardening so you'll know when to plant and in what order. These charts will guide you along, providing seed-to-sprouting times at certain soil temperatures. I've also included calendar charts that show, based upon area frost dates (assuming you have a frost), how soon before or after a frost you can plant a given crop. You'll find that some plants are very frost-hardy and can be planted much earlier than those that are just on the borderline. Turn to page 262 to 269 to see the charts.

PLAN ON A FALL CROP

As soon as the summer crop is finished, you're ready to plant cool-weather crops for the upcoming fall. These crops are frost-hardy, meaning that both young and mature plants withstand frost. The seeds you plant at the end of summer will sprout quickly since the soil is warmer. Transplants can begin outdoors and grow much faster than the same thing planted in the spring. Look at the charts; compare sprouting times for the same seeds in both spring and summer temperatures.

The fall crop gains an extra advantage from late summer weather. The problem with cool-weather plants in the spring is not cool weather but warm weather at harvest time. A plant's purpose in life is to reproduce seed, and the rising temperatures of an approaching summer make this happen sooner. As it does so, the plant's whole character changes. Many people don't realize that plants like lettuce put up a flower stalk, which then goes to seed. If you wait too long to harvest lettuce, the stalk will shoot up, and the same thing happens to other crops like cabbage. The head splits open, a stalk shoots up, develops flowers, and then turns to seed. It's nature's way of allowing the plant to reproduce, but the plant changes taste when this happens. All the energy goes toward the seed and the plant itself, as far as taste is concerned, becomes rather tough, coarse, and bitter.

In cooler weather, this process is delayed. The plant feels no urgency to complete the growing cycle. So in the fall, the plant slows its maturation process, allowing it to maintain flavor for a longer length of time as temperatures continue to grow cooler and cooler. If it's frost-hardy, it doesn't matter if it is the middle of fall and you start getting frost. Some plants can endure some freezing and still provide a crop for harvesting. Fall is a great time to plant if you put in the right crops.

SOIL TEMPERATURE

Soil temperatures vastly influence sprouting times. For example, if you plant carrot seeds in the summertime when the temperature of the soil is between 60° and 80°F, the seeds will sprout in less than a week. But if you plant the same seeds in early spring when the ground temperature is perhaps 40 degrees, they will take a month and a half to sprout. Just another 10 degrees warmer and they will sprout in a little over two weeks. The chart shows that when the soil is cold and freezing, no seeds will sprout. When it warms up to 40 only half of them will sprout; but as soon as it gets to 50 degrees, suddenly almost all of them will sprout and will continue right through the warmer temperatures of summer and fall.

What happens to seeds when they don't sprout because the ground is cold? They could rot, or fungus could attack them. They could break their dormancy and then go dry. They could be attacked by insects, or dug up by animals or birds. So, the quicker you can get them to sprout the better off they will be.

SPRING, SUMMER, AND FALL CROPS

Some crops, like the cabbage family, take so long to grow that there isn't enough time to plant seeds directly in the garden and wait for the harvest. So you have to buy from nurseries or raise your own transplants indoors ahead of time.

The same situation applies to the warm-weather summer crops like tomatoes, peppers, and eggplants. They take so long to produce that you must plant your garden with transplants. The charts show this all in detail, indicating when to start seeds and when to transplant.

The fall crop is better for raising your own transplants because you will be able to start the seeds in the summertime, raise the

Although it's a great idea to start your own transplants from seed, this is an example of what not to do. It's not necessary to sow so much when you practice the SFG method.

transplants outdoors in your garden, and then move them into their permanent spot in the early fall for late fall harvest.

STARTING SEEDS AND GROWING SEEDLINGS

There are plenty of advantages to growing your own transplants and storing the remaining seeds in their packet until next year. First, seeds cost pennies, while transplants cost dollars. There are many more varieties offered in seed catalogs than as transplants at the nurseries. The only setback is time because growing your own transplants depends on the time and work you can spare. If you're a brand new gardener, however, you may want to wait until next year to start your own transplants. Like everything else in life, we tend to go overboard and do too much and then it becomes a chore. Don't let it happen to you!

Storage of Seeds

If your seeds are stored properly, they will last for many years. Contrary to what the gardening industry would like you to believe, it is not necessary to buy fresh seeds every year or to pour out that whole packet of seeds all at once. SFG teaches you to plant just a pinch of seeds. Then store the rest. By planting just a pinch of seeds instead of a whole packet, you can save a lot of money by saving the excess seeds for next year's crop, and the next year's, and so on. Some seeds will last up to five years. Seed companies guarantee that a certain percentage will sprout; this number is always very high, usually up into the nineties. Of course the seed industry wants you to buy a fresh packet of seeds every year so they can stay in business. There's nothing wrong with that! But there's also nothing wrong with saving money with a more efficient system.

How to Store Seeds

What is the ideal storage condition for seeds? It is just the opposite of the moisture and warmth that make them sprout. You'll want to store them in a cool, dry place—the driest, coldest place in your home. Some people freeze their seeds. But I find they get moisture even if they are in a zip-lock bag because it never seems to be totally airtight. I prefer refrigerating them in a wide-mouth jar with a screw lid. Label your containers and store them in the refrigerator on a back shelf. In each jar place a desiccant packet from a medicine vial, or add a little powdered milk wrapped in a tissue to soak up any excess moisture in the jar.

GERMINATION RATE

What happens to seeds that are in storage? As they grow older, their germination rate (the percentage that sprouts under ideal conditions) gradually diminishes. But the solution is very simple. Plant a pinch of seeds—just two to three—instead of only one to ensure that at least one will sprout. If your seeds are many years old, test the germination rate yourself or just plant three or five or however many seeds depending on how well they sprouted the year before. If you marked the sprouting rate on the packet, you can reasonably estimate how many to plant the next year.

Special Section: Children & SFG

SQUARE FOOT GARDENING WITH CHILDREN

I've always considered Square Foot Gardening a family-friendly activity. It's a great way to get children out of the house, away from video games and the computer, get them some fresh air and exercise. It's also a wonderful way for children to learn everyday lessons from nature as well as become more self-sufficient. It's really fulfilling to see your child's eyes get big as she says, "Look what I grew!" Of course, getting kids involved in SFG means keeping in mind that you're dealing with little people that have short attention spans, unlimited creativity, and tons of energy.

I always try to encourage parents to see all the learning possibilities from a garden and that carries over to inside the house. There are lessons about math, science, biology, nature—all kinds of things your child can learn from his or her SFG. Always keep an eye out for teachable moments because they pop up all the time in Square Foot Gardening!

Off to a Good Start

Start as you would any SFG, with the location. Let your child pick a location but guide them toward one that gets all the sun the plants

This 3 x 3 box is full of quick-growing salad crops sure to keep the young gardener engaged and excited with the harvest.

With SFG, every member of the family can have his or her own box, including the kids!

will need and is as close to a door that your son or daughter regularly uses as possible. (Don't forget, it can be the front door as well as the back!) You want your child to pass it often and be able to see it out of the house—that way they are more likely to interact with their SFG. I think it would be great if you could position their box so that your child can see it from her room. Wouldn't that be wonderful—she looks out her window and sees it every day. That would work especially well for a child's bedroom on the second floor. It's just a real treat if you can send your child out to pick strawberries for her cereal in the morning. That's a special way for kids to learn the value of a garden.

Boxed Fun

With the location selected, you'll want to build the box. I try to let kids do as much as possible in creating their SFG. That's why I say include

Putting together a prefab SFG box like this one found on the Square Foot Gardening website is so easy . . . a child can do it!

them in the whole process of building the 3 × 3 SFG box. Help them in shopping for the lumber, cutting it, drilling holes, and screwing the box together. Even with you helping them out, it gives your child a real feeling of accomplishment, that they did it.

Of course, if you don't have tools or your child is too young you may want to use a pre-fab box, rather than building from scratch. You can still keep them involved with the construction process, even if it's just joining the sides together with a corner block. (Remember to buy a 3 × 3 box for kids less than eight.)

Children often like to personalize their boxes, which is fine, as long as they don't get any toxic materials on the inside of the box or underside of the grid. Let them paint the box with soy paints or other non-toxic paints. Or here's an idea: Let them stamp the sides of the boxes with their own rubber stamps that you can find in a crafts store. You can even help your child stencil her name on the outside of the box! Just let their imagination go (preferably before assembly) and you're sure to see some interesting designs.

Growing a Child's SFG

Children really become engaged in an SFG when they start thinking about what they'll plant. Start with a seed catalog. It's fun to sit down with a child on a rainy day or at night inside and look through those beautiful pictures and wonderful descriptions. Make a list of the things that your child wants to plant, and then sort through the different varieties available. Or go to a nursery with the list and look through the seed packets on the rack.

If you want to get a jump on the season and start building excitement in your son or daughter for their new garden, start some seedlings on a sunny windowsill. Fill small cups with vermiculite, plant the seeds and keep the vermiculite moist. You can imagine the delight on children's faces when they see those seeds start sprouting. They'll be checking them every morning when they get up.

Here's a list of some of the best plants for kids—the ones that will yield the most and grow the fastest.

Radishes. An all-time kid pleaser, radishes grow in as few as three weeks. There are cool and hot-weather varieties and one square provides 16 radishes. Plus, they are pretty much fail-safe.

Lettuces. You might not think this would be such an interesting crop for kids, but they love it. That's because it's quick-growing and gives little ones a way to interact with their garden using their scissors (cutting that dinner salad every night). Choose leaf varieties, which mature more quickly than head types. You can also select from different colors, which are sure to grab a child's interest!

Cherry tomatoes. Every gardener loves tomatoes, but younger gardeners will really appreciate these smaller varieties. When the fruit ripens, your children can just pop them in their mouths for a healthy, tasty treat as they run around playing in the yard. Cherry tomatoes are started by transplants, so take your little gardener with you when you head to the nursery and discuss the different labels on the transplants to pick out the variety that will provide the most interest. Regardless of which you choose, the cherry tomatoes are abundant when they mature, with all those little fruits on a long stem. It's very impressive and worth bragging about. Your child can bring his or her friends over and say, "Look, I grew that!"

Bush beans. Easy to grow, quick, and high yields all make this a kid's garden favorite that grows in many colors and sizes. Kids also get a kick out of growing pole beans up a vertical support. You can teach about different seasons and the natural crop rotation of SFG by replacing the bush beans with snow peas in the fall.

Carrots. Just like radishes, kids seem to love carrots. You'll have to temper their anticipation and desire to pull the carrots before they are mature. But even if they do, you'll just enjoy baby carrots for dinner! I think this is a great opportunity to bring some math into the garden. Carrots take two or three times as long as radishes, so if a radish takes twenty days, ask your little Jane or Johnny how long the carrots will take. How many months is that?

Corn. Choose short varieties and don't be afraid to choose unusual types with multi-colored kernels for added fun. This is also a great way to teach children how to protect their garden bounty from birds and other thieves! But for success, you'll need at least several squares of corn so that they can pollinate. You may even want to plant a whole separate box of corn (and maybe a square of sunflowers for an attractive pairing). One thing's for sure: corn on the cob never seems to go to waste! As fun to eat as it is to grow.

Sunflowers. Beautiful and fun to grow, kids flip over these tall garden flowers, and will enjoy eating the seeds after the flowers are dried. Choose short-stalk varieties so you and your child don't need to stake the sunflowers, and the flowers will be closer to the child's eye level.

Nasturtiums. These are considered prime flowers for including in a children's SFG. They are easy to grow, durable, pretty, and as a bonus, the blossoms can be tossed onto a salad to really amaze your kids!

The Tiny Hands Planting Plan

As you've learned, you can use your fingers to divide up individual squares for planting. So can your children. When I'm working with little ones in the garden, I like to teach them my "Zip, Zap, Bing, Bing, Bing" method.

For instance, for nine per square foot, take two fingers, spread them apart, and draw two lines horizontally (zip), which divides the square into thirds, and then two vertically (zap), so that you've got nine sections. Folks from Texas like to use the "hook-em-horn" sign using the trigger finger and little pinky finger.

For those with smaller hands (kids love doing this), have them use their thumb and the trigger finger, or take one finger and draw two lines separately going each way. Poke nine holes (bing, bing, bing) in the middle of the drawn squares and you're ready to plant your seeds.

It's even more fun marking the sixteen plantings per square foot. Remember, there is no measuring. Divide the square in half each way (eyeball it) by drawing lines in the soil with your finger, the same zip zap (one vertical line and one horizontal line, each dividing the square in half) as described for four per square foot. Then, take two fingers, your trigger and middle fingers, and punch holes in the soil.

They should be spaced about 3 inches apart. Give your kids a ruler and show them how to read it so they can practice their finger spacing. In each of the four squares, go bing, bing, with your fingers, marking two holes each time so there are four holes in each small square.

You'll probably need to help out with smaller seeds, because unreliable motor skills and excitement can lead to way too many seeds being planted. We don't want that, because we want to show our children that gardening is fun—not the unpleasant backbreaking toil that my mother's row garden was for me!

You can make a fun game out of practicing picking up a pinch of smaller seeds indoors, on a table over a piece of white paper. The kids can count how many they picked up and dropped.

Watering

Keeping plants from getting thirsty is a great way to teach kids proper watering methods. You can actually show them how wasteful standing around with a hose spraying everything is. Or how wasteful a sprinkler system is, because they were meant for lawns, to spread water over wide areas, not SFGs. The way we water in SFG is also a chance to teach children about treating plants gently, as they pull aside the lower leaves and slowly pour a cup of sun-warmed water right over the roots. And it's a great time to discuss why we use sun-warmed water—wait till you hear some of the answers they'll come up with!

The Zap, Zap, Bing, Bing, Bing planting system is perfect for the young at heart and the just plain young.

KID QUIZ

Here's a good question for children to think over. Which part of a seed sprouts first? Is it the top stem with its leaves? A fun children's book would have the tops popping out of the ground—looking around and if it likes what it sees and wants to stay, calling down to the root and saying, "Anchor me in." But that's a fairy tale. For all seeds, the root sprouts first and goes down. How does it know to go down? Gravity! After the root gets started and secured with little feeder roots so it can start taking up moisture and nutrients, it calls up to the top and yells "all clear below," then the top sprouts and goes straight up against gravity. It is not because of darkness or light or any other reason—strictly gravity, and the all-clear signal, of course.

For young SFG enthusiasts, the fun in their box doesn't end when the season comes to a close. Decorating their boxes is yet another way for children to have fun in the garden with SFG.

Enjoying the Crops

Harvesting an SFG is the really fun part, and it's the most rewarding stage for children. You can amaze them by pulling up a bright red radish, swishing it around in the sun-warmed water bucket, and popping it into your mouth. Just imagine the look of delight on their faces when they learn that everything in the garden is ready to eat . . . right now. You'll have to show them how to determine if a fruit or vegetable is mature (without dampening their enthusiasm), but after that, they'll get in the fun habit of harvesting salad makings every night.

They'll be able to say with pride, "I grew that!"

WHAT DID I DO WRONG?

Knowing that roots sprout first will help your seeds successfully grow. Here's why. Traditionally, gardeners hoed open a long row, planted a whole packet of seeds, covered, watered, and then walked away from their garden hoping for the best. If nothing grew, they thought the worst: "Maybe they were bad seeds. Or, maybe I'm a terrible gardener!" What these gardeners did not realize was that the seed might have already sprouted, perhaps after a week or two, and the root was heading down before the top could come up and break the surface. If the gardener gave up and quit watering, it is possible that their seed did die. Why? Because if the soil dries below the seed—in the root zone only 1 or 2 inches below the surface—the root will wither and die from lack of moisture. But if the gardener had kept the soil moist, then the seeds would have had a good chance to put the root down to support the plant and its new shoot.

KEEPING RECORDS

Many gardeners keep planting data—when, what, and where they plant, how long it takes to sprout, and how well their plants grow. It may sound like a lot of bookkeeping, yet some people enjoy recording their garden data and even set up computerized spreadsheets to make computations from this information. I don't bother to keep all these details myself, but if you enjoy it, this may help you learn faster and measure the progress more effectively.

MOVING PLANTS

A SFG garden is small, and I've been able to change things around once they were all planted. It doesn't take much to move and replant something from one square to another if you think it would look better somewhere else. It's kind of like arranging a room of furniture and pictures on a wall. You can make all kinds of layouts and drawings even to scale, but I guarantee you once everything is in place, you'll change your mind.

DROP A PINCH

We have learned about seed size and shape and storage and sprouting conditions. The next thing is to practice planting. You can do this indoors in the winter before you start your garden. Take different kinds of seeds from the tiniest to the largest and practice picking up and dropping a pinch of seeds onto a piece of white paper to count your results. This is really a lot of fun, almost a family game.

There is a very practical reason for doing this. When I tell people to just plant a pinch of seeds—two or three—I think I have given them all the instructions they need. But I always find so much variation in how many seeds they end up planting. It's in your finger dexterity, and you may need a little practice. If you are having trouble, you may even want to use a spoon for picking up that pinch of seeds. A white plastic spoon usually works great, especially if you're using darker colored seeds. If you scoop up too many, you can just shake a few back into the palm of your hand.

> Some seeds require special preparation or planting methods. These seeds are so few, though, that it's not worth going into detail. It's not something you have to remember or study because the seed companies, bless them, print any special instructions or requirements right on the back of the seed packet.

HOW DEEP?

How deep should you plant a seed? This depends a lot on the size of the seed and the soil you plant it in. Generally speaking, a seed's depth is two to four times the thickness of the seed. It's important to place your seeds

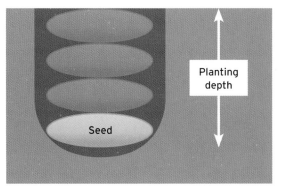

Plant seeds two to four times the depth of their size. When they've sprouted, transplant them into four packs. When they're large enough and the right time comes, move them into their own square foot.

below a moist surface to prevent it from drying out. Too close to the surface and it can dry out from the hot sun. Once a seed receives moisture and begins sprouting (known as "breaking dormancy"), it will die if it dries out, so don't forget to water regularly.

Too Deep Isn't a Problem

You don't have to worry too much about placing your seed too deep, in part because your Mel's Mix is loose and friable. If the seed is planted too deep for the kind of seed it is, as soon as it begins to receive moisture, nature will tell it, "Get going, buddy, put some roots down and start growing." That sprout can push right up through Mel's Mix because there are a lot of nooks and crannies and the soil is very easy to move. This is one of the hidden advantages of starting with perfect soil. It almost guarantees that all of your seeds will grow into plants.

TIME TO SPROUT

How long does it take to sprout seeds? The chart in the Appendix shows how many days it takes various types of seeds to sprout at various temperatures. In addition, what percentage can you expect to sprout? This chart can be valuable to you and should be used whenever you plant seeds. If you know ahead of time it's going to take ten days for the seeds to sprout at the average outdoor temperatures, then you won't be a nervous Nelly every day wondering when, but you will know to keep that soil moist for those number of days. You can also judge from the percentage that will sprout at that temperature, how many extra beyond two or three seeds to plant to ensure one good healthy plant.

PRESOAKING

Before planting your seeds, give them a jump-start by presoaking them. While some can be soaked overnight, some fall apart after only an hour; it depends on the seed. Big seeds should be soaked for only about a half hour to an hour. Bean and pea seeds, which might look shriveled up, swell up and break in half if you soak them too long. Beware, water makes some seeds slippery. A plastic spoon can help you handle them.

INDOOR SEED SPROUTING

The easiest way to sprout seeds indoors is to place them on a moist paper towel. Then put the paper towel and seeds in a very shallow tray or dish; keep it moist (a plastic bag would be handy to maintain moisture) and in a warm place in the house. Check daily; when you see roots, it's time to plant. Rather than handling the seed at this point, carefully cut the paper towel into little squares, and lift each one out with a knife. Now you're ready to take it outside, plant it in

Modular trays allow roots to develop in their own cell of growing medium, this means they don't get tangled up with neighbouring roots and so transplanting young plants is easier and there is less of a check to growth.

How to Start Seeds

To start seeds for growing your own seedlings, poke some holes into the bottom of a container. (This is a leftover plastic container shown in the photo.) Fill the container with vermiculite and pour water around the rim of the plate.

Add enough water until you notice a very slight color change to the vermiculite (it becomes darker). Pour a few seeds into the palm of your hand.

Pinch a few seeds with your thumb and forefinger.

Sprinkle the seeds across the surface of the vermiculite.

Cover the seeds with a thin layer of vermiculite (unless they need light to germinate; check the seed package).

your SFG filled with Mel's Mix, cover it, and give it a drink of water. You've just given your plant a head start—in about half the time. Instead of fourteen days, you may see a sprout coming up in just six.

Starting Transplants Indoors

Now it's time to decide whether you want to grow your own transplants indoors rather than direct seeding out-of-doors. To raise your own seedlings, you need a little bit of paraphernalia: Mel's Mix, a few cups and saucers, four-packs, and trays. Start your seeds in a little cup of vermiculite and transplant them into four-packs filled with Mel's Mix after they begin growing.

Seed Leaf

When you're sprouting seeds in a cup of vermiculite, I suggest you transplant them into the four-pack as soon as the tops have sprouted and you see the first two leaves called the seed leaves. Most garden experts say to wait until you have two "true" leaves, but I have found that if you wait until the set of true leaves develops, the roots have already grown so long and tangled that it's almost too late to transplant. The seed leaf comes first, and it's usually a fairly flat, large leaf that doesn't look like the plant's regular leaves. The first set of "true" leaves comes out next as the stem grows higher.

Lift By Its Ears

When the seeds have seed leaves and you're ready to transplant to the four-pack, carefully lift the plant by holding on to one of the seed leaves between two fingers. Then with your pencil, dig in the vermiculite, loosen it up, and lift the whole plant out—root and all—from the bottom while your other hand is holding the top of the plant by one of the seed leaves. Don't touch the plant stem, just the leaf. If the roots are very long, trim off the bottom third with a pair of scissors. Don't worry . . . you won't kill the plant. For every root you cut off, two new roots will sprout as it branches out, creating a much stronger plant.

After the seeds sprout, take your pencil and make a hole in one cell of your four-pack, or outdoors in your garden soil. Then lower the plant root down into the hole. Make sure the hole's big enough to hold the whole root. Take the point of the pencil and push the Mel's Mix around the plant. Plant it a little lower than when it sprouted. Give it some water, either from above for outdoors or from below for indoors in four-packs, and then give it shade immediately. Sun will kill that young seedling. In fact, if you're outdoors, always work in your own shadow, then make sure the plant has shade for at least a couple of days. (Refer to Chapter 4 for information about how to build shade cages.) Then you can let it have brighter light and then finally full sunlight.

Trim the Roots

When you place transplants into the garden, take a look at the roots to see if they are rootbound, in other words, if they've grown in a circle. My solution for a rootbound plant is to take that same pair of scissors and just cut off the bottom roots. Yes, the whole thing—the mass of roots and the soil. Then all the ends of the roots, wherever they are, will branch and send out little feeder roots. Lower the whole plant into the hole at the proper spacing in your outdoor garden.

You can trim excess roots by snipping them off with your scissors. Trim off only the excess though.

Push the mix around the seedlings to form a slight saucer shape in the mix. Because of the saucer shape, water is directed straight down to the roots.

Water Well

One caution: the plant and root should be very wet before you transplant into your SFG. Take your four-pack and let it float in a bucket of warm water until it sinks and there are no more bubbles coming up. That's when you know the plants are totally saturated with water. Then take it out, pop each plant out of its container, cut the root bottoms off, and plant it. Your garden soil should be moist, so you're not putting a wet plant into dry ground. Dry ground will suck the moisture right out of the roots.

> "I was surprised at how much I could get from such a small area."
> – Michael from Georgia

Saucer-Shaped Depression

Next, push the soil back around the plant to form a slight saucer shape in the soil. Make sure you plant at the level of the soil, factoring in the slight depression of the saucer. Because of the saucer shape, water goes straight down to the roots. We don't want to water the rest of the square foot if we don't have to. How's that for conserving water?

OUTDOOR SEED SPROUTING

The procedure for outdoor seed sprouting, transplanting into four-packs, watering, and then planting into the garden is all the same, just in much nicer weather. Late afternoon on a cloudy day is the best time.

Hardening Off

Hardening off is the process of getting the plant adjusted to a new environment—like going from indoors to outdoors. It's important that your plants are acclimated gradually so they can get used to their new location and different weather conditions. This requires some effort because you don't want them out at night when it's cold or freezing and you also don't want them out in the burning hot sun in the daytime.

Regulate Sunlight and Heat

To help harden off plants, regulate the sun exposure. If it's hot out, place your plants out in the sunlight in the morning, but at noontime provide some shade. Let them receive direct sunlight in the early morning, shade at midday, and perhaps, when the sun starts down, a little more direct light in the afternoon. Now that's really pampering your garden plants. And don't forget the little drinks of water every now and then. Actually all that sun, then shade, then sun can easily be done with a shingle stuck in the ground at the right place and the right angle.

Can't Dry Out

To keep your newly planted seeds from cooking in the hot sun, cover the square with a piece of cardboard cut to fit in the grid. Estimate the soil temperature and sprout time (see the charts in the Appendix), then write the sprout date and the date you planted it on the cardboard with a magic marker. Weight down the cardboard to keep it from flying away in the wind. Of course, you'll need to lift the cardboard before you sprinkle water on the soil surface to keep the soil moist, and then remove it a day or two before the sprout date.

> If you are planting something that may need a plant support later as it gets fully grown, you might consider other plants that could share the same support and plant them in adjacent squares.

SPACING

How many plants will fit into a square foot? The numbers are so simple and easy to remember: 1, 4, 9, or 16. If you like math, and who doesn't, you will recognize right away that these numbers happen to be the squares of 1, 2, 3, and 4. And, in addition to the fact that we're gardening in square foot plots, that's how Square Foot Gardening got its name . . . because it's as simple as one, two, three, four. The number of plants you grow in a square foot depends on a plant's size when it's fully grown. (Go to the chart in the Appendix to see mature plant sizes.)

You can also figure it out very easily from the "thin to," directions on a seed packet. (Now, every time you read "thin to," you will think of me and say to yourself, "Why do the seed packets tell me to plant so many seeds only to go back and thin to just one plant?")

Store surplus seeds in jars, grouping similar seeds together so that you can find them easily next time you plant the crop. Label the jars and it's even easier finding the seeds you need! Keep the jars in the back of your refrigerator and you won't need to buy more seeds anytime soon.

A newly-planted bed of quick growing salad crops, all correctly spaced so the plants can grow away without too much competition.

A TYPICAL GARDEN

Let's plant one 4 × 4 and see how much we will grow in those 16 square feet. We'll start with tall plants on the north side of the box so they don't shade shorter plants. Then put some colorful flowers in each corner. Let's assume it is still springtime, but that we're past the last frost, so we could put four pansies in each corner using our favorite colors.

Carrots require little care until they're harvested. So let's plant two squares of different carrots in the center squares, one square of sixteen onions and a low-maintenance square of sixteen radishes in the center. Then we'll put one square of nine beets in an outside square because we'll harvest their leaves during the season and then finally pull the beet bottoms later. We can plant two or three varieties of leaf lettuce on the outside, depending on your tastes. In another square we could put sixteen chives, and four parsley plants in another, which would provide us a continual harvest. For more color we might want to put a square of red salvia along the back. And perhaps in one corner some dwarf dahlias, one per square foot. Or perhaps some nasturtiums spaced at one per square foot. One of the first things we would have planted in the spring is one or two squares of spinach, nine per square foot. Then depending on your family's taste we could have one or more squares from the cabbage family. That could be red or green cabbage, broccoli, or cauliflower. Keep in mind this is not the only 4 × 4 in the whole garden. So we don't have to put all the cabbage into one SFG. It's better to space them out throughout the garden—makes it harder for the cabbage moth to find them all.

PLANS AND DRAWINGS

Remember I mentioned that some people feel a desire to think ahead and draw up a list of everything to be planted in their garden. Then there are even some people who want to assign those plants to spaces ahead of time. So it means drawing a chart, more or less to scale, of your garden and assigning those particular crops to each square foot. Despite being an engineer who loves charts and diagrams, I don't usually do that. I just like to plant as I see fit. It's very easy to stand in the garden and as the square becomes vacant you just look around and decide it's time to plant another square of radishes. Or maybe you'd like to have some more beans, but this time you'll put in the yellow variety instead of green. It's also very easy to spot and plant where you'd like some color. I find it very easy to just bring home a four-pack of flowers I liked at the nursery and decide by looking at the garden where they would look best. But it's your Square Foot Garden, and you should do whatever makes you happy.

REPLANTING

Keep in mind that, as soon as you harvest, it won't be a big deal to replant because you're going to do it one square foot at a time. Once your newly planted garden starts maturing in the spring—for example, that square foot of radishes will be ready to harvest in four weeks—you'll be ready to replant just that one square. The season has changed and it's warmer, and most of your summer crops can now be planted. So your choices have increased and also most of the summer crop is fairly long-lived and will be in that spot through the whole summer season. As you replant you keep the same criteria in mind—taller plants on the north side to keep them from shading other plants, working your way to cascading flowers on the front corners to look pretty. Place plants that don't need much attention and only occasional harvesting like peppers on the inside, and shorter plants and those that need constant care or harvest to the outside just to make them easier to tend.

WEEDING

This could be the shortest paragraph in the entire book. To start with, your Mel's Mix has no weed seeds in it, and any weeds that do sprout are easily observed because they're not in the proper space and they look different from the plants that are there. Because the soil is so soft and friable weeds come out easily—root and all. You have to weed about once a month. End of paragraph; end of story.

HARVESTING

Keep in mind that we harvest many of the crops continuously, if possible. For example, a leaf lettuce is not allowed to wait until it forms

This is a good example of a rootbound container plant. You'll want to trim the matted roots before planting. (Don't worry, it's better for the plants anyway.)

a large, mature head, but with a pair of scissors and a salad bowl you can continuously trim the leaves from such things as lettuce, chives, beets, Swiss chard, spinach, parsley, and even onion tops. As long as you don't take too much at one time, the plant will easily survive and thrive. Filling your salad bowl each day should not diminish the garden in any way. In fact, right after you harvest you'll find it hard to notice where you got everything and if anything is missing.

YOU'VE LEARNED THE BASICS

You've now learned all the basics of Square Foot Gardening. You've learned how it got its name—from the squares of one, two, three, four. You have also learned how many and what kind of plants fit into a square foot by memorizing, calculating, or by looking it up on the chart. You've learned how to zip zap in the soil to get the proper and exact spacing then start planting your seeds and transplants. Are we having any fun yet? Next chapter we're going to discuss how to maintain and harvest your SFG.

Okay, now it's time to go out to your garden and do something outrageous that will amaze or dumbfound any neighbor who might be watching you. Do you know how to do a rain dance?

7

Growing and Harvesting

This is going to be a fairly short chapter because SFG requires so little maintenance once your garden is prepared and planted. You'll experience a continuous cycle of nurturing, harvesting, and replanting each year with no soil preparation and no weeding to do ever again. How does that sound?

You'll be amazed at the bounty that comes from your compact, no-maintenance SFG box.

Bringing in Your Crops

All of the nurturing you'll need to do in your SFG consists of providing necessary structural support for plants, ridding the garden of any tiny, occasional weeds or pests, and watering. You'll enjoy observing your garden's growth until harvest; every square is different because it was planted with a different crop at a different time. That's what makes SFG so interesting.

CARE

When asked to name the greatest advantage of the All New Square Foot Gardening, most say it's tending their garden from aisles and never stepping on their soil. Like many others, I always wondered why we were taught to loosen soil with rototillers, shovels, forks, and hoes, only to walk all over it again packing it down.

So why are the experts still teaching us to do this? I say, just stop walking on your growing soil—it's that simple.

KEEP IT LOOSE

Let's think of some of the advantages of not packing your soil down. The plant roots need air and moisture, just like people. If you pack the soil down, it becomes more and more compressed (called compaction) and it becomes harder and harder for air to circulate through the soil making it more difficult for roots to grow. They may not die, but they certainly won't grow well. So why not provide them with nice, loose, friable soil like Mel's Mix? This way, water can percolate down and air can circulate.

THREE TOOLS

Another big advantage of SFG is that the number and cost of tools is reduced to almost nothing—you will only need three tools. Just think, you no longer need a rototiller! Eliminate that cost and you now have an extra thousand dollars in your pocket. And you don't have to hire someone at fifty dollars every year to plow for you. You don't even need a shovel or rake or any of those special digging tools that have been invented to dig up the tough soil. Gardening "experts" will tell you to go out and buy the best tools you can find because they will last longer, but they also cost more. With SFG, you no longer need any of those big, expensive, heavy-duty tools that take so much energy to maneuver—they're suddenly obsolete.

GROWING AND HARVESTING RULES

- Don't walk on your growing mix
- Only three tools needed
- Support your plants
- Weeds and other pests are not a problem
- Water the right way

These are the only tools you need for your All New Square Foot Garden. A trowel, a pencil and scissors—that's it.

A TROWEL, A PENCIL, AND SCISSORS

The first tool of the three tools you need is a trowel. I've found that the one-dollar variety is really the best buy. They're attractive, strong, and neat looking. They have all the features of a six-dollar trowel. So instead of just one, now you can afford six—one for every SFG box! Why not buy an assortment of colors? You can have one in every box just sitting there waiting so that you don't have to go looking for a tool when you walk by and see a square that is ready for replanting. Of course, if you see an occasional weed, your big, strong weeding tools are your own thumb and forefinger!

The trowel is for transplanting, for mixing in an added trowel full of compost when you replant each square foot, and for loosening up and turning over the Mel's Mix in an individual square foot or even an entire 4 × 4. In the spring you won't believe how perfect the soil will be if you follow the Mel's Mix formula and start with a perfect soil.

The other two tools you'll need are a pencil (yes, that's a tool) for poking holes and lifting out young seedlings for transplanting, and a pair of scissors for harvesting beet, lettuce, or Swiss chard leaves for supper, cutting off dead blossoms, and snipping off extra seedlings if more than one seed sprouts in a hole. Because SFG tools are so simple and inexpensive, I love to splurge and keep one of each at every 4 × 4. That way, I never have to look for a tool.

PENNY PINCHER

I like to buy children's pointed scissors in August when you can find back-to-school sales. Usually I can purchase them for about fifty cents—an affordable price that allows for several pairs around the garden.

It would be fun to list all the tools that you no longer need if you have a SFG. In fact, you could probably just go into your garage or toolshed and see them all right there—poor, lonely tools. Maybe you have some old-fashioned single-row friends who just can't give up all that hard work and could use some extra heavy-duty tools. You could rent them out and maybe make a few bucks.

OPTIONAL ACCESSORY

Although you only need three tools, you might want to invest in a kneeling pad. Unless your boxes are placed on tabletops, your most frequent position while gardening will be kneeling. For less than four dollars, you can buy a kneeling pad that is comfortable and durable. There's no need to buy the fancy ones that strap to your knees. They're terribly uncomfortable and will end up hanging in your tool shed along with the other lonely tools.

WEEDS

SFG has few or no weeds. But how? Weeds plague every garden, right? First, there are no weed seeds in peat moss or vermiculite. Next, any seeds that were in the ingredients you added to the compost pile will get cooked and killed in that 150°F temperature as the pile heats up. If you prepare the bed properly and line the bottom of the box with landscape fabric, no weeds will sprout from the bottom. Since we are not using our ground soil, which is filled with weeds, the only possible weed seeds in our SFG might have blown in, and as soon as they sprout, you will see them because they are out of place. Your two fingers will do the rest, pulling out the weed, roots and all. Compare

First, remove any weeds or grass from inside your box, then lay down landscape fabric as a weed barrier. This will be your "best friend" against future weeds.

Weeds are a rare occurrence in an SFG, but if you do find one it will stand out because it won't be in proper plant spacing. Any weed will be easy to pluck out because of the nature of Mel's Mix.

that to what you've experienced with your existing soil. Anytime the existing soil anywhere in the country is left alone, it sprouts weeds. Which system would you like to have in your backyard?

I See You

How can you tell if a new sprout is a weed? First, it's not in the proper space among your little transplants. Remember one, four, nine, and sixteen.

If it is out of place (and I'll bet you were careful to make sure your spaces were correct in that square foot), you'll pull it out of that soft Mel's Mix without a problem.

PESTS AND PLANT PROBLEMS

The only way to intelligently answer the questions we get about pests and plant problems requires knowing the weather, growing conditions, history, and present gardening condition in an area. If the question came from my county, I'd give a great answer. But when it comes from across the country or anywhere in the world, it's difficult to give an accurate answer.

County Extension Agents

There is a good solution. Some of our tax dollars go to train and maintain a staff of horticultural experts in every county in the country—the county extension service agents. In addition, the county extension agents train another group of neighborhood volunteers called "Master Gardeners," who then go out in the community helping others by answering their questions. It is a great service, and we often refer questions to the agents and their staff. If your question is about pests or problems or even the best varieties to grow in your area,

GUIDE TO COMMON PEST SOLUTIONS

The treatments are listed in the order of severity and the order in which they should be used.

Insect	Affected plants	Treatment
Aphids (tiny, pear shaped bugs, usually found in groups; can be many different colors, slow-moving, found on underside of leaves and tender stalks of plants)	Wide variety of plants; attacks leaves and new growth	Wash off with hose spray; homemade garlic spray; insecticidal soap
Cabbage worms (adults are white or cream-colored moths, with dark spots on wings; damage-causing caterpillars are fuzzy green and slow-moving)	Cabbage, broccoli, cauliflower, kale, and similar crops	Floating covers early in the season; handpick worms and drop in soapy water; spray with neem oil; for serious infestations spray with bacillus thuringiensis (Bt)
Corn borers/Ear worms (striped green, brown, or pink caterpillars [ear worms], pink or reddish caterpillars with darker spots)	Corn, peppers, and beans	Plant resistant hybrids if corn borers or ear worms are an ongoing problem in your area
Flea beetles (dark, shiny—sometimes metallic—greens and blacks on small bodies; these beetles can hop when disturbed)	Beans, squash, lettuce, turnips, broccoli, sunflowers, corn, and other plants such as mustard and eggplant	Sticky traps; beneficial nematodes at the start of the season (experts recommend pyrethrin spray for severe infestations, but I don't believe this is ever needed in an SFG)
Japanese beetles (large-bodied iridescent insects with winged but slow moving and slow flying)	Roses and a wide variety of vegetables and flowering plants	Hand pick; insecticidal soap; Neem oil at first sign of beetles; pheromone traps (use carefully to avoid drawing more beetles into your yard)
Slugs & Snails (soft-bodied slugs are green to yellow, slimy and 1 to 2 inches long; snails are similar, brown, with brown shells and prominent antennae)	Tender young seedlings and transplants	Go out at night to detect them in the garden; hand-pick and drop in salty or soapy solution; set out flat beer in shallow saucer near susceptible plants
Cutworms (ugly gray-brown worms, about 2 inches long, with a noticeably greasy appearance)	Most vegetable and garden plants, as seedlings or transplants	Protect seedlings and transplants with cardboard collars such as toilet paper tubes or wrap the stalks in aluminum foil; apply beneficial nematodes to the soil
Tomato hornworms (green worm with white bands and red horn)	Tomato plants, eggplants, peppers, and potato plants	Cut off affected leaves with hornworms on them and dispose of the hornworm and leaf in the garbage; do not try to pick off hornworms because they can leave an awful smell on your hands
Spider mite (green or amber insects about the size of a pencil lead; amber or white eggs; wispy white webs)	Most leafy plants	Garlic spray; spray of equal parts water and alcohol

you couldn't find a more informative source. To find your local extension agent, look in your phone book in the Government blue pages, find your county, and then look for the heading "Extension of (your state) University;" don't look under "Agriculture."

The only problem I have with the county agents is that most of them are trained in our agricultural colleges, which still teach single-row farming and hand-me-down gardening. So, they are not the best source for answers to SFG questions. You'll have to come to us for those questions.

Built-In Resistance

The truth is that many of the changes I've made to Square Foot Gardening not only make the method easier and more trouble-free, they also protect your plants from pests and diseases. For instance, when you raise your SFG up and fill it with Mel's Mix, you completely separate your existing soil from the soil in your new square foot garden. That eliminates any possible contamination, like lead, that might be in your existing soil, from getting into your garden. This would be especially true in a community garden, built on an empty lot in a city. SFG is the only gardening method that would protect you from that danger.

That alone is going to eliminate many of the diseases and pests that overwinter in the soil. We also prevent diseases and pests with "selective separation"—by not planting two squares of the same crop next to each other. Pests don't like to work—they prefer to have their meals all lined up, as they are in a row garden. Diseases are less likely to transfer between plants, when the same type of plants are grown in different boxes. It's just one of the reasons that we plant every square foot with something different and separate the same crops into different boxes. All in all, Square Foot Gardens are just far less susceptible and inviting to pests and diseases than row gardens are.

The healthy, strong plants of a properly planted SFG are just as likely to attract beneficial insects such as this lady beetle (who will take care of any aphids that dare try to hurt your plants) as they are to attract harmful pests.

Preventing Pest Problems

PHYSICAL BARRIERS

Floating covers are an easy way to protect young and immature plants from pests that lay their eggs on the undersides of leaves.

The wire cage described on pages 70-71 is the best solution to keep wildlife, pests and the occasional soccer ball out of your SFG.

A simple perimeter of crushed eggshells can keep most slugs and snails away from your plants. Epsom salts (above) can serve the same function.

If you're not sure what type of pest you have, you can't be sure what type of homemade spray will work. That's why it's always wise, whether you're dealing with a diseased plant or a pest, to take a sample to an expert. You can clip off damaged leaves, but a live critter is the best way to determine exactly what you're dealing with. Your local nursery professional will usually be able to tell you what you've got, but the County Extension Service agent will definitely be able to identify the pest and give you guidance on the best spray (or other treatment) to use on it. Actual samples are great, but these days, you can just whip out your smart phone, take a closeup picture, and e-mail it to the local Extension Service office. That way you save on gas—one more way that SFG is saving you money and time!

PREVENTATIVE SPRAYS

Make a pest spray by boiling ingredients for several minutes—in this case garlic and cayenne pepper (one of the most effective sprays). Allow the liquid to cool to room temperature, then strain it into a spray bottle, using a strainer or cheesecloth over a funnel.

When spraying plants, be sure to spray the undersides of the leaves, where many pests like to hide. Spray every day or so, and as soon as possible right after rainfall.

Troubleshooting Process

But nature being nature, every once in a while you may have to deal with a pest of some sort or a disease that affects your harvest. You'll use one of three strategies to fight these problems.

Physical Barriers

Remember that old saying, "An ounce of prevention is worth a pound of cure?" Well, barriers are all about preventing problems before they become problems. You can stop most garden invaders by simply not letting them get to your plants in the first place. Larger invaders such as deer, raccoon, squirrels, and other wildlife are easy to foil with the simple wire cage on pages 70-71. (It's also a great way to keep family pets and even the occasional soccer ball away from your plants!) But even insects can be blocked from access to your SFG. Floating covers are fine mesh nets that you place over early season plants to prevent insects like the cabbage moth from laying eggs on the leaves of your plants. You can cover individual square feet by just wrapping the floating cover around the plant. Air and light and water can still get in, but the insects can't. Similar garden netting placed on more mature plants such as corn can keep hungry birds away. You can wrap more mature plants, such as corn and tomatoes, with the floating cover held in place with two small rubber bands or clothespins.

Removal

Sometimes though, you don't realize you have a problem until you see it on the plant. In these cases, you'll move onto the second strategy: cutting away infected leaves and fruit. Insects tend to be pretty

Physical removal is one of the most effective and easiest ways to head off problems at the first sight of trouble. This strategy works for many insects as well as diseases.

Neem oil is a common non-toxic spray that works on a range of insects as long as it is used at the right time. As with all over-the-counter products, follow the label directions to the letter.

slow-moving creatures. Many bugs, such as that common villain the aphid, can be washed or picked off plants. There are traps to remove many flying insects. Diseases can often be nipped in the bud (excuse the pun!) when caught early enough, simply by removing affected leaves and fruit, and keeping the box clean of leaf litter.

Treatments

Sometimes though, a problem is a little more advanced. Where simple removal doesn't take care of things, you'll need to use the third strategy: active treatments. These include both homemade formulas, such as the ever-useful garlic spray (insects of all kinds just hate it) and over-the-counter solutions.

The Last Resort

You'll choose solutions, just as you will pest-fighting strategies, by starting with the mildest. Only when simpler tactics fail should you move on to the more serious treatments, such as pesticides. However, I avoid chemicals of any kind in my SFG. Chemical treatments are unpredictable and can stay in the soil for a long time. I'd rather lose a few tomatoes or even a whole harvest than risk growing produce with potentially harmful toxins.

The chart on page 144 lists the most common pests gardeners deal with. But keep in mind that many are local; the best place to start whenever you have a problem in your garden is with the local Cooperative Extension Service agent in your county. Go to http://www.csrees.usda.gov/Extension/ to find contact information for your local office. The first step is to call your local agent and describe what you have. They may be able to help you right over the phone and you can save time and the gas it takes to drive over there. If you have to take samples of the plant damage or actual pests in for identification and advice on how to eradicate the problem, put them in a zip-top plastic bag.

To summarize pest problems, try not to worry about them. Enjoy your garden. If one square gets devastated, pull it up and replant it with something else. If you didn't use the protective structures of Chapter 4, try them out next season to help eliminate your problems.

WHICH PLANT VARIETIES?

Quite often people will ask questions like, "Which are the best varieties of potatoes or carrots to grow in my corner of the state?" These questions can only be answered by your local expert—the county extension agent. They are always up-to-date on all the new varieties and what grows best in their area. Keep in mind if you have a question about any of the vine crops, you will want to train them up a trellis, while most single-row gardens allow them to sprawl.

SUPPORT YOUR LOCAL PLANTS

Some plants, such as root crops and low-growing salad crops, need no support, so there is nothing to do for them. The taller crops might need a little help, however, depending on whether they are a leaf or head crop like Swiss chard or cabbage. If a heavy wind and rain or hailstorm knocks them over, simply straighten them up and push a little extra soil around the stem.

Too Top Heavy

The plants that usually need a little support are the summer crops like peppers, okra, eggplant, corn, and bush tomatoes. Those can easily be supported by installing nylon netting so it is suspended across the entire 4 × 4 garden, held tight by four corner posts. (See Chapter 4 for construction details.) The same support technique will also work for tall flowers like gladiolus, giant marigolds, and tall dahlias. One of the reasons we provide plant support is the soil mix is so loose and friable that the tall plants need a little help.

WATERING

Plants need water just like people do. Everyone asks, "How do you water and how much?" My ideal way to water is ladling out a cup of sun-warmed water from a bucket that can be left in the sun next to your garden. Gently lift the bottom leaves of the plant and, with your other hand, ladle a cup of that water into the depression around the plant. With a saucer-shaped depression in the soil, the water will soak right down to the roots instead of rolling away from the plant into other parts of the garden.

We do get a few people who say, "Oh that would take too long." But they've failed to think about the fact that, first, their garden is only a fraction of the size that it used to be. That means 80 percent of the watering you used to do is no longer needed and was actually wasted. Next, you're not watering the tops of the plants or the leaves, so you're not promoting fungal diseases and other problems. You're keeping the water where it will do the most good—around the base of the plant where it can travel down to the root system.

The soil consistency of your Mel's Mix is already 100 percent of materials that hold moisture. When you water, it goes right into the soil around the root system and stays there. The root system is going to be able to drink up the water in the amount and time needed. Is this a major advance in water conservation or what? Hello, conservationist, are you listening?

And why sun-warmed water? One answer is that it's for the same reason people don't like to take a cold shower. The more scientific reason is plants can absorb nutrients in the soil much faster and grow better if the soil and water temperature are warmer. In spring and late fall, sun-warmed water helps warm the soil. Remember the chart in the Appendix showing sprouting times in various temperatures. The warmer the weather, the faster they'll grow and the quicker you'll harvest. That's why people have greenhouses. If you build a structure to form a miniature greenhouse around your SFG, the radiant heat

A bucket of sun-warmed water is the ideal source of water for your SFG. Keep it near the box and full, and you'll be able to water any time you notice your Mel's Mix is drying out.

When your plants need a drink, just dip your cup in the bucket and pour the water directly into the saucer-shaped depression at the base of each plant. Keep the cup with the bucket at all times.

from the sun will warm the soil from the surface down. But simply pouring warm (not hot) water into the soil means the warmth tends to go a little deeper—and even quicker—than the sun baking the surface of the soil.

Don't Drown Me

Invariably gardeners water plants too much, perhaps out of kindness or fear that they will fail. So they think, "Oh, I'll give it a little extra. It won't hurt." Usually it did hurt with local soil that didn't drain well, but it won't if you are using Mel's Mix, where the soil drains excess water. Most people don't realize that plant roots need air as well as moisture. Lucky for you, Mel's Mix allows air into it because it's loose and friable. (Chapter 5 tells you how to make Mel's Mix.)

With Mel's Mix you cannot overwater. Remember the sponge? Each little piece can hold moisture so a plant root can grow around that piece and take out the moisture when needed. When that little sponge gets saturated, the rest of the water drains right out through the bottom. That's how Mel's Mix works, and that's why you never have to worry about giving your plants too much water.

With Mel's Mix you cannot overwater. I repeat: you cannot overwater.

But because your soil mix drains readily when saturated, it also has a tendency to dry out more quickly than most garden soils. Regular soils stay saturated, so single-row gardeners may be used to turning on the sprinkler or flooding the garden twice a week and that's it. Your All New Square Foot Garden is different. You have to water a little more often and pay more attention to watering.

The secret, of course, is looking at the plants. After a while you'll be able to walk past your 4 × 4 garden box and immediately spot any square foot that needs water. Perhaps the plants will be slightly wilted. Maybe they'll be just a little droopy or their color will be a little off. You merely water those square feet right then and there because your bucket of warm water is always right next to your garden. And because you're dipping a cup in the bucket you're not going to get yourself all wet and dirty.

Think of your plants in your garden the same as you do your children. If they've been out in the hot sun and playing hard and one of them looks a little droopy and wilted, you know right away to inspect that child a little closer to make sure he or she is properly hydrated.

Too Much

Existing watering systems give all different types and sizes of plants the same amount of water at the same time. This is not only very impersonal; it's also very inefficient. If our farmers did that we'd have water shortages all around the country. Hey, wait a minute, we do have water shortages all around the country!

How Much

In conclusion, only water as much as each plant needs. And the best way to tell is from experience—the same way you know your child needs a drink. Yes, it does take a little bit of experience to raise a family, but gaining this experience brings a lot of pleasure.

"I've lived my life doing the backbreaking work of single row gardening—this is so much better!"
– Gina from Kentucky

ALTERNATE WATERING METHODS
A Hose

For those who want to use a more traditional method, there is always the hose. Yes, it's a nuisance to get out or put away, and in row gardening it always seemed to be knocking plants down as it has to be dragged around the garden. Another advantage to SFG boxes is the hose won't do that anymore as the box corners keep the hose from crushing the plants.

If you do use a hose, make sure you have one of those shut-off valves right at the end of the hose so you have complete control of the force and amount of the water. There are many short and long extension hand wands that come with a spray nozzle. This also allows you to water directly under your plants, and the nozzle on the end of the wand can be poked down and worked around the lower leaves of the plant so that most of the plant remains dry.

Leave an extra length of hose coiled in the sun to help warm the water up a little, maybe just to take the chill off tap water, but you have to be careful at the start if it's hot out and a hose full of water has been laying in the sun for some time. You don't want the water to be too hot. Do what you do when giving the baby a bottle—test the water on your wrist.

Drip, Drip, Drip

A very efficient way to water your SFG is with a drip irrigation system. I know it was designed for row gardeners, but it can be adapted for SFG just as easily. The only problem I have is it sort of takes away the nurturing and close attention paid to your

NURTURE YOUR PLANTS

I suggest watering by hand because it allows you the time to nurture your plants. You're able to stop and notice how your plants are growing. You can appreciate their beauty and color, notice their blossoms and fruit. It tells you when the plant is going to be ready for harvest. It's a satisfying feeling to work in your garden with each plant. You're not standing off in the distance with a hose, which is very impersonal. You're not opening a big valve and letting the sprinkler system take over or the irrigation water come in. (And guess what? Irrigation water is filled with weed seeds. Have you folks who live in states that irrigate ever wondered why you have to weed your single-row garden so often?) Even a drip irrigation system is impersonal–though, I must admit, efficient.

plants. If you just turn a valve or worse yet, a mechanical timer turns the water on and off, you never get close to your plants and they will miss you. But I must admit the watering gets done very efficiently and effectively. Try running small soaker tubes spaced every 6 inches the length of your box for complete coverage of every square foot.

Lawn Sprinkler Systems

Some people tell me they have located their SFG on the lawn, and they have an underground sprinkler system that goes on and off automatically. What should they do, they ask? What can you do—rip

up the lawn or turn off the system? No, you just live with it. I tell them to make do with what they have and just keep a bucket or two around for special plants as needed.

HARVEST

Harvesting your crop is the culmination of the gardening experience. The harvest should be a joyful and exciting time because, after all, this is why you're growing all these plants in the first place.

A SFG box frame fitted with automatic drip irrigation is an efficient, low-maintainence solution. The equipment seen here can be purchased from the SFG website.

Too Much

The problem with traditional gardening is that there is too much to harvest all at once. If you plant an entire row of something all at once, it's all going to be ready to harvest all at once, and it becomes an overwhelming task. Not so great for the home gardener who just wants dinner tonight, not a month's worth of lettuce in one day. So, after the first few pickings, the rest becomes all drudgery.

Control That Planting

Everything is different with a SFG. Now, every time you begin to plant something in your SFG, look the item up in your SFG book to find how many to plant per square foot. Prepare the soil, smooth it out, do the zip, zap, bing, bing, bing, bing to mark the spacing. Now, select the varieties you want from your seeds, pour some into the palm of one hand, and plant a pinch in each hole. As you smooth the soil over the seeds, water with a fine spray. Then ask yourself, "Do I want any more than sixteen radishes all at once? They'll be ready in four weeks and they'll all come to harvest within one week." Usually the answer is "No. I really don't want any more than this. I'll wait a week or two to plant another square foot of radishes somewhere else." Right then and there you can see one of the huge advantages of your grid establishing boundaries and SFG giving you automatic control—simple and easy.

Remember that the SFG theory is to visualize the harvest. Ask yourself, "How much do I need for one or two weeks?" Then only plant that much. It takes about a minute.

A Little of This, A Little of That

You don't have to wait for the plant to mature to its maximum size. Go out at harvest time (which might be a half an hour before lunch or dinner) with your pair of scissors and a small basket or salad bowl, and cut off a few outer leaves, perhaps one from each plant. To harvest a varied salad, just take four lettuce leaves, parsley leaves from another, and perhaps beet greens from another. Each square may contain a different variety and color of lettuce. You might pull one radish and one carrot, even though they've only grown to half size, wash them off in your bucket of sun-warmed water, put the tops in the compost bin, and then continue around your Square Foot Garden taking just a little bit here and a little bit there of this and that. Soon your harvest basket is full and you look at your garden and cannot even see that anything is missing.

Snip, Snip

Continually harvest any type of leafy vegetable—like leaf lettuce or Swiss chard—by snipping a little here and a little there throughout the season. This can't go on forever because the plant, especially cool weather plants, will eventually go to seed. When it sends up a seed stalk, the plant has completed its growing season and its use for harvesting. Take one last harvest, remove what's left over, and prepare that square foot for replanting—unless you want the kids to see how a lettuce or radish plant produces seed.

> "I had always been a little afraid of composting, but Mel makes everything so logical and easy to understand."
> – Karen from Utah

HARVEST AND REPLANT

With Square Foot Gardening, you're only dealing with 1 square foot at a time. To paraphrase the words of Dr. Robert Schuller, "Inch by inch, anything's a cinch." With SFG, our saying is going to be "square by square, you'll soon be there." As soon as you finish harvesting 1 square foot, it's time to prepare the soil and plant a new crop. Just take out any debris like dead leaves, stems, or roots—you can place these in your compost bin—then add a trowel full of compost (hopefully it's homemade) to the square, turn the soil over with the trowel, smooth it over, and you're ready to replant. You can do all of that in 60 seconds!

Harvest only as much lettuce as you need for your meal. Cut one or two outer leaves from each lettuce plant.

Replanting

Now it's getting more interesting and fun because you will be able to choose what you want to replant in every single square foot all through the garden season. Remember, you can get at least three crops a year in every square foot. So, multiply your number of square feet by three and there are a lot of choices to make! Every choice is going to be fun, exciting, and interesting. Of course, what you select depends a lot on what time of the year it is and what you can use and enjoy.

A LITTLE NOW

Whether you're planting, harvesting, maintaining, or watering you don't need hours and hours to enjoy your garden. Because you can do a little bit here and a little bit there, you can do it any time of the day—even on your way out the door! If you see a few tiny weeds growing, pluck them out; give a drink of water to any plants that appear a little droopy or wilted (remember your bucket of sun-warmed water is right there and so is your trowel if you need to loosen the soil). It's like straightening a crooked picture as you walk down the hall, jotting a note to someone who will be coming home soon, or putting something away in the refrigerator. These are things you can do right then and there. And they're fun things to do. No heavy work. No getting all dirty and sweaty.

A WONDER

If your garden is close to the back door or kitchen door, you'll probably use it much more. You'll enjoy the fresh greens and salad more often, eat healthier, and feel better. SFG could be part of a weight-loss program, if you ask me! On top of all that, you'll have fun doing it! Don't forget to share the fun with your spouse, children, or grandchildren— the wonder of growth and harvest is priceless. Harvest a few small plants with a child, and that child will remember the experience forever.

NEXT CROP

When the summer is finished, you're ready to plant a fall crop, which will be a cool-weather crop. Go through the whole quick process of picking out any debris, adding a trowel full of compost, mixing it in, smoothing it over, and deciding what's next. There goes another minute out of your busy life. How about spinach? Check the spacing, get the seeds out, soak them for a little while, pop them in the ground, smooth them over, water, and you're all finished. Another minute gone, but you are creating life. You've now planted three crops in one square foot in only one year. You started with a root crop, replaced it with a fruit crop, and finally, in the fall, added a leaf crop. In addition, you practiced soil improvement three times in one year—square by square.

ROTATION NOT CRITICAL

The nice thing about SFG is you are also practicing crop rotation without even knowing it. Crop rotation is very important in traditional row gardening when dealing with existing soils that have very few nutrients in them—nutrients that can quickly be depleted by planting and replanting the same crop year after year in the same soil.

When you begin gardening with a healthy, rich soil like Mel's Mix, crop rotation is really not critical. Mel's Mix gives you a garden soil that is 33 percent compost, which has all the nutrients and trace elements that plants need. But crop rotation is still a good idea for insect and pest control in addition to soil nutrients. If you grow the same thing continuously in the same place, eventually pests or diseases may take over since they have lived and played in that spot for so long. But if you replant every square three times a year, SFG is going to be no picnic for them. They will have to move every two months. I'll bet they will go somewhere else to set up residency. How about your row gardener next door who laughed at you when you started building your boxes?

ADD COLOR

One more thing. Now that you've become an accomplished gardener one square at a time, you've improved the look and landscape of your garden and perhaps even your yard and patio. When you decide you need a little color over here or there, you may put in a summer crop of flowers—perhaps pink petunias—you become a designer. Just think— you're enjoying a painting in progress when you garden the All New Square Foot Gardening way!

What are some of your favorite flowers or herbs? Plant them among your veggies for added color and interest.

8

Vertical Gardening

The vertical gardening we do in our SFG boxes ensures the best production from different vining and bush-type plants, keeps the box looking tidy, and is as easy and foolproof as can be!

In SFG we go up, not down, including growing a whole bounty of crops on the sturdy vertical support shown here.

Gardening with Support

By now, you might feel that the 80 percent reduction in size, the no fertilizer needed, the growing in only 6 inches of Mel's Mix, or even the no digging of your existing soil ever again are all that you could ask from your All New Square Foot Garden.

In addition, you might say that most people would think that all of the above is amazing and earth-shattering (well, okay, how about just impressive), but this topic, "Vertical Gardening," is downright spectacular.

HOW IT HAPPENED

Here's a quick flashback to 1976 when this retired engineer took up gardening. I developed SFG but as I looked at tomato plants growing in pots on decks and in single-row gardens, I knew my work wasn't complete. Tomatoes are not only America's favorite vegetable to grow, but they also take up the most room and cause quite an unsightly mess by the end of the season if they are allowed to sprawl all over the ground. There are also the complaints of slugs getting in and ruining all of the tomatoes as well as gardeners stepping all over the vines and

WHY SHOULD YOU GROW VERTICALLY?

- It's spectacular.
- It saves space.
- You grow better crops.
- It adds a third dimension to your SFG.
- It costs less than you could imagine!
- It lasts for years.

HOW DO YOU GROW VERTICALLY?

- Build a super strong steel frame
- Attach nylon netting

WHERE DO YOU GROW VERTICALLY?

- Along the north edge of your 4 x 4
- Next to any fence or building wall

WHEN DO YOU GROW VERTICALLY?

- Anytime before vine crops start sprawling

crushing them when trying to harvest the fruit. The whole idea of growing tomatoes this way seems very non-productive. At the time, the only cages available were too short and too weak to solve the problem.

I said, "This is no way to treat a tomato. We can't let it lie down and sprawl all over the ground. It should be allowed to stand up straight and tall so that it can be proud of itself and a benefit and credit to the community."

Six months later my vertical frame was designed, tested, and put into operation. It was an All-American model made from rigid German steel conduit and Japanese twine. It was so strong that it held up through rain, sleet, snow, and heavy September storms when the tomato plant filled the entire frame and was loaded with red, ripe tomatoes.

After growing tomatoes this unique and attractive way for several years, I began thinking about the other vine crops that spread all over the garden. Could they be grown the same way? First I tried pole beans (a no-brainer), then cucumbers and peas. Then even winter and summer squash. They all worked and grew well, and they looked just great growing on a vertical frame. And I was so pleased with the results of growing vine crops this new way that I said, "This is a good thing," and included the method in my first book on SFG.

But since then—Wow! You should see the vertical gardens now. The pumpkins, all kinds of melons (including the new smaller watermelons), and all of the really big squashes grow 7 feet in the air.

VERTICAL GARDENING

A few years ago at our display gardens in Utah, we were growing 35-pound pumpkins 7 feet in the air. We made the vertical frames 8 feet above the ground for no other reason than we wanted to show off and demonstrate how tall they can be! Now this was a spectacular sight, and many people have wanted to know how they could accomplish this same feat in their own backyard.

We usually refer to vertical gardening as "Advanced SFG." But, really, as soon as you master the basics of Square Foot Gardening, you can enjoy growing crops vertically. And you will be the envy of the neighborhood when you do.

Picture This

Can you just picture a wall of green in your garden filled with vine crops like tomatoes, cucumbers, pole beans, even melons and squash?

Installing a Vertical Frame

MATERIALS

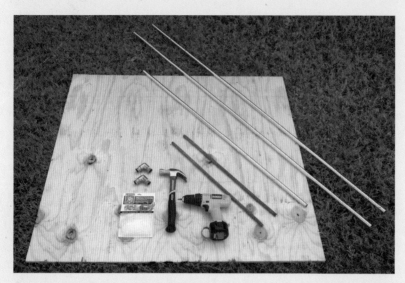

To construct a vertical frame, you need: two 5-foot electrical conduit pipes (½-inch diameter); one 4-foot conduit pipe (½-inch diameter); two 18-inch long rebar supports of ½-inch diameter; screwdriver; hammer; two elbow connectors; and trellis netting.

ASSEMBLY

Once you've attached the elbow connectors to your 4-foot conduit pipe, lay it against the north-facing board of your SFG. Next, hammer the rebar where the elbows are located. You'll want to drive the rebar in about half its height.

Slide the 5-foot conduit pipes over the rebar for a standard strength vertical frame. Or use a short steel fence post instead of the rebar for an extra-strong frame.

Attach the top conduit to the legs and tighten the screws in the elbows.

All the colorful fruit just hanging there waiting to be picked! No sprawling plants all over the ground with their fruit lying on the soil getting all dirty and eaten by slugs. These walls of green can even be located so they hide any unsightly areas of the yard or garage. They can even give you some privacy to keep neighbors from peering over the fence to look at your SFG. It's not only a spectacular sight, but those plants will be up in the air getting better sunshine and air movement. They'll produce a more useable harvest for you with nothing wasted. To top all that off, each plant will only take 1 or 2 square feet of garden space and grow perfectly well in your 6 inches of Mel's Mix. Another big advantage is you can do all this standing up—no bending, kneeling, or squatting down to tend your plants.

CONSTRUCTING SUPPORTS

I experimented through the years with all different types of materials and frames, and I finally settled upon one that was so simple, easy, and inexpensive to use that it was almost ridiculous.

I found that electrical conduit is the cheapest, strongest, and best material to use for the vertical supports. I do not like PVC pipe or wood because it eventually will bend and break and destroy your whole vertical garden. When you first build and plant a vertical frame out of just about anything, it looks sturdy and strong. But, near the end of the growing season, when your plants have grown to the top and filled up all the open spaces, that frame acts like a sail on a boat. Just when your tomatoes are getting ripe and ready to pick, along comes a late summer storm with lots of wind and rain, and the next thing you know the whole thing is flat on the ground.

Using electrical conduit and a steel ground rod (rebar) will prevent this from happening. And the two posts and top are simple and inexpensive to buy and install.

The conduit itself costs a few dollars for a 10-foot length, so you can see we're not talking about big bucks here, and you should be able to talk the clerk at the store into cutting it in half. For the corners you can buy elbows, pre-bent rounded corners or bend your own if you have a conduit bender (about twenty bucks at the same store). It's kind of fun to bend the conduit, and once you get the knack of it, it comes out nice and smooth with good curves (see the photo on page 30). The

HOW MUCH ROOM?	
Plants Per Square Foot	**Plants Per Two Square Feet**
Gourds (1)	Melons (1)
Tomatoes (1)	Pumpkins (1)
Cucumbers (2)	Summer Squash (1)
Pole Beans (8)	Watermelon (1)
	Winter Squash (1)

straight pipes are connected with a simple metal coupling (see the photo on page 163) that has two set screws that tighten each pipe together, and they both usually cost less than a dollar.

Placement of Vertical Supports in the SFG Garden

When you're deciding where to place your vertical frames, keep in mind that you don't want the vines to shade the rest of the garden. So, the frames work best when placed on the north side of each box. If you want more vertical crops than one frame per box, you can make double or triple boxes and turn them east and west so the frames can go all along the north side. You could also devote a special-sized box just for vertical crops. Make a 2 × 12-foot or any length box with a vertical frame continuously on the north side. This could stand against a wall or fence. You could even plant the front squares with pretty flowers or any low-growing crop like peppers or eggplant that will look great and will hide the bottom stems of the vertical vines.

INSTALLING THE VERTICAL FRAME

Your vertical frame should be installed outside the box, so it sits on the ground. Aside from driving the concrete reinforcing bars (rebar) into the ground, and slipping the conduit over them, you could also attach the vertical frame to your box with pipe clamps on the side. This would give them even more stability.

Securing Vertical Supports In the Ground

To secure the vertical frame, pound two ½-inch diameter pieces of concrete reinforcing bars (rebar) into the ground. These bars can be purchased already cut at any building supply store and should be anywhere between 18 to 24 inches long depending on your soil. The looser (sandier) your soil is, then the longer the bar should be. Drive the rebar halfway into the ground, keeping it nice and straight; I suggest you wear gloves for this. The two electrical conduit legs slip right over those ½-inch rebars and are securely in place. We never pound on the conduit itself because the ends will bend and then they won't fit into the coupling or over the rebar.

Extra-Strong Frame for Heavy Crops

To make the vertical frame extra strong for watermelons, squash, and pumpkins, drive a steel fence post into the ground first instead of the rebar. A fence post can be just the shortest 3-foot tall size. Once the fence post is in the ground, then the conduit is attached to it with three pipe clamps. The whole frame then becomes so strong that it will hold up any weight no matter how high you go.

Attaching Vertical Frame Netting

To attach the trellis netting to your frame, first hook the netting on the two corners. Next, cut the netting at each connection. This will give you one long strand. (Be careful to cut on the same side of the connecting strand each time.)

Loop the long strand over the top of the frame and firmly tie a simple knot. Try to keep the length uniform so your netting isn't crooked.

Make the same cuts down the sides of the frame and firmly tie knots around the supporting pipes.

Tie the netting tight and your vertical frame will look neat and trim for many years.

VERTICAL SUPPORTS ON A PATIO, BALCONY, ROOFTOP, OR WAIST-HIGH GARDEN

Vertical supports can also be added to patio, balcony, or waist-high gardens. They are constructed in the same manner. However, we suggest that they be no taller than 4 feet.

Instead of using rebar in the ground to secure the supports, they are fastened to the garden box using special clamps screwed into the sides of the box. Buy those when and where you buy your conduit and lumber. In this situation, there's not a great strength with the vertical frame, so it would be necessary to put the struts from the top down to the south side of the box, and depending on how high, and your location, the wind, and the plant growth, you might have to provide additional support, such as guy wires.

NYLON NETTING ON THE SUPPORTS

Now that the vertical frame has been constructed, it is time to add something for the plants to grow on. I used to use either special wide-opening fencing or good strong synthetic twine or cord, but then along came this beautiful, soft, indestructible nylon netting with large openings you can reach through. This nylon garden netting is now the only material I use for vertical gardening. It's white, keeps its color, can't be broken, will last forever, and is easy to work with. The netting is tied tightly and securely to the top and sides of the vertical frame, and the plants can then be gently woven in and out of the netting as they grow. The netting comes in 4- and 5-foot widths and various lengths and is available at most garden centers and catalogs. When we teach our classes, it is always fun to ask two of the strongest men to come up front and try to break the netting; they just can't do it!

> At least once a week, gently take the new growth on your vertical crops, and carefully weave it in and out of the netting. The wide squares in the netting make it easy to reach through and guide your plants without breaking them.

ARBORS AND WALKWAYS

If an upside-down, U-shaped metal vertical frame works so well for one box, just think of all the various shapes, sizes, and arrangements you can make with more vertical frames.

You can put two together in a straight line, turn a corner, or even zigzag. You can put four together to form an arbor. You can put netting on two sides so it's a walk-through, on three sides so it's a sitting area, or on four sides with one little opening for the kids to play in. That would be a secret place, and you could put netting across the top or run two sets of vertical frames down a pathway, creating a wall. You could even create a whole maze with dead ends, turns, and twists. All of the types of plants that would grow on it produce huge leaves, and make a very interesting visual pattern for your yard.

And don't forget vining flowers. If you want something that blooms every year with little care required, instead of an annual vine, you might want to plant something more permanent like a perennial flower such as clematis, honeysuckle, climbing roses, trumpet vine, or thumbelina. Another good summer vining crop is New Zealand spinach. If you had long walkways with the vertical frames down each side, you could build 2-foot-by-any-length boxes and have them on the outside giving you plenty of walking room. You could also put them so that 1 foot is inside the path, and 1 foot is outside. I would plant the vine crops on the outside so they would climb up the netting, and plant flowers along the inside that will do well in the eventual shade of the pathway—perhaps something like impatiens or coleus.

PLANTS THAT GROW VERTICALLY

Seed packets and catalogs often do not indicate whether a variety is a vining or bush type. The seed companies are constantly changing and adding new varieties, and in order to find out the best ones that vine, I would suggest that you call (if they have a toll-free number) or e-mail the various seed companies to find out. Tell them you are doing Square Foot Gardening and want to grow crops vertically and that you want to know which of their varieties are vines which need trellising and support.

Planting Seeds or Transplants

Remember, tomatoes are the only vine crop you cannot start as a seed directly in the garden. They take so long to grow into a sizeable plant that in most cases we have to grow or buy transplants to put into the garden as soon as the last frost of spring is over. The rest of the vine crops can be started from seed directly in the garden. The seed planting chart in the Appendix shows when to plant them at the best time, and Chapter 9 shows you how to start the season earlier or extend it later.

EASY CLIMB

One of the particularly desirable points of vertical gardening is that there's very little maintenance to do for the plants. Aside from watering, it's a matter of once a week tucking the tops of the plant in through an opening in the netting, and back through another one, so

With tight netting and a strong frame, you'll be able to grow all sorts of vining crops.

they keep climbing up the netting. Some of the vertical crops, like pole beans and cucumbers, will do all the climbing themselves, but tomatoes have to be helped through the openings and pointed to the top. The netting is so strong that it will easily hold up the plant and, in fact, after further studies I found out the netting will also hold up all the fruit, including small watermelons and pumpkins. Some of the winter squashes got so heavy I was afraid late summer storms would blow over the whole contraption. It depends on how strong the ground rods are and how tough the soil is. But if your frame is located outside the box and the ground rod is pounded into your existing soil, it would require bending the rebar, or the electrical conduit, before the frame would come down.

TOMATOES

The most popular home garden vegetable is tomatoes, and when you're vertical gardening the SFG way, there are a few things you can do to increase your yields.

Tomatoes and the Single Stem Method

The theory behind pruning to one single stem is that all the energy goes straight up the main stalk, and you will have more tomatoes per square foot than if you allow it to put energy into branching out.

Nature has already taught some vines to climb. You basically just need to plant the seeds and watch them go!

Because tomato plants aren't natural vining crops, you'll need to train yours up through the vertical netting.

That means you have to cut off the branches, and the best time to do it is when they're tiny. Unfortunately, most gardeners don't. They look so small and cute, and as they grow bigger and bigger, they begin to take on the appearance of a productive plant and it becomes hard to cut them back.

To help convince you to prune off those suckers, remember that the nice thing about them is once you prune them, you can root them, and they can become another plant for a late crop.

No matter how large the sucker or side branch, you can stand it in a glass of water and transplant that into the ground as soon as the roots sprout. Or, you can stick those suckers in a cup of vermiculite, and keep that in a saucer of water, and they will also sprout roots. They are great, free plants for a late harvest for canning, juice, or preserving.

Get in the habit of inspecting and pruning your tomato plants once a week to a single stem, and weave the top in and out of the netting. At the same time, check the overall appearance of the plant to make sure you have no tomato worms visiting.

You have to use your own judgment, but after you get accustomed to bending plants, you'll get used to their resilience. You'll know how far they can bend and when not to push them. Remember, though, if you're bending a plant near the top or in through the netting, the end is very supple and easy to maneuver. However, if you're trying to bend the stem closer to where it's planted, the vine will be hard and fairly rigid. So, if you have to bend it there, you might stuff something under it like an old wadded-up tee shirt. In a few days, you can retrieve the shirt after the stem has taken the new shape.

Lay Tomatoes Down

Since a tomato plant can sprout new roots along its main stem, I have found that the best way to plant the main crop of tomatoes is to lay them down horizontally in a shallow trench. They will develop an enormous number of roots, all along that hairy stem, which will sustain a larger, more productive plant. Pick your best-looking plants, and pinch or cut off the lower leaves (at least two or three) so you have a tall skinny plant ready to plant in a lay-me-down position.

To do this, you first locate the square foot it's going to be in, take your hand or a trowel, and dig out a long shallow trench, perhaps 3 or 4 inches deep in the middle of the square and as long as your tomato plant is. Make the trench long enough so you can lay down the plant with the root ball at one end. Dig a little deeper for the root ball and then lay the stem on the bottom of the trench. At the other end where the top is (remember you cut off most of the lower leaves), very, very carefully bend the top so it starts pointing up. You can take the Mel's Mix, and push it underneath that bent top to act as a pillow (see, this is really a bed), and if you're very gentle, you'll end up with the top sticking out of the soil at a slight angle. It does not have to point straight up; it just has to be aboveground. Fill in the rest of the trench and water well.

In just a few days that top will straighten itself up, and at the same time all the new roots will start sprouting out from the main stem. If you noticed the root system when you put the plant in the ground, depending on what size pot it was growing in, it probably had a very small rootball, perhaps only 1 or 2 inches wide, and 1 or 2 inches long. But now for the average transplant you're going to develop a 6- to 8-inch rootball along the entire length. This procedure will not take any strength from the plant, and it will not delay any of the first tomatoes you're going to harvest from that plant. In fact, because of its extra root strength and size, it will be a more vigorous grower than before.

Some books may advise you to dig a deep hole, and plant the tomato straight down deep so just the top leaves show, thus burying the entire stem with the idea that the roots will still sprout along the stem. This is okay, but that puts the plant quite deep in the ground and usually it's still springtime and the ground is still fairly cool. So I've found the lay-me-down method will make the plant grow much faster, because the soil at that level is warmer, by perhaps as much as 10 degrees. After the plant is heading skyward, you treat it the exact same way as any other tomato transplant. This method of lay-me-down planting also will give you more fruit because the first fruiting branch to form along the main stem will be closer to the ground, allowing you more distance to the top of your vertical frame to have fruit.

> *"More manageable, enjoyable, and bountiful than I'd ever imagined."*
> *– Manja from Oregon*

Tomato Worm

If you see some of your tomato leaves are chewed up, you may have the dreaded tomato worm. Look for little black specks (the droppings from the worms), and check the surrounding leaves to find them. The worms are camouflaged but still brightly colored, large, and beautiful. Usually there are just one or two at the most. (Caution: do not pick it up. Tomato worms emit a very foul smell that will get on your hands and clothes.)

Play it safe. Get your scissors, and cut off the leaf. Put it in a paper bag, seal it, and throw it in the garbage. Tomato worms don't usually harm the tomatoes themselves, but they take strength from the plant as they eat many of the leaves. If your children are interested in a

This vertical garden has bean and tomato plants. They are planted with sage and squash. Think of the harvest!

science project, you might have them come and look at the tomato horn worm and get their ears as close as they can. They can actually hear them crunching the leaves. (Be careful, the worms could jump on your head—no, I'm only kidding!)

Over the Top

What do you do when the tomato plant gets to the top of your tower, and there is still a lot of growing season left? You have two choices, depending on how many tomatoes you've picked so far and how many green ones are coming. You can either cut the top right off, stop its growth, and allow a good part of the energy to go into the existing tomatoes. Or, you can let the top continue to grow, and let it hang over the side. It will keep growing until the end of the season, which for a tomato plant is the first frost. If you want to protect this plant from the first frost (and everyone does), the vertical frame is designed so all you have to do is gently lay a tarp or blanket over it. Next morning take it off, fold it up, and you're ready until the next threat of frost. This way you can keep your tomato plants growing and producing for several more weeks.

PRUNING CUCUMBERS, MELONS, AND MORE

The other vine crops can have their side branches continue to grow until the whole plant takes up too much space. In general you want the plant to spread out to be approximately 1 to 2 feet wide on the vertical frame netting. If you plant one plant per square foot, it can fill that 12-inch wide square, going right up the netting. If the spacing for that particular vegetable (for example, cucumbers that are spaced 2 per square foot), you would trim the side branches back so that each one is from 6 to 9 inches wide outside of its space. Squash is a little different because the leaves are so large that it's hard to judge where the stem is and how much room the entire plant is taking. That's why we give squash a lot more room (2 square feet per plant) in the vertical garden. Although most squash plants will grow on one central stalk, some do branch. Those with branches take longer to have fruit, so if you cut them off all the energy will go to the main branch and the flowers and fruit on that main branch. When it grows to the top, let it hang down until it gets near the bottom, put it through the netting, turn it up, and start all over again.

All the vining plants are very vigorous, energetic, and sturdy, so there's not much you can do to deter their growth. But whenever you're bending a stem to poke it through the netting or over the top, hold it with two hands and be careful so it doesn't break.

SAFETY PRECAUTIONS

If your crops are growing thickly and have covered the 4-foot-wide frames, you might want to play it safe and put guy wires on the vertical frame when you get near the end of the season. This requires tying something like fishing line or strong cord from the top bar down to the south side of the box. For the north side, you could always prop the top up with a 12-foot board cut out with a notch to fit into the top bar. That would hold the frame up from both directions.

COLD-SEASON HANDLING OF A VERTICAL FRAME

After the growing season is over, the frame can be removed intact and hung out of the way in the garage to wait for the next growing season.

STEP-BY-STEP VERTICAL FRAMES

Materials	Assembly	Install	Maintenance
Legs One 10-foot length ½-inch steel electrical conduit	Cut in half with pipe cutter or the store may cut for you	**Step 1** Assemble elbows to top	**Winter Storage** Slip vertical frame off ground rods and hang on fence or garage wall
Top One 4-foot length ½-inch steel electrical conduit	Cut or buy 4-foot long from 10-foot piece	**Step 2** Measure location for ground rods	Mark and protect ground rod with brightly colored tape or paint
Ground Rods Two 24-inch long ½-inch reinforcing bar	Nothing to do	**Step 3** Hammer ground rods halfway into ground	
Connectors Two 90° elbows	Nothing to do	**Step 4** Slip pipe legs over ground rods	
Netting Nylon trellis netting Openings 7 x 7-inch Size: 4-feet wide x 5-feet tall	Cut outside netting squares to create long tie strings	**Step 5** Assemble top to legs **Step 6** Tie netting tight to top and legs	

Some people leave their vertical frame up all winter, and during the holiday season, weave brightly colored ribbon or even lights in and out of the netting to decorate for the holidays!

CONCLUSION

We have seen how beneficial and easy vertical gardening can be. Not only can you grow vining crops in less space, but harvesting becomes much easier and crops don't get soft and mushy from resting on the ground. Vertical frames add beauty to a garden as well as that unique, upward dimension.

So, we encourage you to add this innovative feature of Square Foot Gardening to your own garden. You will be so glad you did!

Extending
the Seasons

We gardeners like to bend reality a bit.
Nature says, "You can't plant now, it's too
cold." But we say, "Wanna make a bet?" This
chapter will show you how to get the most
out of your garden each year by pushing
the envelope on nature's conditions.

Floating covers like
this material, draped
over a support such
as the "wagon frame"
hoops shown in this
SFG can significantly
extend your growing
season—and the time
you can enjoy fresh
fruits and vegetables.

With a variety of easy-to-make implements, your garden can grow 30 to 50 percent more produce each year. And in addition to the extra food, it extends the beauty of the garden and the satisfaction of the gardener. However, this idea isn't necessarily for the first-time gardener unless you've got a lot of time, a natural talent, and a lot of confidence.

Nature gives us our gardening cues as the seasons change. We're going to use those seasonal cycles as our framework for this chapter. But first, why would you want to extend your seasons? Well, would you like to pick the first tomatoes on the block? Would you like a garden-fresh salad on Thanksgiving? Your answer to these questions will help you determine how much work you want to put into extending the growing season because growing out of season does require more time and effort.

LENGTHEN SEASON BY 50 PERCENT

In most parts of the continental United States, the average growing season runs from May to September. This means that most gardeners grow vegetables during an average of six months out of a possible twelve. When these six months are extended by an additional two months, the growing season is extended by 33 percent. A three-month extension provides a 50 percent increase—a worthwhile goal that can be achieved easily and inexpensively. Gardeners gain a great sense of accomplishment from these increased yields, and modern homesteaders and food preservers find it an absolute blessing.

Square Foot Gardeners don't have the negative experiences associated with doing all that hard work when they garden, so they look forward to more gardening and want to lengthen the growing season. For them, gardening isn't a test of endurance. It's a pleasant experience. They don't want to know how soon they can quit, but how long they can continue experiencing the joy of gardening!

Don't think you must extend the season to be an accomplished gardener. Sometimes it's just as good to sit back, relax, and just "go dormant" for a while. Instead of gardening you could be satisfied and save time and work.

KID'S SCIENCE PROJECT

If you want to be really scientific, get a thermometer to measure the soil temperature at the surface, but be sure to cover the thermometer so the sun doesn't shine directly on it. Also take the temperature of the soil at a depth of 2 inches. Then measure and record the same information in a 4 x 4 that has been covered with black or clear plastic. Use the charts in this book to find how long it takes seeds to sprout at certain temperatures. Plot all that information, and then use the charts to compare the quicker seed sprouting time. Not only is this a fun project for the kids, it will enable you to get an earlier, more successful start on your garden.

It's your decision. But if you think it's time to trick nature into feeding you year-round, then read on! The rest of the chapter will explain what to do each season to extend your harvest from cool-weather and warm-weather plants.

Extend the Harvest by Growing Out of Season

The obvious way to extend the garden year is to start earlier than usual and keep the plants growing later. Cool-weather crops can be grown in two extra plantings for a longer season. The first planting is made in the early spring and will mature in the cool weather of late spring. The second crop of cool-weather plants can be planted in late summer to mature in the late fall.

Since early spring and late fall can bring some rather severe weather, growing out of season is simply keeping the cold temperatures away from your plants. To do this, it's important to provide these crops with the extra protection they need from the elements.

By covering and protecting your crops, you are basically creating an artificial environment. After all, that is what a greenhouse does—it keeps the cold air out but lets the sunlight in. What more could a plant want?

In addition, all of the summer or hot-weather crops can be started two to three weeks earlier than normal and they, too, can be extended up to a month beyond their normal season in the fall. Then, an extra planting of lettuce, spinach, and radishes can be grown during the hot summer months that are normally considered out of season for these two crops. Sound like a lot of work? With Square Foot Gardening, it's easier than you think. It all depends on you providing protection from the sudden and harsh temperatures and weather.

Box with Cage

Since a Square Foot Garden takes up so little space, it is relatively easy to protect your crops.

While special techniques that provide extra protection may vary with the season and the variety of vegetable, they are quickly learned and easily practiced. Chapter 4 explains how to build a special box and the various kinds of protective cages. These structures make it possible to moderate the climate in that box so you can stretch your growing season at both ends.

EARLY SPRING

A great time to extend the growing season is early spring before anyone else is out gardening. Begin by warming up the soil in your SFG boxes. Spread clear or black plastic over the top of the soil, and

It's okay to start seeds inside to get a jump on the season, but you still have to practice good SFG methods. This gardener planted too many seeds—remember, a pinch is two to three seeds, not ten.

weigh it down with a brick in each corner. After a couple of sunny days, take the cover off, lift the grid out, and mix up the soil with a trowel so the warmer surface soil is moved down below and the colder, deeper soils are raised to the top. Then replace the plastic covers. This is no big deal since your Mel's Mix is loose and friable at all times of the year. Besides, the soil is only 6 inches deep. How much work could that be?

JUMP START YOUR SEEDS

If you want to get a quicker start and earlier growth, try sprouting your seeds indoors, and then transplanting them into individual containers when they are very young. Before the plants get too large, harden them off before planting them outdoors in your spring box.

SPRING

For your first spring planting, set up a spring box with a storm window cover or the PVC type structure over any garden square where you'll be planting an early crop so the sun will start warming the soil. Do this about four weeks before it's time to plant your seeds. For a double-quick soil warm-up, cover the soil with clear or black plastic, and then remove it before planting. Or you can use plastic covered cages over individual squares around the garden instead of the entire 4 × 4-foot area. When the weather is warm enough, transplant the plants you've grown into the open garden squares. They can also be left to grow where they were planted by removing the protective cage from the squares.

Climate Control

When you're using a spring box on your early crops, remember that fresh air has to get in and you have to vent out the hot air that builds up on sunny days even in cold or freezing weather.

Heat builds up quickly in the boxes on sunny days. As the weather warms up, slide or lift the cover open a little farther each week until you can remove it entirely. (Don't try to prop up a glass storm window with sticks; believe me, the wind will blow it down whenever you're not around.) A light frost won't hurt most cool-weather crops, but too much heat will cook them. It takes a little experience to learn how to control the heat and moisture inside your frame. Keep in mind these precautions when trying to grow out of season.

> You must check your spring plant boxes every day in sunny weather. If your plants begin to wilt or if the soil dries to a depth of 1 inch, it's time to water. Water with a cup of sun-warmed water.

Extending Cool-Weather Crops into Summer

In addition to lettuce and radishes, you might also try growing spinach or even cabbage out of season into the early summer. Spring crops can be grown from seeds or from transplants started indoors a few weeks ahead of time. When choosing varieties of cool-weather crops to grow into summer, look for words like "long standing," "slow to bolt," and "heat resistant" in the seed catalogs or packet descriptions.

SUMMER

As the spring season progresses, it's time to give some summer vegetables—such as beans, squash, and cucumbers—a head start. For earlier harvests, try starting the seeds for these warm-weather crops right in their permanent location under a protective cage two weeks before the usual planting time. They will be much hardier and stronger than seedlings grown on the windowsill. When all danger of frost is past, remove the covers.

There is an entire industry with all kinds of protective devices and products to help the gardener be successful in early gardening. They vary from water-filled walls around the plant to special ground covers designed to heat up the soil quicker. Try some of these products and see what happens. I always like to place an unprotected plant right next to the protected one for comparison.

Shade and Water

If you're the type of person who doesn't like hot, sticky weather, and you literally wilt in the sun, then the obvious solution is to move into the shade with a large pitcher of your favorite cold drink. Well, lettuce and radishes are no different. If you can provide shade for these spring crops (especially during the noon sun), along with some extra water, you will be able to harvest throughout most of the summer. Look for special hot-weather varieties of your favorite plants in your seed catalog.

Cover the square with a shade cage, and give the plants plenty of water—as a general rule, water twice as often as you usually would. Remember, one of the best aids for growing a good crop is Mel's Mix—our soil mix that combines equal parts peat moss, coarse vermiculite, and blended compost. It holds lots of moisture so the plant roots can take up all that's needed, yet drains well so the roots can't become waterlogged.

Shade Screens

The shade cage will admit enough light for proper growth while keeping the temperature down considerably. A layer of thick mulch will also help moderate soil temperatures. You can also make use of natural shade or sun screens by locating a planting of spring crops behind (to the north of) your vertical growing frames.

Keep in mind that you're growing out of season, which means it is not the plant's natural inclination to grow then. You are urging these plants on, so be generous with your help and attention and don't expect too much. Just enjoy the challenge and experience!

Summer Plants into Fall

Gardeners sometimes wonder whether the extra effort involved in protecting summer crops from the first fall frost is worth the effort.

SUMMER LETTUCE

Did you ever notice that just when all of the good summer salad vegetables are ready—like tomatoes, cucumbers, and peppers—the lettuce and radishes are all gone? In the hot, long days of summer, these spring crops bolt and set seed, becoming bitter and unappetizing. However, there is a way to get around this and still "have your salad and eat it, too!"

1. Cover lettuce with a shade cage (see Chapter 4 for instructions).

2. Give it twice as much as water as you normally would.

3. Cover the ground surrounding the lettuce with a thick layer of mulch.

I think it certainly is, if you want an extra two or three weeks worth of harvest from all those warm-weather crops. Quite often the first frost is followed by a long period of clear, warm weather before the next frost. If you can protect your garden from that first frost, you can enjoy green plants and fresh vegetables during one of the most pleasant periods of the year—mid-autumn. Since most of these crops have a six to eight week harvest season, the extra two to three weeks gained amount to quite a bit—more than a 25 percent extension of the season.

All Together Now

To protect your crops from frost, you can start with a PVC arch or covered wagon frame, and then cover it with a large sheet of plastic, floating cover, or light blanket. Fasten down the corners so it won't blow off during the night. Or, the low-growing crops can be readily protected with a loose covering of hay that is easily removed the next morning.

To protect vine crops from frost, just throw a blanket or tarp over the vertical frame so it's hanging down on all sides. This is one of the prime advantages of growing squash, tomatoes, cucumbers, pole beans, pumpkins, and similar summer crops on a vertical frame.

When all the summer crops grow in the same box it's easier to protect them from frost.

1. Cover summer crops with a PVC arch or wagon frame (see Chapter 4 for details).

2. Add a plastic cover and fasten down the corners, or

3. Cover the crops with loose hay.

FALL

When fall arrives, you and your garden have three options: to store food for the winter, extend the harvest, or stop your garden. Whichever you choose depends on your time and desire.

PLANTING BEFORE FIRST FALL FROST	
Five to Ten Weeks Before Frost	**Zero to Five Weeks Before Frost**
Broccoli	Lettuce
Cabbage	Radishes
Cauliflower	
Beets	
Carrots	
Lettuce	
Spinach	

Extending the Harvest by Storing It

Let's look at the easiest and least-known way to extend the harvest—storing it. There's the old-fashioned but economical canning, preserving, and freezing for the future, and it has a place. But I think the most economical and environmentally correct way to extend the season is to store the harvest. There is almost no work and money involved, and the flavor and nutritional value of each vegetable is greater than if it was frozen or canned.

HANDLE YOUR HARVEST GENTLY

The only secret of successful storage is actually very simple—learn each vegetable's best storage conditions and provide it. There are really only two: cool and dry, or cold and moist. The list of vegetables that need cool and dry conditions is easy to remember because there are only a few—pumpkins, winter squash, and onions. The temperature should be around 50° to 60°F, and the humidity needs to be fairly low—at about 50 percent.

Try to find a cool corner of your garage or basement where the temperature stays above 35 but below 60°F. If you think your storage area might freeze or get too warm at times, you can build two walls to enclose a corner to provide an even-temperature fruit closet. Add some insulation, and remember to allow plenty of air circulation. Don't stack produce up in a big pile, but spread your vegetables out evenly on a shelf (not on the floor).

Handle produce as gently and infrequently as possible. When you're out harvesting, treat each vegetable as if it were an egg. Any bruise or cut will be the first spot to spoil. Lay each harvested vegetable separately in a box of sawdust or crumpled newspaper; don't pile them all together. Do not wash or scrub the produce.

These carrots were lifted from their growing beds in autumn and stored in trays of moist peat moss or similar mix, kept in a garden shed. Stored this way, they'll last until spring.

Leave the bottom of the root on root crops, and at least an inch of the top growth. For crops such as vine crops, leave as much of the stem on as possible. Only store produce that is in really good condition.

Vegetables in the group that need cold and moist conditions are all root crops—beets, carrots, turnips, white potatoes, and winter radishes plus all of the cabbage family. This group also includes fruit—especially apples. The ideal storage temperature for them is as cold as you can get without actually freezing—35° to 45°F.

Actually, the simplest way to store root crops is not to dig them up at all. Roll a bale of hay over the planted area; this will break their tops and stop the plant's growing cycle while keeping the ground from freezing. When you're ready to harvest, simply roll the bale over, dig up a few vegetables, and then replace the bale. Regular radishes won't hold up too long in freezing weather while the winter radish will last almost indefinitely. Carrots and leeks also do quite well through the entire winter. If you're feeling adventurous, you can experiment with leaving different root crops in the ground to see which last through the fall and winter so you'll know what to expect the following year.

Cozy Cover

Cabbage and other leaf and head crops can also be stored in the garden, but they won't do well under a solid bale of hay. Instead, it is better to use a loose, fluffy covering of straw or leaves. To keep the wind from blowing this loose covering around, try placing a 2-foot-high fence of chicken wire around your garden areas and anchoring the wiring at each corner with stakes.

DIG IT IN

Another storage method for root crops is to bury a container in the ground and pack your vegetables in layers of moist sawdust, peat moss, or sand. You can sink a plastic or metal garbage can straight into the ground while keeping the top a few inches above the surface so no water gets in. Make sure the cover fits tightly; then pile at least 12 inches of hay or leaves over the top. Keep everything

---

DON'T FEED THE ANIMALS

There is one problem with using hay bales as winter mulch—they can provide a cozy nest for ground mice and voles that love to eat crunchy root crops. So keep an eye out for these pests and any damage they may be doing. If they do infest your winter storage plot, it's best to harvest everything and store your produce in a different place.

dry by covering it with a weighted-down plastic sheet or tarp. Watch out for leaks in the container that can allow groundwater to seep in. If you can, select an area on high ground to locate the storage container. The ground will not freeze under or around this container, and your vegetables will be maintained in a very even and moist condition.

TEMPERATURE DIFFERENCES

On a cold night you can walk around your property and actually feel the differences in temperature. The cold air virtually rolls down the slope and settles in low-lying areas; in fact, this is called cold air drainage. Surprisingly, this will happen even where there is not a great difference in elevation. Once you get the knack of watching out for frost and covering your plants when it threatens, you will see the advantages of locating a garden on the top or south side of a slope rather than at the bottom of a low area. You will also see the advantage of grouping your crops according to their weather requirements. This makes it easier to protect them from either frost or freezing in both the spring and fall. One of the greatest advantages of SFG is how easy it is to protect your garden since it is condensed into small, uniform areas.

It's much simpler and more cost effective to grow cool-weather crops for an extended season using a sun-heated box that protects plants from just the severe weather fluctuations.

Frost

Frost forms when the outdoor temperature drops below the freezing point, resulting in the deposit of ice crystals. Plant material will freeze when there is an accumulation of cold air, 32°F or below, at ground level. Frost can, and does, occur in low areas while the hills and slopes right next to them might be frost-free. This is because hot air rises and cold air sinks. If a body of water is nearby, it can greatly reduce the occurrence of frost as water holds heat very well.

In general, frost usually occurs in the very early morning hours, particularly after a still, calm night when the weather is dry. The

WRITE IT DOWN

Don't forget to draw a diagram of what's left in the garden and where so you won't be frantically digging around on a cold winter afternoon looking for the carrots but finding only radishes. The entire garden looks the same once the snow covers everything.

GROWING WINTER VEGGIES

1. Select fast-growing varieties with superior cold resistance.
2. Select the sunniest sheltered spot in your yard (it can be temporary).
3. Plant in a sheltered box.

chances of frost are also increased following the passage of a cold front, indicated by an intermittent and changing weather pattern of broken clouds and occasional precipitation; this is in contrast to the steady or continuous rain and the heavy, low-hanging clouds that accompany a warm front.

When frost is predicted, be ready. Your best bet is to catch the evening weather forecast, particularly the local one. Another (perhaps better) source is the Internet. One of the best websites is www. weather.com. Click on "Lifestyle," then "Home and Garden," then "Lawn and Garden" and enter your zip code. You'll get all the information you need to be ready for that first frost.

Light Versus Hard Frost

A light frost blackens the outer leaves of most summer flowers and vegetables. It is indicated by a white covering on the lawn in very early morning. Summer vegetables can still be harvested if eaten right away.

A hard frost will blacken and kill all summer flowers and vegetables. Plants that were bushy and colorful the day before are now just droopy skeletons with blackened leaves hanging like rags from the stems. This can be very disheartening for gardeners who come out in the morning to find that the garden has been devastated. A hard frost is indicated by a crunchy feel to the ground and a thin film of ice on the birdbath. This is the time when most gardeners declare an end to the season. But if you have planted some colorful fall-blooming plants (mums, asters, and some hardy daisies) along with the fall vegetables, and you clean up the garden right away, your garden will still look attractive and inviting after a hard frost. Your spirits will be lifted and you can go on to enjoy an autumn garden.

WINTER

Gardeners who are particularly ambitious and want to continue growing something all winter will need additional tools for providing special protection to a very select variety of plants. If you can keep the ground from freezing solid and provide sunlight in just a small area, in many parts of the country you can continue growing special varieties of lettuce and spinach, hardy leaf crops such as kale, and a number of oriental vegetables all winter long. It's also possible to plant some members of the onion family in the fall in order to get a larger or early crop next spring and summer. Call your county extension service for local advice and conditions.

As you continue gardening, you'll learn which vegetables are hardier in your particular area. Wind and rain have a lot to do with plant survival and how much protection you need to provide.

Special Cold Varieties

Salad from your garden during the coldest months of winter? You bet. A fall box (that's just a SFG box that's used during the fall) can provide fresh salad each week during the winter without a greenhouse. Here's how: select fast-growing vegetables for your winter garden. Try any of the hardy salad greens and root crops, but look for special cold-tolerant varieties. Every seed company offers different varieties so look through catalogs and select those that are recommended for cold and winter growing. Look for names that have words in them like "Arctic," "Frost King," or "Snow Man" (I just made that last one up).

PICK A SPOT

Now, pick the sunniest, most sheltered spot you can find for your winter garden. It doesn't have to be in the main garden; next to the house or garage is better, especially if you have white painted brick or stucco walls, since they will reflect quite a bit of heat into your miniature garden. Remember that the sun is very low in the sky during the winter, and the place that may have been in full sun during the summer could now very well be a very shady place in the winter. Don't place the box under the roof or gutter line, or you'll risk the chance that rain, sleet, or snow will fall on it. You'll be in good shape if the area is sheltered from strong winter winds and if it gets a maximum amount of winter sunlight. It doesn't have to be a permanent spot either. First, lay down a sheet of plastic or sturdy weed cloth and in the spring you can pick everything up and return the area back to its former use.

> *"Fantastic! It very much appeals to my innate sense of organization and efficiency."*
> *– Jeff from North Carolina*

Snuggle Up

Install your winter box, fill it with Mel's Mix, and start your planting. Since the plants will grow very slowly compared to spring and summer and since you'll be harvesting every leaf almost as it is ready, you can plant your produce closer than the usual spacing, even as close as one-half the recommended distance.

Insulate

Provide some insulation around the winter box, by banking the outside with soil or placing bales of hay all around. Provide a tight-fitting cover or make a double-layer cover with plastic to keep the soil and air from losing heat at night. Throw a blanket or tarp on the box for those extra cold nights.

> "Best book on gardening I've ever read, wish I'd found it years ago."
> – Mindy from New Jersey

PUTTING YOUR GARDEN TO BED

When it is time to put the SFG to bed, we do this the same way we put our children to bed. You wouldn't think of sending them to their room and paying no attention to them would you? Instead, we encourage them to prepare for bedtime—to brush their teeth, get one last drink, fix the bed just the way they want it, and then spend some time reading a bedtime story. Then it's finally lights out.

Well, treat your garden the same way. Don't leave it a mess with dead plants and debris lying about. Tidy it up and make it look good. Now is an excellent time to mix a little extra compost in each box and smooth and level it out so it will be all ready for the spring planting. That's never happened before with single-row gardening. Now it's not only possible, but also very practical.

The little extra work you do in the fall will keep your garden attractive and neat-looking all winter and make your springtime garden easier to begin. You'll simply go out, rake off the mulch cover (remember your rototilling neighbor?), and start planting either at the regular time or early.

Grids in Winter

You can remove, clean, fold, and hang up the grids now or leave them on the boxes all winter, which will remind you of how much fun you have now with gardening. What I'm suggesting for the end of the season is really no different than what I recommend you do all season long. Keep your garden neat, tidy, and attractive. If you keep it in tip-top condition (and that's not too difficult with a no-work garden), you will enjoy it so much more.

TAKE NOTES

The only thing you might want to do is record in a notebook or journal some of the highlights of this past year—notes for improvements, special varieties of plants, and tips for next year.

DECORATE FOR THE HOLIDAYS

You'll enjoy SFG much more if you keep your garden neat and attractive at all times.

Since you no longer have to hoe the weeds or dig and cultivate the soil, you'll have time and energy for the pleasant things like trimming off yellow or dead lower leaves, dead blossoms, removing plants, or dead and pest-damaged leaves or entire plants.

But what about winter? Not much work to do after putting the garden to bed, but you might think about decorating the garden so it still looks nice all winter long or at least for the holidays.

Thanksgiving

Make a nice arrangement in one or more boxes of a fall scene, like a stack of corn with pumpkins. Some of the boxes could just have a bale or two of hay or straw. Maybe even a scarecrow in a box. Those boxes could be covered with cloth (like white garden floating covers) or old colored sheets tacked or stapled down.

Christmas or Winter

Here are some ideas that will make your SFG festive during the bleak winter months.

1. Make Christmas boxes out of your garden boxes by using old colored or striped sheets, a tarp or table cloth, or floating garden covers.
2. Think ahead when you go to yard sales or the thrift shop. Many covers could serve double duty as frost covers in the fall, then decorative covers in the winter.
3. Use wide, colorful ribbon, rope, or contrasting colored strips of sheets to tie bows on the boxes. Tuck in greens and pine cones, even lights if you can get an extension cord to the garden. (Remember now, your garden no longer needs to be way out back; it can be right near your back door where you'll see it more often.)
4. Decorate your vertical frames with decorative lights, pine branches, pine cones, and bird feeders.

After Christmas, stick a discarded Christmas tree in the center of each box, and make them into bird feeders, with or without lights. Tie a string from each box corner to the treetop for support.

START SMALL

This chapter has taught us how to extend all the seasons and how doing that can give us an extra 50 percent of gardening time. How exciting! If you read through all this and felt a little discouraged or glazed-over, don't worry. If you have never grown out-of-season, add just a few features here and there as you gain more confidence. It can be a really fun challenge to any gardener—regardless of experience. As with all new gardening projects, my recommendation is to start small in order to gain experience, confidence, and pleasure—then expand. And just in case you need more convincing, remember that All New Square Foot Gardening eliminates so many gardening tasks that you have the time and energy to extend the seasons.

OUT WITH THE OLD

Old Way	New Way
1. Clean off summer residue	Do this daily and it won't accumulate
2. Turn over the soil	No longer necessary
3. Perform a pH test	No longer necessary
4. Add all the humus you can get	No longer necessary
5. Add peat moss if no humus	No longer necessary
6. Add new 3 to 6 inch layer	No longer necessary
7. Dig in manure or leaf mold	No longer necessary
8. Add some fertilizer	No longer necessary
9. Use a fork, shovel, spade	No longer necessary–use trowel
10. Dig as deep as you can	No longer necessary
11. Deeper is better	No longer necessary
12. Break up clods, remove stones	No longer necessary

Special Gardens and Gardeners

Not every yard is the ideal flat and sunny surface for gardening. Some are sloped, some are shaded, and some are oddly shaped. Gardeners, too, come in many different forms, from the very young, to the very old, the healthy and strong, to the physically disabled. But regardless of the specific conditions in your yard, or what type of gardener you may be, SFG is designed to accommodate all kinds.

Bringing the SFG method into schools with the "Square Yard in the School Yard" program has helped teach many, many youngsters about the benefits of gardening and SFG in particular.

No Yard

Sometimes a property may have limited space for a garden. If you're in a no-property situation, think creatively and closer to your front or back door. For instance, patios, decks, and balconies always have room for a small garden. A corner of a patio or balcony could contain several 2 × 2-foot boxes. These could be stacked up creatively at different heights to form a very attractive corner garden that would use less space than a 4 × 4-foot area. The boxes could be placed on low tables of different heights or on something like milk crates or cinder blocks in order to give each one a different height. If you install a vertical frame with netting along both walls or just tack the netting to the walls, it could fan out so it gets larger as it gets higher to expand the garden area even larger. Another option, of course, is at the base of and even on top of a balcony or deck railing. You could install 6- to 12-inch wide boxes on the floor or bolted to the top of or hanging from the railing on both sides. This would create almost a wall of gardens ending up in quite a few available square feet.

WOODED YARD

If you have a heavily wooded yard, then you don't have too many choices. One solution is to locate several boxes around the house wherever they might receive enough sunlight. Your boxes could be on the ground or even on legs next to the house. If you had a southern exposure with enough sunlight, you could put a double-decker long box against the house. Other than that, the only choice would be to make a clearing in the woods, but that would have to be a fairly substantial area to get your SFG boxes out of the shade. If these suggestions don't work—it's shade gardening for you.

HILLSIDES

What if the only space you have for a garden is on a hillside or fairly steep slope?

If it's facing south, it may be worthwhile to develop it for your All New Square Foot Garden. The limiting factors are how steep the slope is and how big your garden is going to be. You're in luck with a SFG because you can build boxes that will fit into the lay of the land.

Basically, in order to have a level garden so your soil and water don't run off, you're going to cut a path into the hillside wide enough to make a garden area. If you want a 4-foot-wide bed, you will have to

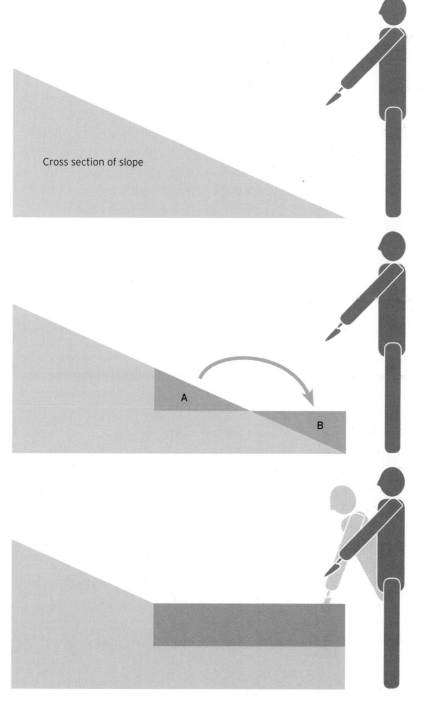

SFG ON A SLOPE

Cross section of slope

A

B

1. The "cut and fill" technique is an effective way to install an SFG box on a sloping yard. First, decide exactly where you want to install the box.

2. The beauty of this method is that the minimum amount of earth is moved around. A section is dug out (a) and then placed at the foot of the slope to create a base (B).

3. The ground is leveled off and you can now place a box frame there, line it and fill it with Mel's Mix.

reach in from both sides and that can be too much of a stretch from the uphill side. However, with a 3-foot wide box, which will be higher than the downhill aisle, you will be able to reach in the full 3 feet from the downhill side because you are standing up rather than kneeling down next to the box.

To get a 3-foot wide level spot, you just cut into the hill and move the soil downhill to form the 3-foot wide areas.

Think ahead about water availability, time, and the cost to dig and then level a pathway wide enough to hold both you and your garden. The steeper the slope, the harder it becomes.

DECKS

When creating deck gardens in an apartment or condominium, be sure to consider the people below you and how you're going to water. Your garden may not be a problem when it rains, but when it is sunny and bright and your garden water drips down on the neighbors while they are at their barbeque below, they may not look favorably upon you or your garden.

There are several things you can do about this situation. First of all, since Mel's Mix holds water so well, it's highly unlikely you will overwater, which will prevent a lot of dripping or excess water leakage. Just in case, though, you can always choose not to drill drain holes at consistent intervals over the entire bottom of your SFG, but only a couple in one corner. Then, slightly slope the box towards this one corner and put a decorative vase or other container underneath to catch any drips that may leak out.

RAILINGS

Another popular location for a garden is on a railing—particularly on a wooden railing. Railing boxes make a very decorative and excellent garden, particularly if you include trailing plants that add some color and character. If you have railings that are flat, it is very easy to set a box right on top of it. For stability, it should be bolted down. If you can't bolt your boxes to the railing and you're higher than the first floor, I would place the boxes on the floor. Consider the strength and size of your railing and the surrounding environment to make sure your railing boxes aren't too big. There are various holders sold at home improvement stores that snap onto your railings and can accommodate standard-sized boxes. These boxes can hang over the outside or inside of your railing, depending on your preference. One advantage of having the box hang over the outside edge is the box won't take up any of your valuable deck space. In addition, should it drip when you're watering, the water will bypass the deck below. There is one safety concern and that is anything falling. If your box is on the inside of the railing, it doesn't have far to fall and won't hurt anyone.

GRANDPARENTS

One of the greatest bonds that I have found between grandparents and grandchildren is formed during a gardening project, even if the visit is short. Give your grandchild a garden or just a square, let him write his name on the grid, encourage her to plant her garden, and you may find your grandchildren will keep in touch more often just to find out how the garden is growing. This, of course, can work just the opposite way when the grandparent visits the child's home and they plant a garden there. And, of course, there will be great anticipation for the next visit and what has happened in the garden. Selecting plants for children is quite simple; plants should be easy to grow, fast growing for quick results, and something that will produce an exciting result.

GARDENING FOR SENIORS

Some people find it difficult to do hard, manual labor like digging up the existing soil, as well as getting down on the ground and then getting back up again. With SFG, the simple answer is to just raise the garden up to the gardener's height. It can be a sit-down garden, which is particularly adaptable for a person in a wheelchair or someone that wants to sit and garden. A little higher would be a stand-up garden if that makes it easier to tend; since there is very little maintenance— just nurturing—you are not standing for long periods of time. And the gardens, once they have a plywood bottom installed, can be moved to any location for the convenience and pleasure of the gardener.

You can now put various sizes of boxes on patios, near the pool, the back door, or any pleasant area around the house that is easy for a senior to attend to their garden. Of course, there is no longer the need to walk way out back carrying a bunch of heavy-duty tools. Now, it is just a matter of going to your garden and tending it with the minimal amount of effort, work, and tools. There is no weeding, and because we are starting with a perfect soil mix, there is never any heavy

SFG FOR SENIOR CITIZENS

As we get older, it may become harder to do certain things. With SFG, you'll see another big advantage when you harvest 1 square foot and add that trowel full of compost. There's no heavy digging! You can readily visualize how conventional gardening would become too much work and too much effort, causing someone to give it up. SFG has the advantages of small space, no heavy equipment, and raised boxes. Wheelchair, sitdown, or standup gardening is now a real possibility. The best support for a tabletop garden is a strong table with four legs, giving all-around access. The less desirable method is the use of sawhorses, which may be sturdy, but limit the access. The least desirable method is a table with just a center support, which could be unstable. But in any case, it almost boils down to just planting a few seeds, growing, and caring for them. Gardening then becomes a very simple, easy, and pleasant, task. So you'll never have to stop gardening if you're using the All New Square Foot Garden method.

digging. There is no need to even have shovels or forks or any large tools, just one trowel.

Sometimes seniors enjoy out-of-season gardening because they have the time to tend their gardens during the tricky, out-of-season weather. This also gets them moving about out of doors more often, which is another asset.

SPECIAL NEEDS GARDENING

SFGs have gone a lot of places over the years. They've been placed on wheels; we know of a veteran's hospital where a SFG was built on a gurney and wheeled from the roof down the service elevator so it could be taken to bedridden patients. The SFG Foundation has taught the blind; I designed a SFG for the Helen Keller Institute on Long Island where blind students learned gardening. We have also taught at the school for the deaf in Salt Lake City, Utah. Other worthwhile places we have installed SFGs are in prisons and troubled youth facilities. Building a small portable garden (in sizes from 2 × 2 up to 4 × 4 with a plywood bottom added) allows people to participate who otherwise might not have been able to garden.

GARDENING IN SCHOOLS

One thing I've learned from teaching SFG over the last thirty years is that kids love to garden. They are so excited about growing plants. From the beginning, it was obvious that SFG is perfect for teaching arithmetic and all kinds of math and, that in fact, anything in the scientific field is easily taught using gardening as the vehicle. But then I began to see that a teacher could readily relate all subjects to gardening.

One of the best examples of this is a teacher in California named Sandy. She teaches every subject in the classroom through the class's Square Foot Gardens. One year, the final project was to have each student write me a letter telling me about their garden. They each described what they liked best and then drew a picture illustrating it. They were learning penmanship, spelling, pronunciation, letter writing, and the ability to describe observations and feelings. During the year, Sandy covered many aspects of science and art, as well as economics, history, language, communication, and the environmental issues. The class produced a play and video about SFG and invited parents and the rest of the school to come learn with them. This, of course, gave Sandy the opportunity to teach play writing, acting, stage presence, costume design and making, advertising, publicity, promotion, and so much more. A side benefit is that, in addition to school subjects, the children learned the important values of sharing, nurturing, and responsibility.

We have worked with all age groups from preschool through high school using gardening as a teaching tool. Suddenly learning begins to have some type of meaning in their lives, and they can begin to see the value of the subjects they have been learning in the past.

A Square Yard in the School Yard

The only change in SFG for children is that we make the box a little smaller because they can't reach in as far. Instead they garden in a 3 × 3-foot box, which equals a square yard. As I mentioned before, this is how we got the name for our school program, "A Square Yard in the School Yard." We have the description and photos of many school programs on our website on the School Gardening page.

A plan needs to be made on what to do with the gardens during the summer vacation period. There are lots of solutions—all you need to do is brainstorm with the students, and the brainstorming itself becomes another learning experience!

COMMUNITY GARDENS

With SFG, it is possible to have pocket gardens anywhere in the community, even right in a city. It doesn't take an entire empty lot now, and it doesn't have to be a huge project to convert space into a community garden. It is now possible to take just a corner of that lot or any other small space—perhaps even in an existing city park—and have a very small community Square Foot Garden. Each person can have from one 4 × 4-foot box up to an area of perhaps 12 × 12, which would enable them to have four or more boxes. One of the best things about using SFG in a community garden is that since there are no weeds, the garden doesn't become an overrun eyesore by the middle of the summer. This means it is much easier to operate and get public and official approval. If you want to start a community garden, I would emphasize the need again to start small, gain experience, become successful, and then expand during the second season or year.

Community gardens do require a set of guidelines for what participants can and cannot grow so they don't interfere with their neighbor's garden; the guidelines should also cover the hours of operation, use of water, and maintenance of the gardens so they look neat and attractive. The use of pesticides and fertilizer was always a big concern with community gardens, but that issue can be totally eliminated with SFG.

In the layout of the garden, it would be nice to have several tables where people in wheelchairs could wheel right up to their assigned garden plot. Also, several benches and some shade are always a good feature.

GROUP PROJECTS

A SFG could be a demonstration project for many different groups, including children's gardens, scouts, 4-H'ers, Master Gardeners, botanical gardens, and garden clubs. A group could create a salad garden with all the fixings—lettuce, tomatoes, root crops, and edible flowers. Each square would have a nice sign stating what is there and how it is used in a salad. Another idea would be an herb display with signs and an invitation to touch the plants.

> *"Your method is awesome. My 3-year-old and I have a blast with two 4 × 6 boxes."*
> *– Rich from North Carolina*

The nice part about the idea of using a SFG is it requires so little maintenance yet produces such a spectacular showcase. It is an easy way of attracting new members or of putting on a demonstration at a function. Another nice thing about it is, at the end of a fair or show, four people can pick up the garden, put it into a van, and take it home. In that situation, you can even include a shortened vertical frame so that it would still fit in the vehicle and yet would add a third dimension to your display.

HUMANITARIAN PROJECTS

For some, gardening is an enjoyable hobby, but for many it can mean the difference between life and death. One step up from starving—the worst condition in the world—is poverty and continual hunger—and that's where SFG comes in. We can help solve the hunger situation. We have a billion people who need help, and the solution is to teach them how to help themselves. They need to be shown how and then helped to start just one Square Meter Garden of their own; the rest will follow. We teach them to use straight compost in their gardens because of the lack of peat moss and vermiculite in many of these areas of the world;

they can create compost for free, while improving their environment. We believe that, instead of our governments and humanitarian organizations sending food, they should start educational programs that teach people how to compost and how to create a SFG garden. It would cost less, produce more, allow people to become self-sufficient, take very little effort, and yet deliver worthwhile results.

That is why the SFG Foundation is so intent on taking Square Foot Gardening worldwide with its international counterpart Square Meter Gardening. We feel it can truly make a difference in the every-day lives of so many millions of people.

On My Soapbox

Well, here I am, on my soapbox trying to solve worldwide problems when you just want to learn how to have a better garden in your yard. But what this book is all about is how SFG can reach and help so many more people.

That's the significant and imperative message I want to bring to the world. Will you help me? You can—by encouraging others to start a SFG. Get involved in your community or stretch your involvement to the entire world. Anyone, anywhere in the world can now have a small square meter garden right at their back door. The nutritional value of the children's diet will improve dramatically and step-by-step, and as they expand their garden, that family will be closer to self-sufficiency and independence from government and private aid programs. You know the saying, "Give a man a fish and you feed him for a day. Teach a man to fish and you feed him for a lifetime." The world hunger problem can never be solved until we help people help themselves, step-by-step, square-by-square. Then, maybe the saying will be, "Show a family how to Square Meter Garden, and they will feed themselves forever."

Appendix

That just about wraps up the SGM method, apart from this summary.

AT A GLANCE

VEGETABLES

Name	Family	Height	Spacing per Square Foot	Growing Season	Weeks from Seed to Harvest	Years You Can Store Seeds
Asparagus	Lily	4-6 feet	1 or 4	spring, summer	3 years	3
Bean, Bush	Pulse	12-18 inches	9	summer	8	3-4
Bean, Pole	Pulse	4-7 feet	8	summer	10	3-4
Beet	Goosefoot	12 inches	large - 9 small - 16	spring, summer, fall	8	4-5
Broccoli	Mustard	18-24 inches	1	spring, fall	16	5-6
Cabbage	Mustard	12-18 inches	1	spring, fall	16	5-6
Carrot	Carrot	12 inches	16	spring, summer, fall, winter*	10	3-4
Cauliflower	Mustard	18-24 inches	1	spring, fall	14	5-6
Chard, Swiss	Goosefoot	12-18 inches	4	spring, summer, fall, winter*	8	4-5
Corn	Grass	5-6 feet	4	summer	9-13	1-2
Cucumber	Gourd	vine	2	summer	9	5-6
Eggplant	Nightshade	24-30 inches	1	summer	19	5-6
Lettuce	Composite	6-12 inches	4	spring, summer*, fall, winter*	7	5-6
Melon	Gourd	vine	1 per 2 sq. ft.	summer	12	5-6
Okra	Lily	18-24 inches	1	summer	12	2
Onion	Lily	12 inches	16	spring, summer	20	1-2
Parsley	Carrot	6-12 inches	4	spring, summer, fall, winter*	14	2-3
Pea, Sugar Snap	Pulse	vine	8	spring, fall	10	3-4
Pepper	Nightshade	12-24 inches	1	summer	19	4-5
Potato	Nightshade	12-24 inches	4	spring, summer, fall	12	Plant last year's potatoes
Radish	Mustard	6-12 inches	16	spring, summer*, fall	4	5-6
Spinach	Goosefoot	6-12 inches	9	spring, fall, winter*	7	5-6
Strawberry	Rose	6-12 inches	4	spring, fall	perennial	Use plants

VEGETABLES (continued)

Name	Family	Height	Spacing per Square Foot	Growing Season	Weeks from Seed to Harvest	Years You Can Store Seeds
Summer Squash	Gourd	bush vine	1 per 9 sq. ft. 1 per 2 sq. ft.	summer	8	5-6
Winter Squash	Gourd	vine	1 per 2 sq. ft.	summer	12	5-6
Tomato	Nightshade	bush vine	1 per 9 sq. ft. 1 per 1 sq. ft.	summer	17	4-5

HERBS

Name	Family	Height	Spacing per Square Foot	Growing Season	Weeks from Seed to Harvest	Years You Can Store Seeds
Basil	Mint	1-2 feet	small-4 large-1	summer	12	5
Chive	Lily	6-12 inches	16	late spring, summer	16	2
Cilantro	Umbellifer	1-2 feet	1	late spring, summer	5 (leaves) 12 (seeds)	N/A
Mint	Mint	1-3 feet	1	spring, summer, fall	N/A	N/A
Oregano	Mint	1-2 feet	1	spring, summer, fall	16	N/A

FLOWERS

Name	Family	Height	Spacing per Square Foot	Growing Season	Weeks from Seed to Harvest	Years You Can Store Seeds
Dahlia	Daisy	1-3 feet	small-4 medium-1	summer, fall	10-12	2-3
Dusty Miller	Daisy	12-18 inches	4	late spring, summer, fall	15	N/A
Marigold	Daisy	6-12 inches 1½-3 feet	dwarf-4, large-1	summer, fall	10	2-3
Pansy	Viola	6-9 inches	4	spring, summer (if cool), fall	20	N/A
Petunia	Nightshade	6-18 inches	4	late spring, summer, early fall	14	N/A
Salvia	Mint	1-2 feet	4	late spring, summer, early fall	14	1 (use fresh seed)

*In some parts of the country and under certain weather conditions, these can be grown in this season.
N/A = Not advised to store seed.

Basil and Beyond

Although we associate basil with Italian cooking, it is an important ingredient in Asian cuisine too. 'Siam Queen' is a spicy Thai basil with an intense flavor and fragrance. 'Holy Basil' is a sacred herb in India where it is used in religious ceremonies and planted around Hindu temples. Introduced to Europe in the sixteenth century as a culinary and medicinal herb, it made its way to England and America in the mid-seventeenth century.

Basil is used as the perfect complement to summer tomatoes. For a summertime treat, combine tomatoes, basil, garlic, olive oil, and balsamic vinegar in a food processor, spread on crusty bread, and sprinkle with Parmesan cheese.

Six plants of 'Sweet Genovese' will yield enough leaves to make pesto all year without overdosing on it. A mixture of basil, garlic, Parmesan cheese, and olive oil, pesto is a treat with a distinctive Italian flavor. Try making pesto bread instead of garlic bread, or use pesto as an imaginative sandwich spread.

- 2 cups basil leaves
- 2 cloves garlic
- ½ cup grated Parmesan cheese
- 2 tbsp. Romano cheese
- ¼ cup pine nuts or walnuts
- dash of salt
- ½ cup olive oil
- water

Combine basil, garlic, cheeses, nuts, and salt in a food processor or blender. With the machine running, slowly add olive oil. Thin with a few drops of water until it reaches the consistency of oatmeal—not too thick but not runny. Let stand 5 minutes before serving. Toss with cooked pasta; gemelli and penne hold the pesto nicely.

For a creamier taste and consistency, add 3 tablespoons of whole milk ricotta cheese. For a color and taste sensation, add ⅓ cup of sun-dried tomatoes.

To freeze basil for pesto, wash and dry 2 cups of leaves (a salad spinner works well), and chop them in a small food processor with ¼ cup olive oil. Scrape the mixture onto plastic wrap, fold it up, and put the resulting patty in the freezer. To use, defrost the patty, and put it in the food processor with all the other ingredients. Just remember that there is already ¼ cup of olive oil in the patty, so be sure to only use an additional ¼ cup to make up the ½ cup called for in the recipe. Stock up during the peak growing season, and use them all year long in the recipe above. Freezing basil in this way does no noticeable harm to the color or flavor, so you can have the taste of an Italian summer all year round.

When planting basil close to tomatoes and peppers, it is thought they will all grow stronger and more flavorful, and the basil will prevent some of the insects and diseases associated with tomatoes. A layer of basil leaves over a bowl of tomatoes will repel fruit flies.

'Spicy Globe' dwarf basil is a beautiful plant. It grows in adorable little balls perfect for a front-of-the-border accent, with the added attraction of having small leaves that are the perfect size for adding to herbed butters or vinegars. Although cinnamon and licorice basil have a delicious scent, they are an acquired taste for some people. The flavor of lemon basil, on the other hand, is an irresistible mixture of sweet and citrus that complements the lighter foods of summer. Try it in place of parsley when cooking rice or chicken. Or make a light, sweet pesto with lemon basil, olive oil, lemon juice, and Parmesan cheese to top summer tomatoes, bread, or pasta. 'Sweet Dani,' an All-America Selections winner in 1998, is as pretty as it is tasty.

Regardless of what you call it or what your heritage may be, if you are going to grow one herb this summer, basil is the one to choose. And if you really must grow only one variety of basil, make it 'Sweet Genovese.'

GROWING AND CARING FOR BASIL

Start basil from seed outdoors after the last spring frost (basil needs warm nights), or indoors about 4 to 6 weeks before. Or choose plants at your local garden center, but keep them sheltered until that last frost. Once hot weather sets in, basil plants will grow quickly, but they won't amount to much if they get chilled early in the season. Basil plants will turn black and die at the slightest hint of frost.

Sow seeds or set transplants in your SFG or a window box in full sun and keep well watered throughout the growing season. Pinch off flower buds to save the plant's energy for leaf growth. Also pinch out growing tips to keep the plants bushy.

To harvest basil, cut whole stems just above a pair of lower leaves. The plant will grow new stems from that point. Only the leaves are used in fresh or frozen recipes; the stems go to the mulch pile.

To dry basil, hang entire stems upside down out of direct sunlight. Remove the dried leaves from the stems and store in an airtight container. Crush dried leaves into your favorite sauces for a subtle basil flavor.

Now let's talk about some other plants.

Herbs like basil are ideal additions to a Square Foot Garden.

ASPARAGUS

BOTANICAL INFORMATION
Family: Lily
Height: 4 to 6 feet
Spacing: 1 or 4 per square

GROWING SEASON
Spring: yes
Summer: yes
Fall: no
Winter: no

Seed to Harvest/Flower: 3 years
Seeds Storage: 3 years
Weeks to Maturity: 12 weeks
Indoor Seed Starting: 10 to 12 weeks before last spring frost
Earliest Outdoor Planting: 2 to 4 weeks before last spring frost
Additional Plantings: not needed
Last Planting: not needed

Description

Fresh, tender asparagus spears from the spring garden have no rival in the supermarket—and can be easily grown in a Square Foot Garden. Because it is a biennial and takes a couple of years before the first harvest, producing only one crop a year, we suggest you plant an entire 4 × 4 box only in asparagus. The plants get very bushy throughout the summer and need quite a bit of room to spread out so leave good aisle space around them. When you invest in an asparagus plant, consider the location very carefully, as it can last for up to 20 years.

Starting

Location: Full sun.

Seeds Indoors: 10 to 12 weeks before last spring frost. Soak seeds overnight and plant at least ½ inch deep.

Transplanting: 2 to 4 weeks before last spring frost.

Seeds Outdoors: 2 to 4 weeks before the last spring frost, plant seeds that have been soaked in water overnight in a hole between ½ and 1 inch deep.

Traditionally, you buy and plant 2-year-old roots, one per square foot. But I've found that if you can afford to buy enough of the roots, four per square foot will produce a much bigger crop earlier.

The conventional way of planting asparagus is to put about 3 inches of your Mel's Mix down, mark your spacing (either the one or four per square foot), make little mounds at the plant location, and then drape the roots (purchased at the nursery or through mail order) over each one of those little mounds. Then pour in the rest of the Mel's Mix (about 3 more inches, to total 6 inches deep), which covers the roots an inch or two.

If you have lots of time but little money, raise your own transplants from seed. It takes an extra year or two, but costs peanuts.

Growing

Watering: Weekly, more in the summer.

Maintenance: Cut the foliage to the ground in fall as it turns yellow and before the berries ripen. Asparagus self-sows readily, often with less than perfect results.

Harvesting

How: Cut the largest asparagus shoots at the surface of the soil with a sharp serrated knife, making a slanting cut.

When: Harvest asparagus in late spring, when the shoots are 4 to 6 inches tall, for about 6 weeks. Spears taller than 6 inches can be tough. Harvest from mature plants only: don't harvest from first-year plants, and only sparingly, say one or two shoots per plant, the second year. Three-year-old plants are considered mature.

Preparing and Using

Asparagus is best used as fresh as possible, but it can be stored for a couple of days in the refrigerator, standing on end on a wet pad or in a jar of cold water. Asparagus can be eaten raw, steamed, boiled, grilled, roasted, or cooked in casseroles and salads. Tall narrow asparagus kettles are designed to cook the spears upright, immersing the stems while the tender heads steam. Cook asparagus briefly as it can become mushy if overcooked.

Problems

Slugs, asparagus beetle, rust, Fusarium root rot.

> ### Hints and Tips
>
> After the spring harvest, the remaining shoots grow into a large, lacy plant in the garden, and the fronds are lovely to use as filler in flower bouquets.
>
> Male plants are the most desirable as they are the most productive and do not set seed.

BEAN

BOTANICAL INFORMATION
Family: Pulse
Height:
Bush: 12 to 18 inches
Pole: 4 to 7 feet
Spacing:
Bush: 9 per square
Pole: 8 per square
GROWING SEASON
Spring: no
Summer: yes
Fall: no
Winter: no

Seed to Harvest/Flower:
Bush: 8 weeks
Pole: 10 weeks
Seeds Storage: 3 to 4 years
Weeks to Maturity:
Bush: 8 weeks
Pole: 9 weeks
Indoor Seed Starting: no
Earliest Outdoor Planting: immediately after the last spring frost
Additional Plantings: every 2 weeks

Description

Prolific and easy to grow, beans—whether of the bush or pole variety—are a terrific crop for any garden. A lot of gardeners think that pole beans have better flavor, while the bush types taste more like "green beans." Bush beans grow lower to the ground; each plant yields one large crop all at once, with a smaller crop a few weeks later. Pole beans, which are grown on a vertical frame, take longer to grow, but provide a steady continuous yield all season long. A single planting of pole types is adequate, while additional plantings of the bush types are needed to have a constant harvest.

Starting
Location: Full sun.

Seeds Indoors: No.

Transplanting: Does not transplant well.

Seeds Outdoors: Presoak seeds thirty minutes for faster sprouting. Water soil and cover square with a chicken-wire cage to keep out birds. Seeds sprout in 5 to 10 days; remove cage after two weeks. For a continuous harvest of bush beans, plant a new square of a different color or variety every 2 weeks all summer long.

Growing
Watering: Beans must have regular waterings. Do not allow the soil to dry out, but keep the leaves dry.

Maintenance: Weed weekly if you see any weeds sprouting.

Harvesting
How: Break or cut each stem holding the bean pod (there's no harm done if the bean breaks and part of the pod stays on the vine). Do not pull on the plant when harvesting.

When: Pick beans when they are still small and tender. Do not allow them to get so large that pods bulge with seeds; the plant will stop producing and the best flavor is past.

Preparing and Using
Wash and refrigerate if not using immediately. Beans do not store well, so try to use them the same day they are picked. In the old days, beans were called string beans and the string had to be pulled off before cooking. Newer varieties—called snap beans—only form strings if you let them get too tough and large. Beans contain lots of vitamins A, B, and C, as well as calcium and iron.

There are probably as many ways to prepare and serve beans as there are varieties in the seed catalogs. Beans are good eaten raw when they are small—remember, the smaller the bean, the more tender it will be. Raw beans can be served whole with a dip or cut into pieces for addition to a salad.

Cook any size bean. They can be steamed, boiled, or stir-fried, then served individually with a little seasoning, grated cheese, or parsley. Beans are excellent additions to soups, stews, or mixed vegetable dishes. Leftovers are easily marinated for addition to a salad or use as a relish; I've even heard of people adding marinated beans to a sandwich, along with lettuce, tomato, and cheese! How does that sound?

Problems

Aphids, Japanese and Mexican bean beetles, birds, rabbits, woodchucks, and deer; blight, rust and mildew. Sounds like a lot but they are still worthwhile.

Hints and Tips

If your square of bush beans gets floppy and starts spreading over adjacent squares, just run a string around them as a group to keep them in their square. It won't harm the harvest.

BEET

BOTANICAL INFORMATION
  Family: Goosefoot
  Height: 12 inches
  Spacing: 9 or 16 per square
GROWING SEASON
  Spring: yes
  Summer: yes
  Fall: yes
  Winter: no

Seed to Harvest/Flower: 8 weeks
Seeds Storage: 4 to 5 years
Weeks to Maturity: 8 weeks
Earliest Outdoor Planting: 3 weeks before last spring frost
Additional Plantings: every 3 weeks

Description

Beets are a wonderful vegetable to grow because they're easy and both the roots and the greens (tops) are suitable for eating. They are mostly pest- and disease-free and resistant to both fall and spring frosts. The root gets very hard when grown in the hot summer season.

Starting

Location: Partial shade or full sun.
Seeds Indoors: No.
Transplanting: Does not transplant well.
Seeds Outdoors: Each seed in the packet is actually a cluster of two to five individual seeds, so several sprouts will come up from each seed planted. Plant one presoaked seed in each space ½ inch deep three weeks before the last spring frost. To have a continuous harvest, plant a new square every three weeks except in the hottest part of the summer. After the sprouts are about 1 inch tall, cut off all except the strongest plant from each seed cluster.

Growing

Watering: Plants need constant and even moisture.

Maintenance: Keep damaged leaves picked off, mulch in hot weather, and weed weekly.

Harvesting

How: Pull up the entire plant with the largest top. If you're not sure of bulb size, dig around the root with your fingers to uncover the top to check the size. To harvest greens, individual leaves can be cut at any time, but don't take more than one or two from each plant.

When: Roots are the most tender when half size, so start pulling when the roots are approximately the size of a Ping-Pong ball and continue until they are full size. Leaves are usable at any size.

Preparing and Using

Use greens whole or chopped in fresh salads, or cook them like spinach. Roots are rich in iron and vitamin B. Serve hot—boiled or steamed. Marinate leftovers for a salad or relish. Try sautéing shredded raw beets quickly and serve hot, or try them cooked and chilled (shredded, sliced, or diced) in salads or mixed with cottage cheese. Small whole beets can also be cooked and served with an orange sauce, salad dressing, or a spoonful of sour cream.

Problems

Cutworms, slugs and snails, leaf miners, rabbits, woodchucks, and deer. Relatively disease-free.

BROCCOLI

BOTANICAL INFORMATION
- **Family:** Mustard
- **Height:** 18 to 24 inches
- **Spacing:** 1 per square

GROWING SEASON
- **Spring:** yes
- **Summer:** no
- **Fall:** yes
- **Winter:** no

Seed to Harvest/Flower: 16 weeks
Seeds Storage: 5 to 6 years
Weeks to Maturity: 9 weeks
Indoor Seed Starting: 12 weeks before last spring frost
Earliest Outdoor Planting: 5 weeks before last spring frost

Description

Broccoli requires cool weather but is great in a Square Foot Garden. It is very frost hardy and grows well in the spring and fall; it doesn't do well in the summer heat.

Starting

Location: Needs full sun.

Seeds Indoors: Plant 5 to 10 seeds in a cup of vermiculite, or place one
  seed ¼ inch deep in potting soil in each individual compartment of
  a seedling tray, approximately 12 weeks before your last spring
  frost. Seed will sprout indoors in 5 to 10 days at 70°F. Keep seed
  warm (70°F) until sprouted; move to full sunlight as soon as the
  first shoots appear.

Transplanting: Plant outside approximately five weeks before the last
  spring frost.

Seeds Outdoors: Not satisfactory, as the season is too short before hot
  weather arrives.

Growing

Watering: Like all members of the cabbage family, you're growing
  leaves and flowers, which need consistent moisture. Never let
  broccoli dry out or wilt.

Maintenance: Weed weekly; mulch in warmer weather.

Harvesting

How: Cut off the main central head at its base with a sharp, serrated
  knife or clippers, leaving as many leaves on the plant as possible.
  Within a few weeks, new side-shoots (miniature heads) will form and
  grow from the original plant to provide you with a second harvest.

When: Harvest as soon as a head appears full and tight. The head is
  actually a flower head, which you want to harvest before the flower
  buds open. If you have several plants, don't wait too long to cut the
  first one after the heads start forming, even if it looks a little small.
  It's still edible when it's small.

Preparing and Using

Broccoli contains vitamins A, B, and C, as well as calcium, phosphorus,
and iron. Wash under running water and soak in cold salted water for
two hours if there's any chance that a green cabbage worm is present
in the head. Refrigerate if you're not using immediately. Broccoli can
be served fresh and raw with mayonnaise, or any dip, or can be
chopped fresh into a salad. To cook it, you can steam, boil, or stir-fry.
Try it plain with just a little dressing, sour cream, or topped with a
cheese sauce. Cooked leftovers can be marinated for addition to salads
or relishes. It's an excellent addition to any stir-fried dish; mix it with
interesting combinations of meats and vegetables.

Problems

Cutworms, root maggots, green worms, and cabbage worms; club root.

Hints and Tips

After you cut the main stalk, don't remove the plant, as new smaller heads will form for a second harvest. Some claim the smaller side-shoots are even more flavorful than the central head.

CABBAGE

**BOTANICAL
INFORMATION**
  Family: Mustard
  Height: 12 to
  18 inches
  Spacing: 1 per square
GROWING SEASON
  Spring: yes
  Summer: no
  Fall: yes
  Winter: no

Seed to Harvest/Flower: 16 weeks
Seeds Storage: 5 to 6 years
Weeks to Maturity: 9 weeks
Indoor Seed Starting: 12 weeks before last spring frost
Earliest Outdoor Planting: 5 weeks before last
  spring frost

Description

Cabbage is a very easy vegetable to grow: it's frost hardy and takes
very little work. Cabbage comes in a variety of shapes, sizes, colors,
and leaf textures, and can be grown as an early- to late-season crop;
the early-season variety is smaller and faster growing, while the late-
or long-season variety is usually bigger. All varieties grow best in cool
spring or fall weather.

Starting

Location: Full sun.

Seeds Indoors: Plant one seed ¼ inch deep in potting soil in individual
    compartments of a seedling tray 12 weeks before your last spring
    frost. Seeds sprout in 5 to 8 days at 70°F. For a second crop in the
    fall, repeat the process anytime in the middle of June (or back up 16
    weeks from your first fall frost date). In most places you can
    usually start seeds of a new crop as soon as you've harvested your
    spring crop. Keep warm (70°F) until sprouted; move to full sunlight
    as soon as first shoots appear.

Transplanting: Don't let transplants get too large before planting them
    outside. Late transplants do not form good heads, and sometimes
    flower the first year if allowed to get too large.

Seeds Outdoors: The season is too short to plant seeds directly in the
    garden for the spring crop, and starting the fall crop from seed
    outdoors would tie up too much valuable garden space that could
    be used more productively. Start all seeds in individual containers
    for transplanting into the garden.

Growing

Watering: Cabbage needs lots of water to head up properly, but after
    the head is formed and while it is growing to full size, cut back on
    watering or the head will grow too fast and split.

Maintenance: Weed weekly; cut away any extra-large bottom leaves if they are yellow. If large lower leaves are spreading to other squares, cut away any portions that are "over the line." This will not hurt the plant.

Harvesting

How: Cut off the entire head with a sharp, serrated knife or clippers.

When: Anytime the head starts to develop and feels firm. If you have several plants, don't wait until all the heads are large. They may split in hot weather and go to seed, and you'll be left with nothing.

Preparing and Using

Cabbage is delicious cooked or raw and contains a lot of vitamin C.

Problems

Slugs and snails, aphids, and cabbage worms (their worst enemy).

Hints and Tips

Cover cabbages with a bonnet of insect netting or floating cover to keep out the cabbage moth. Otherwise, watch for eaten leaves and then pick the green cabbage worms off by hand.

CARROT

BOTANICAL INFORMATION	
Family: Carrot	**Seed to Harvest/Flower:** 10 weeks
Height: 12 inches	**Seeds Storage:** 3 to 4 years
Spacing:	**Weeks to Maturity:** 10 weeks
16 per square	**Indoor Seed Starting:** no
GROWING SEASON	**Earliest Outdoor Planting:** 3 weeks before last spring frost
Spring: yes	
Summer: yes	
Fall: yes	
Winter: yes	

Description

Carrots are related to the wildflower Queen Anne's lace. The seeds are so small that planting them can be very tedious; practice dropping a pinch (2 or 3 seeds) on some white paper until you get the hang of it. Carrots can be either long and thin or short and stubby; pick the shape and size that best suits your garden. There is nothing more exciting for kids (including kids my age) than pulling up a carrot they planted months ago! It's sort of like fishing—you don't know how big it is until you see it, but you hope it's a whopper.

Starting

Location: Full sun, but can stand partial shade.

Seeds Indoors: No.

Transplanting: Does not transplant well.

Seeds Outdoors: Sprouts in two to three weeks outdoors. Seeds are very small; try pelleted seeds if necessary. Plant two or three seeds in each of the 16 spaces in a square. Water soil and cover the square with a plastic-covered cage. Keep the ground moist at all times, even if it means daily spraying in sunny weather.

Growing

Watering: Carrots must have constant moisture until they're almost mature to grow quickly and continuously. Then reduce watering so the carrots don't crack from overly rapid growth.

Maintenance: Weed weekly; otherwise carrots are relatively work-free.

Harvesting

How: Pull up those with the largest tops. If you're not sure which are biggest, dig around the plant with your fingers to test the size.

When: Pick them early, when they're only half size and at their sweetest and most tender.

Preparing and Using

Scrub with a vegetable brush, but don't peel them. Most of the vitamins are in the skin or close to the surface. Rich in vitamin A and thiamine (vitamin B1), carrots also contain calcium. Carrots are delicious fresh and raw—shredded, sliced thinly, or cut into sticks for snacking. They can be cooked by steaming or boiling. They can be served in a variety of dishes, or added to soups and stews, but seem best when served with a dressing, a dab of sour cream, or sprinkled with parsley and grated cheese. Carrots are so versatile you can even make a wonderfully moist cake with them.

Problems

Carrot rust fly, rabbits, woodchucks, deer, and voles. Virtually disease-free.

Hints and Tips

The long and thin ones can be grown in your SFG with the addition of a high-rise box (see Chapter 4). For a late winter harvest, mulch heavily to keep the ground from freezing to protect your fall-planted carrots.

CAULIFLOWER

BOTANICAL INFORMATION
  Family: Mustard
  Height: 18 to 24 inches
  Spacing: 1 per square
GROWING SEASON
  Spring: yes
  Summer: no
  Fall: yes
  Winter: no

Seed to Harvest/Flower: 14 weeks
Seeds Storage: 5 to 6 years
Weeks to Maturity: 8 weeks
Indoor Seed Starting: 10 weeks before last spring frost
Earliest Outdoor Planting: 4 weeks before last spring frost

Description

Even though cauliflower is a member of the cabbage family, it is not as cold hardy and is more susceptible to the heat. Fall is the best season for planting because the plant will mature in the cool weather. White cauliflower is the most popular variety but the purple one is considered to be more flavorful and does better in the heat. The white variety needs 14 to 15 weeks to mature while the purple variety can take up to 19 weeks.

Starting

Location: Full sun, but will tolerate partial shade.

Seeds Indoors: Will sprout in 5 to 10 days at 70°F. Plant 5 to 10 seeds in a cup of vermiculite, or plant one seed ¼ inch deep in potting soil in individual compartments of a seedling flat ten weeks before the last spring frost. For a second crop in the fall, repeat the process anytime from June 15 to July 1. Keep warm (70°F) until sprouted; move to full sunlight as soon as first shoots appear.

Transplanting: Set out in the garden four weeks before the last spring frost. Place a cutworm collar around the stem, water, and provide a shade cage. Be extra careful when planting; cauliflower suffers more from transplanting than any other cabbage family member.

Seeds Outdoors: Not satisfactory; season is too short before hot weather arrives.

Growing

Watering: Never let plants dry out.

Maintenance: Weed weekly; mulch in hot weather.

Harvesting

How: Cut off the entire head at its base with a sharp knife or clippers.

When: Harvest as soon as the head enlarges, is firm, and has a nice white color, before the buds separate or open. Do not delay harvest, as the head will grow fast and pass the ideal harvest point in just a few days.

Preparing and Using

Serve florets fresh and raw with any salad dressing or dip. Chopped cauliflower is excellent in tossed salads. Cook by steaming, boiling, or stir-frying. Serve hot with cheese sauce, salad dressing, or just sprinkled with grated cheese. It makes a marvelous addition to any soup or stew; cauliflower soup is superb and quite unusual. Marinate any leftovers for addition to salads or relishes.

Problems

Cutworms, root maggots, occasionally cabbage worms, and cabbage loopers; club root.

Hints and Tips

For white varieties that are not self-blanching, bend or break large leaves over the top when heads start to form. Then tie or hold with a rubber band to cover and protect the head from exposure to the sun, which can turn the head yellow.

CHARD, SWISS

BOTANICAL INFORMATION
  Family: Goosefoot
  Height: 12 to 18 inches
  Spacing: 4 per square
GROWING SEASON
  Spring: yes
  Summer: yes
  Fall: yes
  Winter: yes

Seed to Harvest/Flower: 8 weeks
Seeds Storage: 4 to 5 years
Weeks to Maturity: 8 weeks
Indoor Seed Starting: 7 weeks before last spring frost
Earliest Outdoor Planting: 3 weeks before last spring frost

Hints and Tips

Harvest the outer leaves continuously. Plant a square each of all the colors and get out your camera for great ground-level shots.

Swiss chard will survive several frosts even if it's unprotected, allowing a fall harvest. If mulched with loose hay it can be harvested into the winter in most climates. With a complete mulch cover, it will also winter over and resprout the second year for a very early spring harvest. Gradually remove the mulch in early spring and be rewarded by the first fresh greens from your garden. Plants will only produce a crop in early spring the second year; later they will go to seed, so start new plants every year.

Description

Swiss chard is known best for its vitamin-rich leaves and its succulent stems. It's one of the easiest vegetables to grow in any part of the country, and can be grown in the sun or shade, all spring, summer, and fall for a continuous harvest. In most climates it can even be carried over the winter. Chard is available in white- or red-stemmed varieties and is also available in many rainbow colors. It can have either smooth or crinkled leaves, whichever you like; try both! It is also virtually pest- and disease-free.

Starting

Location: Does best in full sun, but can grow in partial shade.

Seeds Indoors: Plant 10 seeds in a cup of vermiculite, or place one seed ½ inch deep in potting soil in individual compartments of a seedling tray 7 weeks before your last spring frost. Seeds will sprout in 5 to 10 days at 70°F. Keep warm (70°F) until sprouted; move to full sunlight as soon as first shoots appear.

Transplanting: Plant into the garden three weeks before the last spring frost. Water and cover with a plastic-covered cage.

Seeds Outdoors: Plant presoaked seeds ½ inch deep in each square three weeks before your last spring frost. Seeds sprout outdoors in two to three weeks. Water and cover with a plastic-covered cage.

Growing

Watering: Weekly, or twice weekly in hot weather. Like all leaf crops, Swiss chard needs lots of water for luxurious leaf growth.

Maintenance: Weed weekly; cut off any yellow or overgrown outer leaves.

Harvesting

How: Carefully cut off each outer stem at the plant base with a sharp knife when the leaves are 6 to 9 inches tall. The smaller inner leaves will continue to grow.

When: Start harvesting when the outer leaves are about 6 to 9 inches tall (approximately eight weeks after planting seeds), and continue harvesting outer leaves (stalk and all) every week or so. Don't let outer leaves get too large before harvesting.

Preparing and Using

Both leaves and stems are edible; leaves are very rich in vitamins A and C, calcium, and iron. The stalks can be cooked and served like asparagus; the leaves are used fresh or cooked, and are similar to, but milder in taste than, spinach.

After harvest, rinse and pat dry like lettuce or spinach; refrigerate if not using immediately. Cut out the central stalk and use the leaves as fresh greens for salads, or boil or steam as you would spinach. Add freshly chopped greens to any appropriate soup for a garden-fresh taste. Chop the central stem or stalk into convenient-size pieces and boil or steam like asparagus or celery. Serve with your favorite salad dressing, covered with bread crumbs, or grated cheese. Marinate leftover stalks overnight for a salad or appetizers.

Problems

Slugs and snails, cutworms, and leaf miners; occasionally rabbits, woodchucks, and deer. Free of most diseases.

CORN

BOTANICAL INFORMATION	
Family: Grass	**Seed to Harvest/Flower:** 9 to 13 weeks
Height: 5 to 6 feet	**Seeds Storage:** 1 to 2 years
Spacing: 4 per square	**Weeks to Maturity:** 9 weeks
GROWING SEASON	**Indoor Seed Starting:** no
Spring: no	**Earliest Outdoor Planting:** immediately after last spring frost
Summer: yes	**Additional Plantings:** every 2 weeks
Fall: no	
Winter: no	

Description

Corn is a long-time favorite of most gardeners. The taste of store-bought corn can't compete with homegrown corn, so many plant a whole 4 × 4 SFG of just corn. Most of the varieties for home use are planted 4 per square foot; only one crop can be grown per season because it needs a long time to mature and lots of hot weather.

There are many colors and varieties of corn. The later season types taste better than the earlier season varieties; the "extra sweet" variety is unusually good and keeps its sweetness even after picking. The most common color of corn is yellow, but the best tasting are the bicolor and white varieties. As new varieties of corn are developed, check with the seed companies for the latest recommendations on how far apart to plant various types of corn so they don't cross-pollinate.

Starting

Location: Full sun; locate corn where it won't shade other crops because it gets so tall.

Seeds Indoors: No.

Transplanting: Does not transplant well.

Seeds Outdoors: Sprouts in 5 to 10 days outdoors. Plant your presoaked seeds 1 to 2 inches deep, depending on the weather, at the proper spacing. Water the soil and cover with a chicken-wire cage to keep out birds. To get a continuous harvest, plant a new crop every two weeks with several varieties of different maturation dates.

Growing

Watering: Weekly, more in hot weather.

Maintenance: Weed weekly; remove the chicken-wire cage when the corn is 6 inches tall. Place a raccoon-proof fence around your squares when the ears are starting to form.

Harvesting

How: Use two hands to harvest—one to hold the stalk and the other to pull down and break off the ear—otherwise you may break the stalk. If there are no other ears left on that stalk it's best to cut it down to the ground. Don't pull it out or you may disturb the roots of the surrounding stalks.

When: Check the ears daily when the silk first browns and the ears feel full and slightly bumpy. The final test of each ear before harvesting is to peel away a small strip of the husk to expose the kernels. They should be plump and full. To see if the ear is ready, puncture a kernel with your thumbnail. If milky juice squirts out, it's ready; if the juice is clear, the corn is not quite ready to pick.

Preparing and Using

Corn loses its sweet taste very quickly after being picked, so try to cook and eat it as soon as possible. If you can't use it immediately, husk and refrigerate it. Up to 50 percent of the flavor is lost in the first 12 hours of storage, more if it's not refrigerated. If you harvest more than you eat, cut the kernels off the cob and freeze them, add to a relish dish, or serve warm with butter and parsley. Of course, corn is excellent added to any kind of soup or stew.

Hints and Tips

Chapter 4 has some great tips on how to keep the critters out of your corn patch.

Since your Mel's Mix stays so loose and friable, protect corn from blowing over in late summer storms with the simple addition of steel fence posts and a little tomato nylon netting. Drive a post in each corner of your 4 x 4 garden and then stretch a 4 x 4 piece of netting between the 4 posts, about 3 feet off the ground. The plants will easily grow right up through the netting, which will support them without any extra work on your part.

Problems

Corn has more problems than any other garden crop, including corn borer, ear worm, birds, raccoons, and squirrels. There are relatively few diseases that bother the home gardener.

CUCUMBER

BOTANICAL INFORMATION
Family: Gourd
Height: vine
Spacing: 2 per square
GROWING SEASON
Spring: no
Summer: yes
Fall: no
Winter: no

Seed to Harvest/Flower: 9 weeks
Seeds Storage: 5 to 6 years
Weeks to Maturity: 7 weeks
Earliest Outdoor Planting: 1 week after last spring frost

Description

The cucumber is a garden favorite, and is very easy to grow in warm weather. Although both vine and bush varieties are available, bush cucumbers take a lot of room and don't produce like the vine types. Use the vertical method to grow your vine cucumbers.

There are many varieties ranging in size, shape, and use, including ones for pickling or serving raw. The pickling varieties are picked much earlier when they are smaller—just the right size for the pickle jar— but they can also be eaten. The slicing types are grown larger and are more commonly used for salads or sandwiches.

Starting

Location: Full sun, although the vine types will tolerate some shade.
Seeds Indoors: Sprouts in 4 to 8 days at 70°F; will sprout even faster at 80°F. Plant one seed in individual paper cups filled with Mel's Mix. Punch holes in the bottom for drainage. Keep warm (at least 70°F) until sprouted; move to full sunlight as soon as the first shoots appear.
Transplanting: Plant the cup and all in the ground at the proper plant spacing. If the cup is waxed cardboard or a heavy paper, tear away the bottom carefully; avoid disturbing the roots. Water and cover with a shade cage.
Seeds Outdoors: Sprouts in five to ten days; place presoaked seeds at proper spacing, water, and keep soil moist until seeds sprout.

Growing

Watering: Weekly; twice weekly in hot weather. Never let the soil dry out. Avoid wetting the leaves, as this spreads any fungus disease that may be present. Cucumbers have the highest water content of any vegetable, so plenty of moisture is required for proper growth.

Maintenance: Weed weekly; keep vines on the trellis; watch out for beetles; mulch in hot weather.

Harvesting

How: Cut (don't pull) the stem connecting the fruit to the vine.

When: Harvest continually! Never allow any cucumbers to become yellow or overly large, or the plant will stop producing. Keep picking even if you have to toss some on the compost pile because you can't use them. Don't try the old practice of eating the large cukes and leaving the smaller ones on the vine, because in only one or two days the little ones will be big. Instead, compost the very large cucumbers and eat the smaller ones.

Preparing and Using

Wash and scrub with a vegetable brush. Serve long, slender burpless varieties with the skins left on. Peel the fatter varieties before slicing, cubing, or cutting into long sticks. Serve fresh, sliced on sandwiches with onions and mayonnaise, or marinate for relish. Many gardeners like cucumbers simply soaked in vinegar overnight and served with lots of pepper. They also go well in any salad or arranged around a spoonful of cottage cheese.

Hints and Tips

Don't let the fruit get too large; pick early and often. Try some of the long, thin varieties for a fun crop.

Problems

Cucumber beetles; mildew, wilt, and mosaic.

EGGPLANT

BOTANICAL INFORMATION	
Family: Nightshade	**Seed to Harvest/Flower:** 19 weeks
Height: 24 to 30 inches	**Seeds Storage:** 5 to 6 years
Spacing: 1 per square	**Weeks to Maturity:** 10 weeks
GROWING SEASON	**Indoor Seed Starting:** 7 weeks before last spring frost
Spring: no	**Earliest Outdoor Planting:** 2 weeks after last spring frost
Summer: yes	**Additional Plantings:** no
Fall: no	
Winter: no	

Description

Eggplant is a nice-looking plant with fruit that comes in a wide variety of colors and shapes; most types yield a rather large, egg-shaped fruit that is black to purple. However, some of the newer varieties are yellow, brown, or white and are smaller and rounder. Eggplant yields a very large harvest and are used in many different styles of cooking. They are easily grown, but take a long time to mature—so you need to start plants indoors in early spring or buy transplants locally.

Starting

Location: Full sun and lots of heat; pick your sunniest spot for eggplant.

Seeds Indoors: Sprouts in 12 days at 70°F, but only requires 6 days at 85°F; won't sprout below 65°F. Sprinkle 5 to 10 seeds ¼ inch deep in a cup filled with vermiculite 7 weeks before your last spring frost. Keep warm (at least 70°F) until sprouted; move to full sunlight as soon as first shoots appear; then pot up in seedling trays as soon as plants are large enough (usually one to three weeks). Keep a careful watch over the plants, especially after transplanting them into seedling trays, because any pause or stoppage of the growth will affect the ultimate bearing capacity of the plant.

Transplanting: Plant into the garden two weeks after the last spring frost; disturb the roots as little as possible. Water and cover with a shade cage. Since eggplant is so vulnerable to cold weather, cover the wire cage with a clear plastic cover as well as a sun shade to provide a greenhouse atmosphere if it is at all chilly. In a few days the sun shade can be removed.

Seeds Outdoors: Not satisfactory, as the season is too short before hot weather arrives.

Growing

Watering: Eggplant needs constant moisture, especially when fruits are forming and enlarging.

Maintenance: Weed weekly; add a thick mulch when hot weather sets in. Provide a wide mesh, open-wire cage support when the eggplant is half grown; the plants will grow right through it, and will be supported without staking.

Harvesting

How: Always cut the fruit from the bush with clippers; watch out for sharp spines on the stems and fruits.

When: Edible almost anytime after the fruit turns dark and glossy (when it's about 6 inches), don't let them get too large. If they turn a dull color they are overripe and the seeds will be large and hard.

Preparing and Using

Peel and slice or dice, then stew, fry, stir-fry, or bake; add to casseroles, or bread and fry by itself. Eggplant mixes especially well with

Hints and Tips

Many cooks use eggplant as a substitute for meat in various dishes. Show the pretty flowers to your children and then have them watch the fruit form and grow bigger every day.

tomatoes and onions. If you're not going to use the eggplant right away, don't refrigerate it; instead, store it on the kitchen counter and enjoy its good looks! Handle carefully or fruit will bruise.

Problems

Cutworms and flea beetles; verticillium wilt.

LETTUCE

BOTANICAL INFORMATION
Family: Composite
Height: 6 to 12 inches
Spacing: 4 per square
GROWING SEASON
Spring: yes
Summer: yes
Fall: yes
Winter: yes

Seed to Harvest/Flower: 7 weeks
Seeds Storage: 5 to 6 years
Weeks to Maturity: 4 to 7 weeks
Indoor Seed Starting: 7 weeks before last spring frost
Earliest Outdoor Planting: 4 weeks before last spring frost
Additional Plantings: every other week
Last Planting: early summer

Description

Lettuce is so easy to grow, very gratifying, and extremely suited for SFG—it grows quickly, prolifically and looks great. While it does grow best in the cool seasons and withstands cold weather, it tolerates some heat and can be grown nearly year-round.

There are several types of lettuce: the solid head usually found in grocery stores; the loose head, or Bibb, a faster growing, and smaller variety of head lettuce; Romaine or cos, which is a loose head with a rougher texture than the leaf types. The Romaine leaf is comprised of many tight, upright leaves and is probably the best pick for home gardeners—but there are also so many great types of leaf and Bibb lettuces that every gardener should try to grow at least four varieties at all times! They do best as a spring or fall crop, but with care and protection, they can be grown in summer and even in winter in many parts of the country. Look for the types that are suitable for summer or winter seasons.

Starting

Location: Full sun to partial shade; shade is welcomed in the hot summer. As with all leafy vegetables, the stronger the light, the higher the vitamin C content will be.

Seeds Indoors: Sprouts in 2 to 3 days at 70°F. Start 5 to 10 seeds of several different varieties in cups filled with vermiculite 7 weeks before your last spring frost date. Keep warm (70°F) until sprouted; move to full sunlight as soon as first shoots appear; then pot up in seedling trays as soon as plants are large enough (usually one to three weeks).

Transplanting: Move plants into the garden anytime until they are half grown. Plant a new square or two of lettuce every other week until early summer. The hot weather, long days, warm nights, and dry soil of summer cause lettuce to bolt to seed. Plant special varieties sold as heat- or bolt-resistant. After summer is over you can start planting the same varieties you did in the spring.

Seeds Outdoors: Sprouts in 5 to 10 days. Seeds sprout quickly outdoors and grow fairly rapidly; however, this method is time-saving but space-consuming. If space is your concern, start all seeds indoors or off to the side of the garden and move plants into the garden when they're half grown. Transplants seem to bolt to seed more easily than direct-seeded plants, so plant the summer crop directly in the garden. Plant one or two seeds in each hole; water daily until they sprout.

Growing

Watering: Try not to wet the leaves; you may spread fungal diseases. Don't water at night; morning is the best followed by noon or late afternoon.

Maintenance: Weed weekly; don't let any weeds grow. Lettuce has such a shallow root system it can't compete with weeds. Provide shade covers for plants in summer.

Harvesting

How: You can cut individual outer leaves or the entire plant. If you're going to cut outer leaves you can start when the plant is half grown. This makes a surprisingly large harvest when combined with a few leaves of beet, spinach, and Swiss chard. If you take just one leaf from each plant, you can still harvest a lot and hardly notice what has been harvested.

When: Harvest leaf varieties at seven weeks, and Bibb varieties at nine weeks, or harvest outer leaves from either one when the plant is half grown. You can also cut the entire plant at any time; it doesn't have to grow to full size to be edible. If you wait until all your plants reach full size you will have to harvest almost all of them at once or they will go to seed.

Preparing and Using

Rinse lettuce under cool water, spin or pat dry, and store in the refrigerator in a plastic bag until you're ready to use it. Lettuce will stay fresh and crisp for several days, although it's even better to harvest almost daily for maximum nutritional value. Lettuce contains vitamins A and B, calcium, and iron (especially the dark green outer leaves).

Hints and Tips

Grow as many different colors and textures as possible to have unusual salads. Pick outer leaves daily to fill your salad bowl . . . in fact, take your salad bowl right out to the garden!

Problems

Rabbits, deer, woodchucks, slugs, cutworms, sow bugs, and wire
worms. There are not many diseases to be concerned about unless the
lettuce is quite wet at ground level.

MELON (CANTALOUPE, MUSKMELON, WATERMELON)

BOTANICAL INFORMATION
  Family: Gourd
  Height: vine
  Spacing: 1 per 2 squares
GROWING SEASON
  Spring: no
  Summer: yes
  Fall: no
  Winter: no

Seed to Harvest/Flower: 12 weeks
Seeds Storage: 5 to 6 years
Indoor Seed Starting: 2 weeks before transplanting
Earliest Outdoor Planting: 2 weeks after last spring frost
Additional Plantings: no

Description

Melons need about 3 months of hot weather to grow, but are a fun and
exciting crop—even though the yield isn't large, when the harvest
finally comes, it all seems very worthwhile. They should be grown on
vertical frames, as they will mature sooner and save space. Of course,
one of the biggest rewards is seeing melons hanging 4 to 5 feet off the
ground on your vertical frame—that's not something you're used to
seeing in your old single-row gardens!

Starting

Location: Full sun; grow on a vertical frame.

Seeds Indoors: Sprouts in 5 to 10 days at 70°F; the hotter the better,
    even up to 90°F for sprouting. Plant single seeds in individual paper
    cups. Plants do not transplant well, so don't start them until two
    weeks before planting outside.

Transplanting: Plant outdoors two weeks after the last frost date. Sink
    the entire cup in the ground after tearing off the bottom.

Seeds Outdoors: Won't sprout in soil below 65°F; takes 5 days in 70°F
    soil. Plant a pre-soaked seed in each square foot, one week after
    last frost. Cover with a plastic-covered cage. Remove weakest
    one later.

Growing

Watering: Mulch heavily in hot weather. Reduce water when melons are almost ripe to develop their sweetness. Keep the leaves dry to avoid fungal diseases and mildew.

Maintenance: Weed weekly; support the half-grown melons in slings; pinch out all new, small melons near the end of the growing season so that all the plant's strength goes into ripening the larger melons that are already set.

Harvesting

How: Twist the melon with one hand while holding the stem with the other. If it resists parting, the melon is not ripe.

When: Harvest whenever it has a strong melon scent, and the netting pattern on the rind (if it's a cantaloupe) becomes very prominent. The stem will slip off easily when the melon is rotated. If each melon is held in a sling it won't roll around and accidentally twist itself off when it's ripe.

Preparing and Using

Some people like melons warm, some, chilled. Cut muskmelons or cantaloupes in half, scoop out the seeds, and cut into wedges, or serve an entire half filled with ice cream, blueberries, or custard. The flesh of all melons can also be scooped out using a melon-baller or cut into cubes and mixed with or added to a fresh fruit salad. They're excellent for breakfast or served as a dinner dessert.

Problems

Cutworms; mildew and wilt disease.

Hints and Tips

Be the first on your block to grow melons! There are so many varieties to choose from—start with the smaller, more common varieties. Melons get very heavy, so make sure your vertical frame is strong and well-supported.

Watermelon: All data and advice above is about the same for this giant of a summer crop. One big caution: make darn sure your vertical frame is strong! It would also be prudent to start by growing the smaller varieties; they produce well, are very sweet, and would be a good trial for your experiment, as they grow well vertically.

Pumpkin: The same scenario will apply to growing pumpkins on your vertical frame. Yes, pumpkins! Be prepared to attract a crowd, and get some good pictures!

OKRA

BOTANICAL INFORMATION
Family: Lily
Height: 18 to 24 inches
Spacing: 1 per square

GROWING SEASON
Spring: no
Summer: yes
Fall: no
Winter: no

Seed to Harvest/Flower: 12 weeks
Seeds Storage: 2 years
Weeks to Maturity: 10 weeks
Indoor Seed Starting: 6 to 8 weeks before last spring frost
Earliest Outdoor Planting: after soil has warmed, 7 to 10 days after last frost
Additional Plantings: not needed

Description

Okra is a tall, warm-season, annual vegetable. It is a pretty plant with large hibiscus-like yellow flowers, heart-shaped leaves, and a thick woody stem. The edible part is a long, ribbed, fuzzy pod that can be yellow, red, or green. Once the flowers have bloomed, the pods grow very quickly, so check the plant daily for young pods as these have the best flavor and texture. Okra loves hot weather, and may not get a long enough period of heat to grow well in areas with a short growing season, but try it anyway as it does grow very quickly during the hottest days of summer. You might also look for smaller, short-season varieties.

Starting

Location: Full sun.

Seeds Indoors: 6 to 8 weeks before the last spring frost. Soak seeds overnight and plant at a depth of 1 inch.

Transplanting: Set seedlings out after the soil has warmed, 7 to 10 days after the last frost.

Seeds Outdoors: Soak seeds overnight, then plant 1 inch deep, 2 weeks after the last frost, and at least 3 months before the first fall frost.

Growing

Watering: Keep soil fairly moist; mulch in very hot weather.

Maintenance: Remove old, hard pods from the plant unless you are saving them for seed or dried arrangements.

Harvesting

How: Cut pods from plants with a pruner or knife. Breaking or pulling the pods can damage the plant.

When: Harvest pods daily when they are young, no more than 4 inches long. Older pods can be too tough to eat.

Preparing and Using

Okra can be stored in the refrigerator in a paper bag or wrapped in a paper towel in a perforated plastic bag for 2 to 3 days; it may be frozen for up to 12 months after blanching whole for 2 minutes. Cooked okra can be stored in the refrigerator for 3 to 4 days. Okra can be served raw, marinated in salads, or cooked on its own, and goes well with tomatoes, onions, corn, peppers, and eggplant. Whole, fresh okra pods also make excellent pickles. And don't forget to make some gumbo!

Problems

Aphids and cabbage worms, verticillium or fusarium wilt.

Hints and Tips

Try something different: barbeque some young pods at your next party.

ONION

BOTANICAL INFORMATION
Family: Lily
Height: 12 inches
Spacing: 16 per square

GROWING SEASON
Spring: yes
Summer: yes
Fall: no
Winter: no

Seed to Harvest/Flower: 20 weeks
Seeds Storage: 1 to 2 years
Weeks to Maturity: 14 weeks
Indoor Seed Starting: 8 to 12 weeks before last spring frost
Earliest Outdoor Planting: 4 weeks before last spring frost

Description

Onions are easy to grow; they don't take much care but are a little unsightly near the end when the tops turn brown and fall over—but that just means they are nearing harvest time. Trim off the brown, dead tops to keep the garden looking good.

Onions can be planted from sets, plants, or seeds; the bulb reaches harvest sometime in the middle of the summer. The size of the bulb is determined by the length of the growing season before the summer solstice (June 21). If you have a short growing season, don't bother with seeds—get the plants or sets (which look like miniature onions). If you live in a milder climate you could try the seed method.

There are many types of onions, from large, fat ones, to small, golf-ball-sized varieties. Some need to be used soon after harvest, while others are fine for storing. Check the seed catalog descriptions and pick your favorites.

Starting

Location: Onions like a sunny spot, but will tolerate some shade.

Seeds Indoors: Sprouts in 5 days at 70°F. Sprinkle about 20 seeds of each variety desired into cups filled with vermiculite 8 to 12 weeks before your last spring frost. Keep warm (70°F) until sprouted; move to full sunlight as soon as first shoots appear; then pot up in seedling trays as soon as plants are large enough (usually one to three weeks).

Transplanting: Four weeks before the last spring frost, shake most of the vermiculite from your young plants and gather them together in small bunches. With scissors, cut off both the tops and the roots so the plant is balanced with about 2 inches of each. Drill a hole at each space in your square with a pencil, and slip in a plant, firm the soil, and water.

Seeds Outdoors: If the season is not long enough for seeds, use sets. Push the tiny onion sets into the ground, pointed side up at the proper spacing, with their tops just showing above the soil. Water, and that's all there is to it.

Growing

Watering: Withhold water when the tops start to fall over.

Maintenance: Weed weekly; when bulbs start expanding use your finger to remove some of the soil around each bulb and partially uncover it. This makes it easier for the bulb to expand. It will not hurt if you can actually see the top of every bulb; in fact, it's kind of exciting to see them getting bigger and bigger every week!

Harvesting

How: Pull the onions out of the ground and place on chicken wire or a window screen laid out in the sun for several days. The tops, roots, and outer skin of each onion will then dry thoroughly. Brush them off and clean off any loose skins, dried tops, or roots by rubbing them between your palms, then store for later use. Any onions with green or thick tops should not be stored but used immediately.

When: About the middle of the summer you'll see your onion tops turning brown and falling over. When the majority have fallen, bend over the remaining ones with your hand. In a short while, the tops will dry up while the bulbs attain their maximum size.

Preparing and Using

You'll find homegrown onions much milder and sweeter than store-bought ones. This makes them more useful, especially for those folks who must be careful of eating too many onions. For a real treat, try an onion sandwich—thin slices of onion with mayonnaise and lots of pepper on your favorite bread. Or add fresh, crisp cucumber slices to the sandwich for a delightful combination. Hang dried onions in a mesh bag, or braid tops together and hang in a cool, dry area for storage all winter.

Problems

Onion fly maggot. Resistant to most diseases.

Hints and Tips

Scallions and green-bunching onions are very easy to grow using your high-rise boxes, which will give you twice the white stalk.

PARSLEY

BOTANICAL INFORMATION
Family: Carrot
Height: 6 to 12 inches
Spacing: 4 per square
GROWING SEASON
Spring: yes
Summer: yes
Fall: yes
Winter: yes

Seed to Harvest/Flower: 14 weeks
Seeds Storage: 2 to 3 years
Weeks to Maturity: 7 weeks
Indoor Seed Starting: 12 weeks before last spring frost
Earliest Outdoor Planting: 5 weeks before last spring frost

Description

Parsley is a wonderful herb that looks great in the garden, yields a big continuous harvest, is extremely nutritious, and doesn't need a great deal of care! Pests don't seem to bother it, and it's disease-resistant too. All in all, parsley is a very easy addition to your SFG. There are many varieties, but basically two kinds: flat-leaved and curly. It's said the flat-leaf varieties taste better, but the curly-leaf types are better looking, and more commonly grown.

Starting

Location: Full sun to partial shade.

Seeds Indoors: Sprouts in 10 to 15 days at 70°F. Seeds are very slow to germinate, and should be soaked in lukewarm water for 24 hours before planting. Sprinkle ten presoaked seeds in a cup filled with vermiculite 12 weeks before last spring frost. Keep warm (70°F) until sprouted; move to full sunlight as soon as first shoots appear; then pot up in seedling trays as soon as plants are large enough (usually one to three weeks).

Transplanting: Move outdoors five weeks before the last spring frost or anytime plants are large enough; plant them at the same depth they grew in the pot.

Seeds Outdoors: Better to start indoors because seeds are slow and difficult to germinate.

Growing

Watering: Never let parsley dry out completely because it becomes tough and bitter and may bolt to seed in the first year.

Maintenance: Weed weekly. Mulch heavily for continual harvest in winter, and for early-spring growing the following year.

Harvesting

How: Cut outer leaves as needed; for a large harvest, cut off the entire plant slightly above tiny middle shoots. Either way, the plant will continue to grow with no harm.

When: Harvest as soon as the plant gets 3 to 4 inches tall and anytime thereafter.

Preparing and Using

Parsley is good in soups, casseroles, stews, and with fish or any kind of meat; it's excellent over boiled vegetables, particularly potatoes. Parsley is loaded with vitamins A and C. Cut up leaves with scissors and sprinkle on food for that decorative gourmet chef look!

Problems

Relatively free from pests and diseases.

Hints and Tips

Pot up a plant or two in the fall for a kitchen windowsill garden, or even plan ahead and pot up several for holiday, birthday, or Christmas gifts.

PEA, SUGAR SNAP

BOTANICAL
INFORMATION
　Family: Pulse
　Height: vine
　Spacing: 8 per square
GROWING SEASON
　Spring: yes
　Summer: no
　Fall: yes
　Winter: no

Seed to Harvest/Flower: 10 weeks
Seeds Storage: 3 to 4 years
Weeks to Maturity: 10 weeks
Indoor Seed Starting: no
Earliest Outdoor Planting: 5 weeks before last
　spring frost

Description

Who doesn't like the taste of fresh peas? Yet until the introduction of sugar snap peas, it was hard to grow enough for much more than a few meals—peas used to take time, space, and effort to harvest, not to mention the shelling. Even when you're all finished, it doesn't seem to add up to much!

The sugar snap peas, or edible pod varieties, have changed all of that. They are extremely high yielding, and you can eat the entire pod. They have about five times the harvest of conventional peas. Sugar snap peas are juicy, sweet, and crisp, and are absolutely wonderful. They can be eaten raw or cooked. They are a must in my garden, and I recommend them as the only pea worth growing. Very few of the pea pods even make it to the kitchen now, because they are such a treat to eat right in the garden—you might need to make a family rule: pick and eat all you want but leave enough for dinner! Once the kids are told they can eat right from the garden, they'll become much more interested in eating vegetables!

Starting

Location: Full sun in spring; shaded toward summer if possible.
Seeds Indoors: No.
Transplanting: Does not transplant well.
Seeds Outdoors: Sprouts in 10 to 15 days outdoors. Mix presoaked
　seeds with legume inoculant powder for an added boost, then plant
　1 inch deep about 5 weeks before the last spring frost. Water and
　cover with a plastic-covered tunnel.

Growing

Watering: Never let the peas dry out.
Maintenance: Weed weekly; keep water off the vines. Keep the vines
　trained up the vertical frame; mulch as weather gets warm.

Harvesting

How: Carefully (with two hands) pick or cut pods off their stems.

When: The beauty of these peas is that you can eat them at any stage of growth. They're just as tasty (raw or cooked) whether their pods are fully mature and bulging with peas, or still thin and barely starting to show the peas inside. Munch on a few every time you're in the garden—what a treat!

Preparing and Using

Just wash and they are ready to eat or cook. Try to use them as fresh as possible; store what you can't use right away in refrigerator. Sugar snaps are rich in vitamins A, B1, and C, and contain phosphorus and iron. As the pods get nearly full size, some develop a string along each edge, but it's easy to remove: just snap off the stem end and pull down, and both strings will easily peel off. The pod is still very crisp and tasty even when full size.

If the pods start to lose their nice pea-green color and turn brown on the vine, they are overripe. Pick them immediately and add them to the compost pile, because if you don't harvest them they will cause the vine to stop producing new peas.

The versatility of these tasty peas stretches the imagination. Try them raw in salads, with a dip, plain, or mixed with other fresh vegetables in vinegar or sour cream dressing . . . or cook them by boiling, steaming, or stir-frying.

Problems

No pests to speak of (except those people in the family that eat too many), but sometimes prone to powdery mildew, especially during warm weather when the leaves get wet.

Hints and Tips

Let the kids grow them and you'll have a vegetarian in the making.

PEPPER

BOTANICAL INFORMATION
- **Family:** Nightshade
- **Height:** 12 to 24 inches
- **Spacing:** 1 per square

GROWING SEASON
- **Spring:** no
- **Summer:** yes
- **Fall:** no
- **Winter:** no

Seed to Harvest/Flower: 19 weeks
Seeds Storage: 4 to 5 years
Weeks to Maturity: 10 weeks
Indoor Seed Starting: 7 weeks before last spring frost
Earliest Outdoor Planting: 2 weeks after last spring frost

Description

Most gardeners love to grow peppers: they're easy to grow, pest- and disease-free, and produce a lot for the space allotted. You can buy transplants locally, or start seeds yourself. They look great in the garden, and some people grow several types for their decorative aspect. If all you've grown are the green bell peppers, give the sweet yellow banana varieties a try. Peppers come in several different shapes, from the bell shape to the skinny, curved, hot chili peppers. They range in color from green and red to orange and yellow. Select the type you want for cooking and go for it!

Starting

Location: Full sun.

Seeds Indoors: Sprouts in 10 to 15 days at 70°F. Sprinkle 5 to 10 seeds in a cup of vermiculite approximately 7 weeks before the last spring frost, cover with ¼ inch more vermiculite. Keep warm (70°F) until sprouted; move to full sunlight as soon as first shoots appear; then pot up in seedling trays as soon as plants are large enough (usually one to three weeks).

Transplanting: Peppers need warm soil so don't transplant until two weeks after the last spring frost.

Seeds Outdoors: The season is too short to start outdoors.

Growing

Watering: Don't wet the leaves; this causes fungal and wilt infections.

Maintenance: Weed weekly; mulch in hot weather; cover half-grown plants with an open-mesh wire cage to support plants without staking. Stems and branches of pepper plants are brittle and break easily, so work carefully among them when harvesting.

Harvesting

How: Carefully cut the fruit from the bush (don't pull or you'll accidentally break other branches). Leave about 1 inch of stem on each pepper for a longer storage life.

When: Harvest at almost any stage of development! Basically, if you want green peppers pick them as soon as they are big enough for your use. You can leave them on the vine and they will turn red or yellow after they become full grown. Peppers can still be eaten when red or yellow; in fact, many people prefer them, as their taste is sweeter and not as spicy when they lose their green color. Of course, the hot chili peppers should turn color before you use them.

Hints and Tips

If you like the hot pepper taste, just look through any seed catalog and pick your poison. Let each child or grandchild pick and grow a different color pepper plant.

Grow enough to have some to grill on the barbecue.

Preparing and Using

Use peppers raw or cooked. Peppers are excellent as a salad or casserole garnish. Cut them into strips, cubes, or thin slices as you would a tomato. Their shape is very attractive as a garnish. Peppers stuffed with a meat, rice, or vegetable mixture and then baked makes a great summer supper. Peppers are high in vitamins A and C.

Problems

Cutworms and flea beetles. No diseases to speak of except an occasional wilt or fungus problem.

POTATO

BOTANICAL
INFORMATION
　Family: Nightshade
　Height: 12 to
　24 inches
　Spacing: 4 per square
GROWING SEASON
　Spring: yes
　Summer: yes
　Fall: yes
　Winter: no

Seed to Harvest/Flower: 12 weeks
Seeds Storage: plant last year's potatoes each year
Weeks to Maturity: 12 weeks
Indoor Seed Starting: no
Earliest Outdoor Planting: in spring when soil has reached 45° F
Additional Plantings: late spring for a second crop to store over the winter

Description

Potatoes need no introduction; we've all eaten them at some point, in a recipe, baked, or out of a bag of chips or container of French fries. But growing your own potatoes is the best way to sample the large variety of potato shapes, sizes and colors. Harvest them early for small, tasty nuggets; or dig them later for large tubers to store over the winter. And the potato plant itself is bushy and pretty, doing double duty as an ornamental and an edible. The white flowers are the indicator that the small, new potatoes are ready to harvest out of the ground and onto the table.

Starting

Location: Full sun.

Seeds Indoors: No.

Planting: Don't plant seeds; cut up potatoes in small pieces and let the eyes sprout, then plant those.

Outdoors: Plant in the spring when the soil has reached 45°F. Use only certified disease-free seed potatoes. Sprout potatoes a week before planting time by placing them in a tray where they will receive light (not sun) and temperatures of about 65°F. A day or two before planting, cut potatoes into "seed pieces" about 1½" square with at least one "sprouted eye" per section. Remove about 5 inches of your soil in that square foot, place four seed pieces at the proper spacing with eyes up, and just barely cover them. When sprouts appear, add enough Mel's Mix to again cover the green leafy sprouts. Keep doing this until the hole is filled back to the top. For an extra harvest, use the high-rise method described in Chapter 4. Cover the plants every week or so with more Mel's Mix, until the plants begin to flower. Make certain any new potatoes that are forming are well covered, as uncovered spuds will turn green.

Growing

Watering: Increase watering during flowering.
Maintenance: Protect from frost.

Harvesting

How: Gently loosen the soil around early potatoes and remove the largest tubers, leaving the smaller ones to continue growing. For later potatoes, gently dig outside the plant and remove the potatoes as you find them. Take care not to stab or cut the potatoes as you dig. If the weather is dry, leave the potatoes on top of the soil for 2 to 3 days to dry. If the weather is wet, bring the potatoes into a garage or basement to dry. This will toughen the skin for storage. Store potatoes in a cool (40°F), dark location for 3 to 6 months. Do not store potatoes near apples, which give off a chemical that will damage the potatoes.

When: Small early potatoes can be harvested as needed in early summer after the plants finish flowering. Later potatoes can be left in the soil until 2 to 3 weeks after the foliage has died back in fall, and can be lifted all at once for storing.

Preparing and Using

Potatoes can be boiled, fried, steamed, grilled, or baked. All potatoes should be cooked or placed in water immediately after peeling to prevent discoloration. To peel or not to peel is generally a result of the preparation method or personal preference. The exception is thin-skinned new potatoes, which should not be peeled.

Choose the type of potato to use in a recipe based on its qualities. New potatoes are moist and waxy and are best for steaming, boiling, and in salads. Oblong mature white potatoes are rather dry and starchy. They are the most popular potato to use for French-fries and they are great for baking and mashing. Round red potatoes have a rather waxy texture, making them ideal for boiling and mashing. Round white potatoes are thin-skinned and hold their shape in salads

Hints and Tips

Let the plant continue to grow for a late harvest of bigger potatoes. The kids will love planting the blue or purple potato variety.

as well as boiling and roasting. Yellow-fleshed potatoes are good for steaming, roasting, and mashing.

Potatoes do not freeze, dry, or can well.

Problems

Flea beetles, leaf hoppers, and slugs; blight, scab, and root knot nematode. Tubers exposed to sunlight while growing will turn green and are mildly toxic.

RADISH

BOTANICAL INFORMATION	Seed to Harvest/Flower: 4 weeks
Family: Mustard	**Seeds Storage:** 5 to 6 years
Height: 6 to 12 inches	**Weeks to Maturity:** 3 weeks
Spacing: 16 per square	**Indoor Seed Starting:** no
GROWING SEASON	**Earliest Outdoor Planting:** 3 weeks before last spring frost
Spring: yes	**Additional Plantings:** every other week
Summer: yes	
Fall: yes	
Winter: no	

Description

Radishes are a great crop for all gardeners—from experts to beginners. Who can pass up a vegetable that matures in only three weeks? Plus, they are zesty and tasty in any dish.

Radishes come in a multitude of shapes from small and round to long carrot shapes. They vary in color from red, pink, white, and even some black varieties. Radishes planted in the spring are normally red or white colored, and will mature in 3 to 4 weeks. Fall radishes take 6 to 8 weeks and store very well; they're referred to as winter radishes.

It's easy to plant too many radishes. They don't like being crowded, so the SFG method is very suitable for this vegetable. Decide how many you can use each week and then plant no more than double that number every other week for a continuous, but controlled, harvest.

Starting

Location: Full sun to partial shade.

Seeds Indoors: No.

Transplanting: Does not transplant well.

Seeds Outdoors: Sprouts in five to ten days outdoors depending on temperature. Plant a square foot every other week for a staggered but continuous harvest. Plant ½ inch deep in spring, 1 inch deep in summer. If you really like radishes a lot, plant some every week of the growing year, even through the hot weather. The plants will still do fairly well then if you give them some shade, lots of water, and a thick mulch. Winter or long-keeping varieties need two months to mature, so start them at least that long before the first fall frost.

Growing

Watering: Don't let radishes stop growing or dry out; lack of water causes hot-tasting and pithy radishes.

Maintenance: Weed weekly; keep covered with screen-covered cage if root maggots are a problem; mulch in hot weather.

Harvesting

How: Pull up the entire plant and trim off the top. Refrigerate edible portions if they're not used immediately.

When: Harvest as soon as they are marble size up to Ping-Pong ball size; the smaller you pull them, the sweeter they taste. The long fall varieties can be left in the ground until frost, then either mulched to keep the ground from freezing, or pulled and stored in damp peat moss or sand after the tops are removed.

Preparing and Using

Slice, dice, or cut into fancy shapes for eating out of hand or to add to salads, and for garnishes. If you have too many all at once, twist or cut off the tops and store in a plastic bag in the refrigerator. Radishes will keep for up to a week before getting soft.

Problems

None to speak of, except possibly root maggots.

Hints and Tips

Teaching a child to garden? This is the perfect first crop; let each child pick a color, and take it from there.

SPINACH

BOTANICAL INFORMATION
Family: Goosefoot
Height: 6 to 12 inches
Spacing: 9 per square
GROWING SEASON
Spring: yes
Summer: no
Fall: yes
Winter: yes

Seed to Harvest/Flower: 7 weeks
Seeds Storage: 5 to 6 years
Weeks to Maturity: 7 weeks
Indoor Seed Starting: no
Earliest Outdoor Planting: 5 weeks before last spring frost

Description

Spinach is somewhat difficult to grow, but a very popular plant. It usually does well if it stays cool in the spring. A rapid grower, it can be grown in a fairly small space and looks great in the garden. It will quickly bolt to seed in the summer heat, but grows very well in the early spring and then again in the fall. Spinach is very cold hardy and in many areas of the country it will winter over; in warmer climates, it can be grown all winter.

There are two types of spinach—the smooth-leaved kind and a crinkly-leaved type called Savoy, which is more popular and more attractive. Neither will endure heat and should be grown in cool weather. Some varieties are more resistant to frost and are particularly adaptable for growing in the fall, and possibly into the winter season. Check your seed catalog for appropriate varieties.

Starting

Location: Any location is suitable, full sun to partial shade.
Seeds Indoors: No.
Transplanting: Does not transplant well.
Seeds Outdoors: Sprouts outdoors in one to two weeks. Plant seeds ½ inch deep, water, and cover with a plastic-covered cage. Plants can withstand any temperature between 25°F and 75°F, so judge your spring and fall planting accordingly.

Growing

Watering: Being a leaf crop, spinach needs constant moist soil.
Maintenance: Weed weekly; mulch in warm weather. Don't work in the spinach square if the leaves are very wet—they are brittle and break easily.

Harvesting

How: Cut outer leaves as needed; small inner leaves will continue to grow rapidly.
When: Harvest as soon as the plants look like they won't miss an outer leaf or two. Keep picking and the plant will keep growing right up until hot weather. If it's a spring crop and you think the plants are going to bolt soon, cut off the entire plant for a little extra harvest.

Preparing and Using

Wash carefully; soil tends to cling to the undersides, especially on the ones with crinkled leaves. Spin or pat dry and store in refrigerator just like lettuce. Better yet, eat spinach right away. Serve fresh in salads, cook slightly for a wilted spinach salad, or cook by steaming lightly. Spinach goes great with any meal, especially when garnished with a chopped, hard-boiled egg. It's high in vitamins A, B1, and C, and is a valuable source of iron.

Problems

Leaf miners and aphids. No diseases to speak of.

Hints and Tips

If you want to grow spinach in the warmer weather, search the seed catalogs for bolt-resistant varieties and provide shade, a heavy mulch, and lots of water in the warmer weather.

STRAWBERRY

BOTANICAL INFORMATION
  Family: Rose
  Height: 6 to 12 inches
  Spacing: 4 per square
GROWING SEASON
  Spring: yes
  Summer: no
  Fall: yes
  Winter: no

Seed to Harvest/Flower: n/a
Seeds Storage: no; seed-started plants take up to 3 years to bear fruit
Weeks to Maturity: n/a
Earliest Outdoor Planting: 4 weeks before last spring frost

Description

Picking strawberries on a clear June day is a treat for young, old, and everyone in between—only about half the harvest actually makes it into the basket! Since strawberries are so popular, most families like to plant an entire 4 × 4 in strawberries—it's easy to protect and harvest. You might also like to build a pyramid box and plant it in all strawberries.

Growing your own strawberries is fun and rewarding. Strawberry plants bear fruit for at least 3 or 4 years, then yields will decrease and eventually the plant will die. Each plant sends out runners that produce a new plant, which can be used as the next generation of strawberries in the garden. However, I recommend you not let them root, as they take so much energy from the parent plant. I'll explain a better way for your SFG.

There are three main types of strawberries: June-bearing, which sets fruit in June; ever-bearing, which will set fruit twice during the growing season; and day-neutral, which is not affected by the length of the day as the others are. And don't overlook the Alpine strawberry, which will reward you with tiny but incredibly tasty fruit over a long period!

Starting

Location: Full sun.

Seeds Indoors: No.

Transplanting: Early spring, as soon as the soil is not frozen. Be sure soil is not wet.

Outdoors: Most gardeners buy strawberry plants in packets of a dozen or so. Soak first, then trim off the roots slightly, and plant 4 per square foot. Leave a saucer-shaped depression around each plant for effective watering. Keep the soil moist; increase water when strawberries are fruiting.

Growing

Watering: Weekly; more during dry periods.

Maintenance: Cut off all the runners as soon as you see them each week; that way all the energy will stay in the parent plant for an increased harvest each year. After 3 or 4 years when the harvest starts to diminish, it is best to pull out those plants and replant, perhaps in a different square with brand-new certified disease-free plants from the nursery. It's true that those runners will produce baby plants and it seems a waste not to use them; some people like to let them grow. However, the problem comes from too many runners producing too many baby plants (because the gardener forgets to cut them off); they take all the energy from the parent, reducing the harvest.

Harvesting

How: Pick the fruit leaving a short piece of stem attached; use scissors for a clean cut.

When: Harvest as fruit ripens, for 2 to 3 weeks.

Preparing and Using

Use strawberries as soon as possible after picking; pop a few right in your mouth. They can be used in fruit salads, on cakes, and in pies. Freeze whole strawberries for use in smoothies—they will be soft when they defrost, but still flavorful.

Problems

Birds and slugs; verticillium wilt. People who put too many in their mouth and too few in the basket.

Hints and Tips

Cover plants with bird netting to preserve harvest.

SUMMER SQUASH

BOTANICAL INFORMATION
Family: Gourd
Height: bush or vine
Spacing:
Bush: 1 per
9 square feet
Vine: 1 per
2 square feet
GROWING SEASON
Spring: no
Summer: yes
Fall: no
Winter: no

Seed to Harvest/Flower: 8 weeks
Seeds Storage: 5 to 6 years
Weeks to Maturity: 6 to 8 weeks
Indoor Seed Starting: 2 weeks before last spring frost
Earliest Outdoor Planting: immediately following last spring frost

Description

Summer squash needs a lot of room to grow, but is unbelievably prolific. It is easy and fast to grow, but needs hot weather to do well. There are many colors and shapes—round, straight, crookneck, and flat—each with its particular taste.

Most of the varieties sold are the bush types, (especially zucchini), so you'll have to assign a larger space (a 3 × 3 area) to just one plant. However, those plants can produce a vast amount of fruit, so most gardeners think it's worthwhile, at least for one or two plants.

An alternate solution is to grow the vining types on vertical frames, which is quite a space saver. (Zucchini can be trained to grow vertically, but it still takes a lot of room because of those huge leaves and prickly stems.) Check the seed packet or catalog to make sure you are getting a vine type; if the seed packet or catalog doesn't say so, call the seed company's toll-free number and ask.

Starting

Location: Full sun.

Seeds Indoors: Doesn't transplant well because of the long taproot. It's best to start seeds outdoors.

If you do want to start indoors, plant one seed in a paper cup of Mel's Mix 1 inch deep. Plant 2 weeks before your last frost date.

Transplanting: Plant outdoors on your last spring frost date.

Seeds Outdoors: Sprouts in 5 to 10 days outdoors. For bush types, plant 2 presoaked seeds in the center of a nine-square space. For vine types, also plant 2 presoaked seeds in the middle of a 2-square-foot space under your vertical frame. Make sure you hollow out a dish shape around the planted seeds to hold plenty of water. Place a plastic-covered cage over the seeds to warm the soil. After sprouting, cut off the weakest plant if both seeds sprout.

Growing

Watering: Keep the leaves dry to prevent powdery mildew.

Maintenance: Weed weekly; keep vines trained up vertical frames or within bounds of the square.

Harvesting

How: Carefully cut through the fruit stem but do not cut the main vine or leaf stems. Handle the squash gently as their skins are very soft and easily damaged by fingernails or if dropped.

When: Harvest as soon as the blossoms wilt, and until the fruits are 6 to 9 inches long. Don't let them grow any longer. Sometimes you have to harvest at least three times a week; they grow that fast. Squash loses flavor as the seeds inside mature.

Hints and Tips

If you need or want to tell the kids about the birds and bees, the garden is the right place to do it—and summer squash is the right plant for you to use. Point out to any eager faces the difference between the male and female flower. The female already has a miniature fruit right before the blossom. The male blossom, which contains the pollen—oh, you know the rest of the story. Didn't your mother or father talk to you in the garden?

Preparing and Using

Rinse lightly and serve sliced or cut into sticks, with a dip, or just as an appetizer anytime. Cook lightly by steaming or stir-frying, in any number of dishes or combinations. Serve squash by itself or with other vegetables, seasoned with a little dressing, grated cheese, or chopped parsley. Squash is high in vitamins A, B1, and C.

Problems

Squash vine borer and squash bug; powdery mildew.

WINTER SQUASH

BOTANICAL INFORMATION
  Family: Gourd
  Height: vine
  Spacing: 1 per 2 square feet
GROWING SEASON
  Spring: no
  Summer: yes
  Fall: no
  Winter: no

Seed to Harvest/Flower: 12 weeks
Seeds Storage: 5 to 6 years
Weeks to Maturity: 12 weeks
Indoor Seed Starting: no
Earliest Outdoor Planting: 2 weeks after last spring frost

Description

A space-hogging plant that many gardeners won't grow because of its large leaves and rampaging vines, winter squash can take over the entire garden. That's why we grow it vertically! The fruit can be picked in the late fall and stored without difficulty to be used during the winter; it retains its delectable flavor long after being harvested.

There are many varieties to select from, but butternut and acorn are the most popular. All winter squashes have thick skins that harden in the fall, and are generally picked after the vines have been killed by frost. You don't get your compensation until season's end, but since there is almost no fresh produce then, the winter squash is very welcomed. The fruit has a mild flavor and is fine grained.

Starting

Location: Full sun, but tolerates a little shade.
Seeds Indoors: No.
Transplanting: Does not transplant well because of the long taproot.
Seeds Outdoors: Since the seeds sprout quickly, you might as well start them outdoors. Plant two presoaked seeds in the center of 2 square feet. Make sure you've left a 2-inch depression around the seeds to hold lots of water during the season. Cover with a plastic covered

cage to warm the soil and encourage fast seed sprouting. Cut off the weakest plant if both seeds sprout.

Growing

Watering: Keep soil moist.

Maintenance: Weed weekly; keep vines trained up the vertical frame.

Harvesting

How: Cut the squash from the vine, leaving as long a stem as possible, at least 2 inches. Then set the fruit out in the sun to cure for a few days, protecting it at night when frost is in the forecast.

When: Harvest after the first light frost, which will kill the leaves and vines, and after the main vine wilts, but before a very hard frost.

Preparing and Using

Peel, cut in half, scoop out seeds, and prepare for boiling or baking. Excellent served mashed or in chunks with butter and parsley. Winter squash can even be added to some soups and stews. Butternut can be used in pumpkin pie recipes (many cooks say it's better tasting than pumpkin itself). Store winter squash in a cool, dry place at 40° to 50°F; check often and use if you see any bruised or rotten spots.

Problems

A few beetles; powdery mildew; and vines too rambunctious to control.

Hints and Tips

Without a vertical frame, winter squash will take over your garden, so make sure you only grow winter squash vertically. This squash is so prolific and vigorous that it is a perfect plant for an arbor or extended vertical structure. When picking the squash, handle the fruit carefully and cut the stem–don't break it off.

TOMATO

BOTANICAL INFORMATION
Family: Nightshade
Height: bush, 3 feet tall; vine, 6 feet tall
Spacing:
Bush: 1 per 9 square feet
Vine: 1 per square foot
GROWING SEASON
Spring: no
Summer: yes
Fall: no
Winter: no

Seed to Harvest/Flower: 17 weeks
Seeds Storage: 4 to 5 years
Weeks to Maturity: 11 weeks
Indoor Seed Starting: 6 weeks before last spring frost
Outdoor Seed Starting: no
Earliest Outdoor Planting: immediately after last spring frost

Description

If you don't plant anything else, you should plant tomatoes—a few different varieties at the very least. There is a huge selection available, some specifically suited for eating, juicing, cooking, or canning. They're available in early, midseason, or late types in different colors ranging from red, orange, pink, and yellow. Size also varies from the small cherry tomato to the extra large 4-pound types that win awards at the county fair.

When choosing varieties, it's very important to consider whether they are pest- and disease-resistant. This is very important, so make a note: resistant varieties are labeled VFN. V indicates the plant is resistant to Verticillium wilt; F indicates it will resist Fusarium wilt; and N is for nematodes, which are tiny, tiny worms that infect the roots. There are some very good non-resistant traditional varieties, but if you are hit with any of these problems and lose your plants virtually overnight just when they're starting to produce, you'll understand the value of the varieties that are disease- and pest-resistant.

The resistant varieties taste great and also mature in early, midseason, or late season. Usually the early season fruits are best suited to the colder climates in the north. If you live in a longer-season climate, you can grow a few different varieties that will produce all season long.

Tomatoes have two different growth habits: determinate and indeterminate (in other words, bush or vine). Bush varieties that grow no more than 3 feet tall are the determinate kinds. Indeterminate types, the vine types, are also the most common and usually mature in mid- to late season. They grow the biggest tomatoes, take the longest to mature, and last until frost kills them. You can amaze your family and friends by remembering the name of the two different types this way: "It is indeterminate how tall the vine types will grow."

Starting

Location: Full sun.

Seeds Indoors: Sprouts in one week at 70°F. Sprinkle 5 or so seeds of each variety you want to grow in individual cups filled with vermiculite six weeks before your last spring frost. Just barely cover with vermiculite and water; move to full sunlight as soon as first shoots appear. Then pot up in seedling trays or individual pots as soon as plants are large enough (usually 1 to 3 weeks). Keep a careful watch over the plants, especially after transplanting them into seedling trays, because any check or stoppage of the growth will affect the ultimate bearing capacity of the plant.

Transplanting: Harden off transplants for one to two weeks, and plant outside on or after your frost-free date. Plant one vine-type plant per square foot. Bush types are planted in the center of a nine square foot area. They take up so much room that I now grow only vine-type varieties. Water and cover with a plastic-covered wire cage for protection from the cold and wind. Leave the cage on until the plants are at least 18 inches tall and pushing at the top.

Seeds Outdoors: The season is too short to start outdoors.

Growing

Watering: Keep water off the plant leaves.

Maintenance: Prune off side branches (suckers) weekly for vine types and guide plant tops up through netting. Prune off lower dead or yellow leaves. Keep adding mulch as the season gets hotter.

Harvesting

How: Gently twist and pull ripe tomatoes so the stem breaks (if it's ripe it should easily break away), or even better, cut the stem so as not to disturb the rest of the remaining fruit.

When: If you're not going to wait until they're red and ripe, why grow them yourself? Some gardeners like to pick them just slightly before that point (say a day or two) if they want extra-firm tomatoes for sandwiches or a particular dish. If you leave them on the vine too long they will turn soft and mushy, so inspect daily; it's one of the pleasures you've been waiting for all year.

Preparing and Using

This is a subject fit for an entire book, and in fact many have been written. What can one say in a few paragraphs? Tomatoes can be used in a multitude of ways. You can enjoy plate after plate of sliced tomatoes seasoned with lots of pepper and sometimes a little mayonnaise; try pouring your favorite salad dressing over that same dish of sliced tomatoes. Soak a plate full in vinegar overnight for the next day's treat. Add thick slices of fresh tomatoes to any casserole and enjoy a flavor not experienced the rest of the year. If you have a lot of tomatoes, use them fresh in cooking instead of canned tomatoes.

Problems

Cutworm, whitefly, and the big, bad, but beautiful tomato horn worm; various wilt diseases.

Hints and Tips

Don't let anyone, anytime ever smoke in your garden. They may contaminate your plants with a tobacco disease. In fact, they should even wash their hands before entering the garden if they are going to handle any of the plants. (Oh, well, there goes all your smoking friends.)

HERBS

BASIL

BOTANICAL INFORMATION
Family: Mint
Height: 1 to 2 feet
Spacing: small, 4 per square foot large, 1 per square foot

GROWING SEASON
Spring: no
Summer: yes
Fall: no
Winter: no

Seed to Harvest/Flower: 12 weeks
Seeds Storage: 5 years
Weeks to Maturity: 4 to 6 weeks
Indoor Seed Starting: 4 to 6 weeks before last frost
Earliest Outdoor Planting: after soil has warmed
Additional Plantings: 3 weeks and 6 weeks
Last Planting: not needed

Description

Basil is a non-invasive member of the mint family. 'Sweet Genovese' is the pesto basil. Basil is used not only in Italian cooking, but in many Asian cuisines. In India, it is planted around the temples and is a part of many religious ceremonies. Basil also comes in flavors such as cinnamon, licorice, and lemon. Go ahead and splurge—grow a few different kinds and discover the wonders of this beautiful and delicious herb.

Starting

Location: Full sun.

Seeds Indoors: Start seeds indoors 4 to 6 weeks before the last frost. Seeds germinate quickly.

Transplanting: Set out after all danger of frost has passed and the soil has warmed. Basil will stop growing if the weather is cool and take a while to catch up, so wait to transplant basil until the weather has settled.

Seeds Outdoors: Sow basil seeds where the plants are to be grown in warm soil. Seeds germinate in 7 to 10 days, and the plants grow quickly.

Growing

Watering: Keep well-watered.

Maintenance: Pinch basil often to keep the plant bushy. Harvesting basil for cooking will also keep the plant strong and bushy. For energetic, tasty plants, remove flower buds as they appear.

Harvesting

How: Pinch stems just above leaf nodes where new stems will sprout. Use only the leaves in cooking.

When: Harvest basil anytime. In fact, the more you pinch off leaves and stems, the more it will grow.

Preparing and Using

Use fresh leaves in cooking, discarding stems. Dried basil does not retain its flavor. Excess basil can be processed with olive oil, wrapped tightly in plastic wrap, and stored in the freezer for up to 3 months.

Problems

Aphids and Japanese beetles; Fusarium wilt.

CHIVE

BOTANICAL INFORMATION
- **Family:** Lily
- **Height:** 6 to 12 inches
- **Spacing:** 16 per square

GROWING SEASON
- **Spring:** late
- **Summer:** yes
- **Fall:** no
- **Winter:** no

Seed to Harvest/Flower: 16 weeks
Seeds Storage: 2 years
Weeks to Maturity: 10 weeks
Indoor Seed Starting: 10 weeks before last frost
Earliest Outdoor Planting: late spring
Additional Plantings: not needed
Last Planting: not needed

Description

This is a fun little plant with a spiky hairdo. The slim, round leaves are hollow and have a mild onion scent when cut. The pinkish-purple flowers are edible and appear in late spring and make a pretty garnish for salads. Chives are a member of the onion family, and oddly enough, it is one herb that hasn't really been used for medicinal purposes during its long history. It is simply a unique garden plant that has enhanced the flavor of savory foods for centuries.

Starting

Location: Full sun.

Seeds Indoors: Plant seeds indoors in late winter. Seeds can take up to 21 days to germinate.

Transplanting: Set plants out in spring. Although chives are cold-hardy, it is best to set new plants out after all danger of frost has passed.

Seeds Outdoors: Sprouts in late spring to early summer.

Growing

Watering: Keep soil moist.

Maintenance: Plants will spread, so divide clumps every few years to rejuvenate the plants.

Harvesting

How: Snip the tips of the leaves as needed to garnish baked potatoes and creamed soups. Don't cut off more than ⅓ of the plant at any one time.

When: Chives can be harvested anytime after the new leaves have reached 6 to 8 inches. To enjoy the tasty pink flowers, don't harvest the plant until you can see the flower buds, then clip around them or wait until they bloom. The flowers make a lovely garnish.

Preparing and Using

Cut ⅓ of the tops off all leaves if you like the flat-top look, or cut a few leaves down to ⅓ of each leaf. Snip the fresh hollow leaves into salads, sauces, soups, or dips.

Problems

Insufficient water can cause leaf tips to turn brown.

CILANTRO

BOTANICAL INFORMATION
- **Family:** Umbellifer
- **Height:** 1 to 2 feet
- **Spacing:** 1 per square

GROWING SEASON
- **Spring:** late
- **Summer:** yes
- **Fall:** no
- **Winter:** no

Seed to Harvest/Flower: 5 weeks (leaves), 12 weeks (coriander seeds)
Seeds Storage: n/a
Weeks to Maturity: 5 weeks
Indoor Seed Starting: no
Earliest Outdoor Planting: after last frost
Additional Plantings: 2-week intervals until early summer for continuous harvest
Last Planting: not needed

Description

The fresh leaf of cilantro is probably the most widely used of all flavoring herbs throughout the world. It is used in Middle Eastern, Indian, Southeast Asian, and South American cuisines. Cilantro is a pretty plant that looks somewhat like parsley. Use it like parsley in smaller quantities for a unique tang. When cilantro goes to seed, it becomes another herb altogether—coriander. Ancients used to chew coriander seeds to combat heartburn (probably after weeding their long single-row gardens). The seeds are sweet when they're ripe, but terribly bitter when immature.

Starting

Location: Full sun to partial shade.
Seeds Indoors: No.
Transplanting: Does not transplant well.
Seeds Outdoors: After last frost.

Growing

Watering: Weekly.
Maintenance: Shelter the plants from wind, otherwise cilantro needs
little care besides watering.

Harvesting

How: Pick cilantro leaves as you need them, even if the plant is only
6 inches tall. For coriander seeds, cut whole plants and hang to dry,
and then shake the dried seeds into a paper bag.
When: Harvest the cilantro leaves anytime after the plant has reached
6 to 8 inches. Harvest the seeds (coriander) after the plants have
turned brown but before the seeds start to fall. Cilantro self-sows
with abandon.

Preparing and Using

Cilantro leaves and coriander seeds are both used in curries and
pickles. The strong, spicy leaves can be added to salads, fish, or beans,
and it is found as an ingredient in many ethnic recipes. The milder,
sweeter seeds can be ground and used in breads or cakes.

Problems

Cilantro is usually pest- and disease-free. The plant does suffer in
humid, rainy weather.

MINT

BOTANICAL
INFORMATION
  Family: Mint
  Height: 1 to 3 feet
  Spacing: 1 per square
GROWING SEASON
  Spring: yes
  Summer: yes
  Fall: yes
  Winter: no

Seed to Harvest/Flower: n/a; perennial
Seeds Storage: n/a
Weeks to Maturity: n/a
Indoor Seed Starting: no
Earliest Outdoor Planting: early spring
Additional Plantings: any time throughout
  growing season
Last Planting: not needed

Description

Mint, and other members of the mint family, has the distinguishing characteristic of square stems. You can see this best by looking at the cut end of a mint stem. Mint plants come in many flavors, such as spearmint, peppermint, apple, lemon, and chocolate, and all mints give off a lovely scent when the leaves are crushed. But beware—mint is invasive. It sends out tough runners that grow roots and leaves every few inches, and will crop up anywhere it can. To keep mint plants in bounds, cut a 6-inch diameter circle around the plants in late spring and again in early fall, and pull out any runners outside the circle. Try not to leave any small pieces in the ground—they too will sprout. In a Square Foot Garden, sink a 12-inch square or round plastic pail or clay pot in that square; don't use a conventional pot with holes on the side or around the bottom. If using a pail, drill some small drainage holes in the bottom. If using a clay pot, cover the bottom hole with a piece of broken crockery or bottle cap. Pull the entire pot up in the fall and take it inside as a houseplant. Don't let this discourage you from growing many different kinds of mints, however, because the benefits truly outweigh the extra work.

Starting

Location: Sun to partial shade.
Seeds Indoors: No, does not come true from seed.
Transplanting: Plant divisions anytime from spring through fall.
Seeds Outdoors: No.

Growing

Watering: Weekly.
Maintenance: Cut back to promote bushiness.

Harvesting

How: Cut mint stems back to a pair of leaves. This is where new
branches will form. Use the leaves as a flavoring and sprigs as
a garnish.
When: Harvest mint anytime after the plant has reached 6 inches tall;
do not harvest the leaves of creeping (groundcover) mints.

Preparing and Using

Use fresh mint leaves in sauces, mint jelly, salads, or to flavor herb teas. Float a sprig of mint in your favorite summer drink, bruising the bottom leaves a little to impart that refreshing flavor. Tuck a sprig of mint into a fruit cup for color and scent.

Problems

Mint is basically disease- and pest-free. Plants may wilt and turn brown without sufficient water, but should spring right back after a good soaking.

OREGANO

BOTANICAL INFORMATION	**Seed to Harvest/Flower:** 16 weeks; hardy perennial
Family: Mint	**Seeds Storage:** n/a
Height: 1 to 2 feet	**Weeks to Maturity:** 8 to 10 weeks
Spacing: 1 per square	**Indoor Seed Starting:** 6 weeks before last spring frost
GROWING SEASON	**Earliest Outdoor Planting:** after last frost
Spring: yes	**Additional Plantings:** anytime throughout growing season
Summer: yes	**Last Planting:** not needed
Fall: yes	
Winter: no	

Description

What would Italian food be without a sprinkling of oregano to give it flavor and color? Oregano is a native of the Mediterranean area and enjoys lots of sunshine. It is a pretty plant with round leaves tightly covering the stems. Variegated oregano is particularly lovely with the leaves edged in white or gold, but the variegated plants are not quite as hardy as the green ones and are used mostly as ornamental plants. Give oregano frequent trimmings to keep it neat and so you can dry the leaves. It is one of few herbs whose flavor is stronger dried than fresh. When the leaves have dried, crumble them lightly and store in an airtight container.

Starting

Location: Full sun.
Seeds Indoors: 4 to 6 weeks before last spring frost.
Transplanting: Plant divisions anytime after the temperatures reach 45°F.
Seeds Outdoors: Spring, after last frost; seeds need light to germinate.

Growing

Watering: Weekly.
Maintenance: Water sparingly; too much water will cause root rot. Harvest or trim mature plants often to keep them in bounds. Divide every 2 to 3 years.

Harvesting

How: Cut stems back to a pair of leaves. This is where new branches will form.

When: Oregano can be harvested anytime during the summer months, but the flavor is best after the buds have formed but just before the flowers open.

Preparing and Using

Oregano loses its distinctive flavor during cooking, so always add it in the last few minutes. Use oregano in salads, casseroles, soups, sauces, poultry dishes, and of course, pizza. Dried oregano has a stronger flavor than fresh and goes especially well with tomato or rice dishes.

Problems

Oregano is usually pest- and disease-free. Too much water can cause root rot.

FLOWERS

DAHLIA

BOTANICAL INFORMATION	
Family: Daisy	**Seed to Harvest/Flower:** 10 to 12 weeks
Height: 1 to 3 feet	**Seeds Storage:** 2 to 3 years
Spacing:	**Weeks to Maturity:** 5 to 6 weeks
small, 4 per square;	**Indoor Seed Starting:** 6 to 8 weeks before last
medium, 1 per square;	frost date
giant, n/a.	Indoor Tuber Starting: 4 weeks before last frost date
GROWING SEASON	Outdoor Seed Starting: not enough time (seedlings
Spring: no	may not bloom until late summer)
Summer: yes	**Earliest Outdoor Planting:** after last frost date
Fall: yes	**Additional Plantings:** not needed
Winter: no	**Last Planting:** not needed

Description

Native to Mexico, dahlias literally come in all shapes and sizes. This gets complicated. They are grouped into nine sizes based on the diameter of the flower, and 18 classifications of form, from the daisy-like decorative form, to pompom, cactus, and the fully double stellar form. Flowers come in every color except blue and green, and multicolors abound. Even the leaves come in colors, from light green to deepest green to burgundy. Plus, they are said to guard neighboring plants against nematodes. There is indeed a dahlia for everyone.

Border or dwarf dahlias grow 12 to 24 inches high and rarely need staking. Garden dahlias are in the 2 to 4 foot range, while giant forms have been known to grow to 10 feet—but not in a Square Foot Garden! Start your own plants from seed (no guarantee what color you'll get), or buy roots (called tubers) for special, especially showy types. In the fall, dig up the newly formed tubers and store in a frost-free area until the next spring.

Warning: dahlias can be habit-forming. If you get hooked (I did), join your local Dahlia Society and you'll fit right in!

Starting

Location: Full sun to partial shade for best results.

Seeds Indoors: Start seeds 6 to 8 weeks before last spring frost. Seedlings emerge in 5 to 21 days.

Transplanting: After last frost date.

Seeds Outdoors: No, time is too short for seeds, but you can plant tubers anytime after the last frost.

Growing

Watering: Water dahlia tubers when first setting them out, then wait until you see shoots before watering again unless the soil is unusually dry. This will prevent the tubers from rotting. Once the root system is established and shoots begin to show, give dahlia plants daily water, especially during the hottest summer months.

Maintenance: When the plant reaches about 3 inches tall, pinch off the growing tip to encourage bushy growth. Mulch dahlias to keep the soil moist. Support tall varieties. Deadhead to encourage reblooming.

Since dahlias are easily grown from seed, you may not want to bother digging up the tiny tubers of seed-grown plants. Simply start them from seed again next year. If you do want to dig up the tubers, after the first frost has killed the foliage, carefully dig dahlia tubers and let them dry for a few hours. Cut off the stems, leaving a 2-inch stump, remove excess soil, and store in a box filled with peat moss or vermiculite, in a cool, frost-free location. Check the dahlias each month over the winter and discard any rotten tubers. Spray any tubers that start to shrivel with warm water.

Harvesting

How: Dahlias have hollow stems, and a sticky white substance will ooze from the cut. This is a nutrient that the cut flower needs to stay alive. To preserve the flower, sear the cut end with a match or candle. After searing, prick a hole in the stem just under the head of the flower. Remove any leaves that will fall below the waterline. Dahlias will last 5 to 7 days in a vase.

When: Cut dahlias when the flowers are fully open.

Problems

Earwigs and slugs; powdery mildew.

DUSTY MILLER

**BOTANICAL
INFORMATION**
  Family: Daisy
  Height: 12 to 18 inches
  Spacing: 4 per square
GROWING SEASON
  Spring: late
  Summer: yes
  Fall: yes
  Winter: no

Seed to Harvest/Flower: 15 weeks; half-hardy annual
Seeds Storage: n/a
Weeks to Maturity: 10 weeks
Indoor Seed Starting: 10 to 15 weeks before last frost
Earliest Outdoor Planting: 2 to 3 weeks before
  last frost
Additional Plantings: after last frost with other
  annuals, or not needed
Last Planting: not needed

Description

One of my favorites for the Square Foot Garden! The charming dusty miller has been grown by generations of gardeners, and for good reason. The soft, silvery foliage is a beautiful addition to just about any garden type, from formal to casual, and the color blends or contrasts with many other leaves and flowers. Its carefree nature, unique color, and interesting texture make it a gardener's favorite. There are a few different kinds of dusty miller, mostly distinguished by the depth of the "cuts" in the foliage—some are scalloped, some are lacy. Dusty miller plants have unattractive mustard-yellow flowers that grow on plants that have overwintered. There are other annuals, and even perennials, that are easily confused with dusty miller. If the plant in question has white daisylike flowers, it is probably Silver Lace. If it has purple flowers, then it is most likely a perennial *Centaurea*. Regardless of which plant you actually have, enjoy it as a lovely garden accent.

Starting

Location: Full sun to partial shade.
Seeds Indoors: 10 to 15 weeks before last frost; seeds need light
    to germinate.
Transplanting: Dusty miller is unique in that it can be set out into the
    garden 2 to 3 weeks before last frost. Waiting until other annuals
    are ready to be planted after the last frost is fine, too.
Seed Outdoors: Only in truly frost-free areas as it is a slow grower.

Growing

Watering: Water regularly when young, weekly once established. Even
    though dusty miller is drought tolerant, it will do best if
    watered regularly.
Maintenance: Dusty miller is fairly hardy and will overwinter in many
    areas, especially if cut back and mulched in the late fall. Prune

second-year plants back severely to maintain the plant's shape and remove any flowering stems as they appear.

Harvesting
Cut branches at any time for flower displays.

Problems
Rot can be a problem in wet soil. Otherwise, dusty miller is nearly problem-free.

MARIGOLD

BOTANICAL INFORMATION	
Family: Daisy	**Seed to Flower:** 10 weeks; half-hardy annual
Height: dwarf, 6 to 12 inches, large, 1½ to 3 feet	**Seeds Storage:** 2 to 3 years
	Weeks to Maturity: 3 to 4 weeks
Spacing: dwarf, 4 per square; large, 1 per square	**Indoor Seed Starting:** 6 to 8 weeks before last spring frost
GROWING SEASON	**Earliest Outdoor Planting:** at last frost date
Spring: no	**Additional Plantings:** not needed
Summer: yes	**Last Planting:** not needed
Fall: yes	
Winter: no	

Description
Just about everyone will recognize the pompom flowers of the marigold. The most common flower colors are orange, yellow, and red/orange bicolor, but they can be found in burgundy, red, and even a creamy white. Flowers can be single, double, or crested, and from 1 to 6 inches in diameter. Marigold leaves are distinctive—slim and lacy—and give off a pungent scent when cut or crushed.

The smaller marigold plants are sometimes called French marigolds, but all marigolds are native to subtropical America and have been grown in Mexico for thousands of years. The dwarf plants range in size from 6 to 8 inches tall. Don't be fooled by the name—dwarf refers to the plant size, not necessarily the flower size.

The larger marigold plants are known as African marigolds, but like their smaller cousins, they are also indigenous to the Americas. Giant marigolds can grow to over 3 feet tall and are a little too big for a Square Foot Garden.

Marigolds are said to discourage nematodes when planted near tomatoes, potatoes, asparagus, strawberries, or roses, especially if they are grown for several seasons in ground where nematodes are suspected. Marigolds also repel the Mexican bean beetle when planted around bean plants. Japanese beetles are attracted to the odorless varieties of marigolds, where they can be trapped and drowned in soapy water placed near the marigolds.

I want to tell you a little story about what is grown around the globe. Whenever we do a humanitarian project overseas, people ask me, "How do you know what crops they can grow in that country?" I answer, "We specifically tell the people we do not try to compete with the farmer or try to grow the basic things they normally eat as part of their Square Meter Garden." We tell them, "We are going to grow new things so your children can have more nutrients and better health than they now have." And still we are asked, "But, how do you know those things will grow there?"

The answer was illustrated when I went to India to attend the grand opening ceremonies of Father Abraham's new Square Foot Garden Training Center. They gave us garlands of their locally grown special flower—and guess what it was? Marigolds! Even more astounding, broccoli turned out to be their most popular and bestselling vegetable. That made me realize that everything we grow in our USA Square Foot Gardens can usually be grown just about anywhere in the world.

Starting
Location: Grow in a sunny location.
Seeds Indoors: Marigold seeds will germinate in about 7 to 14 days, ideal for a child's first foray into the wonders of growing plants from seeds.
Transplanting: After last frost date.
Seeds Outdoors: Okay, but usually not practical as the season is too short.

Growing
Watering: Weekly when young, twice weekly when larger. Don't let marigolds dry out—the plants will wilt and die quickly, and the stress will attract insects and diseases.
Maintenance: Pinch the growing tips back when the plant reaches about 3 inches tall to encourage bushiness. Pinch or cut off spent blooms to prolong flowering.

Harvesting
How: When thinking of flowers to cut for the vase, marigolds don't immediately spring to mind. However, they make a cute bouquet that can last for 7 to 14 days, as long as the stems are not bent.

Marigold stems are short, so try to cut where the flower stem meets a main stem. Remove the leaves that will be under water. To reduce the aroma, add a spoonful of sugar to the water.

When: Cut marigolds when the flowers are one-half to three-quarters open. Fully open marigolds will die quickly in the vase.

Problems
Slugs and mites; Botrytis blight and wilt.

PANSY

BOTANICAL INFORMATION
Family: Viola
Height: 6 to 9 inches
Spacing: 4 per square
GROWING SEASON
Spring: yes
Summer: if cool
Fall: yes
Winter: no

Seed to Harvest/Flower: 20 weeks; short-lived perennial
Seeds Storage: n/a
Weeks to Maturity: 14 weeks
Indoor Seed Starting: 14 to 16 weeks before last frost
Earliest Outdoor Planting: early spring or early fall
Additional Plantings: not needed
Last Planting: not needed

Description
The best word to describe pansy flowers is "adorable." The little "faces" look up at you with hope for a lovely spring after a cold winter, and as a last hoorah of color in the fall. Even the flowers without the actual black blotches look like happy faces. Pansies come in so many colors and color combinations that it's difficult to keep up with the changes and even more difficult to choose which ones to plant. They are easy to grow, as long as you remember that they like cool, moist conditions. When the weather gets hot and dry, plan to either discard or move your pansies.

Starting
Location: In hotter areas, look for heat-resistant types and plant in moderate shade. Pansies can be planted in full sun where summers are cool.

Seeds Indoors: Growing pansies from seed indoors can be a challenge. Sow indoors 14 to 16 weeks before the last frost date. Barely cover the seed, then refrigerate for 2 weeks. Once exposed to room temperatures, seeds should sprout in 10 days.

Transplanting: Set pansies out in early spring as soon as the ground can be worked, and again in early fall to bring the gardening season to a colorful close. In warmer climates, set them out in fall for early spring bloom.

Seeds Outdoors: Not practical.

Growing

Watering: Weekly; water more often if the plants wilt and in the heat
of the summer.

Maintenance: Keep pansies cool and moist. Deadhead pansies for
continuous bloom, and cut back leggy plants to stimulate new growth.

Harvesting

How: Pansies make a cute cut flower; keep in mind that the stems are
quite short.

When: Cut pansy flowers just after they unfurl.

Problems

Slugs and snails; insufficient moisture.

PETUNIA

BOTANICAL
INFORMATION
  Family: Nightshade
  Height: 6 to 18 inches
  Spacing: 4 per square
GROWING SEASON
  Spring: late
  Summer: yes
  Fall: early
  Winter: no

Seed to Harvest/Flower: 14 weeks; half-hardy annual
Seeds Storage: n/a
Weeks to Maturity: 8 to 10 weeks
Indoor Seed Starting: 8 to 10 weeks before first frost
Earliest Outdoor Planting: after last frost
Additional Plantings: not needed
Last Planting: not needed

Description

Petunias are one of the easiest annuals to grow, especially if they are
purchased as plants. The seeds are so tiny, a teaspoon contains over
10,000 seeds! They are branching, creeping plants with light-green,
hairy leaves that can be sticky. The trumpet-shaped flowers come in
just about every color imaginable, even the once-impossible yellow, and
the flower forms range from single to double, ruffled, striped, and
scalloped. Petunia flowers come in a range of sizes—grandifloras have
4- to 5-inch flowers, multifloras have 2- to 3-inch flowers, and millifloras
have an abundance of tiny 1-inch flowers. Pinch petunia plants back by
about one-third before planting, then keep them deadheaded and
pruned throughout the growing season for a nonstop performance.

Starting

Location: Full sun to partial shade.

Seeds Indoors: Start seeds indoors 8 to 10 weeks before last frost, 12 to
14 weeks for slower growing varieties. Don't cover the seeds.
Petunias can germinate slowly, from 7 to 21 days.

Transplanting: Set petunias out when all danger of frost has passed. Pinch at transplanting for better branching.

Seeds Outdoors: No. Growth from seed takes too long to be practical.

Growing

Watering: Weekly.

Maintenance: Deadhead to encourage bloom, and prune back by half if the plant gets scraggly.

Harvesting

How: Petunia flowers make an excellent cut flower for very small containers. Try a tiny vase on the kitchen table or sink area with just one stem in water.

When: Just as the bud is opening.

Problems

Aphids; gray mold and soft rot can occur in humid areas.

SALVIA

BOTANICAL INFORMATION	Seed to Harvest/Flower: 14 weeks; annual
Family: Mint	**Seeds Storage:** 1 year, use fresh seed
Height: 1 to 2 feet	**Weeks to Maturity:** 8 to 10 weeks
Spacing: 4 per square	**Indoor Seed Starting:** 8 to 10 weeks before last frost
GROWING SEASON	**Earliest Outdoor Planting:** once soil has warmed
Spring: late	**Additional Plantings:** not needed
Summer: yes	**Last Planting:** not needed
Fall: early	
Winter: no	

Description

There are so many different salvias that an entire garden can be dedicated to them without duplication. *Salvia splendens* is an annual salvia with tall spikes of red or white flowers, although hybridizers have come up with pink, salmon, and a deep purple that looks almost black. Also known as scarlet sage, salvia is actually a member of the mint family, bearing the trademark square stem. These lovely plants are workhorses in the hot, sunny garden, and are quite drought tolerant once they're established. Cut the plant back by one-third at planting time, to a pair of leaves where you see new sprouts emerging to encourage bushiness, and keep it deadheaded throughout the growing season for a long display of color, texture, and height.

Starting

Location: Full sun to partial shade.

Seeds Indoors: Sow seed indoors 6 to 8 weeks before the last frost. Don't cover the tiny seeds, they need light to germinate. Keep the mix just slightly moist to avoid damping-off.

Transplanting: Set salvia out after the soil has warmed as they can be very frost sensitive.

Seeds Outdoors: No, not enough time.

Growing

Watering: Weekly.

Maintenance: Deadhead often to promote branching and uninterrupted flowering.

Harvesting

How: To encourage a fall crop of blooms, cut all the main stems back to a pair of leaves again in late summer and you'll have a late season showcase of color.

When: As soon as half the buds have opened on the flower stalk.

Problems

Slugs, aphids and whitefly; mildew.

Planting Charts

GERMINATION TIMES AND TEMPERATURES

This chart shows the number of days required for vegetable seeds to sprout at different temperatures.

CROP	32°F	41°F	50°F	59°F	68°F	77°F	86°F	95°F
Beans	0	0	0	16	11	8	6	6
Beets	–	42	17	10	6	5	5	5
Cabbage	–	–	15	9	6	5	4	–
Carrots	0	51	17	10	7	6	6	9
Cauliflower	–	–	20	10	6	5	5	–
Corn	0	0	22	12	7	4	4	3
Cucumbers	0	0	0	13	6	4	3	3
Eggplant	–	–	–	–	13	8	5	–
Lettuce	49	15	7	4	3	2	3	0
Muskmelons	–	–	–	–	8	4	3	–
Onions	136	31	13	7	5	4	4	13
Parsley	–	–	29	17	14	13	12	–
Peas	–	36	14	9	8	6	6	–
Peppers	0	0	0	25	13	8	6	9
Radishes	0	29	11	6	4	4	3	–
Spinach	63	23	12	7	6	5	6	0
Tomatoes	0	0	43	14	8	6	6	9

0 = Little or no germination   – = Not tested
Adapted from J. F. Harrington Agricultural Extension Leaflet, 1954.

PERCENTAGE OF GERMINATION

This chart indicates the percentage of normal vegetable seedlings produced at different temperatures.

CROP	32°F	41°F	50°F	59°F	68°F	77°F	86°F	95°F
Beans	0	0	1	97	90	97	47	39
Cabbage	0	27	78	93	–	99	–	–
Carrots	0	48	93	95	96	96	95	74
Corn	0	0	47	97	97	98	91	88
Cucumbers	0	0	0	95	99	99	99	99
Eggplant	–	–	–	–	21	53	60	–
Lettuce	98	98	98	99	99	99	12	0
Muskmelons	–	–	–	–	38	94	90	–
Onions	90	98	98	98	99	97	91	73
Parsley	–	–	63	–	69	64	50	–
Peas	–	89	94	93	93	94	86	0
Peppers	0	0	1	70	96	98	95	70
Radishes	0	42	76	97	95	97	95	–
Spinach	83	96	91	82	52	28	32	0
Tomatoes	0	0	82	98	98	97	83	46

0 = Little or no germination   – = Not tested
Adapted from J. F. Harrington Agricultural Extension Leaflet, 1954.

SPRING INDOOR SEED-STARTING SCHEDULE

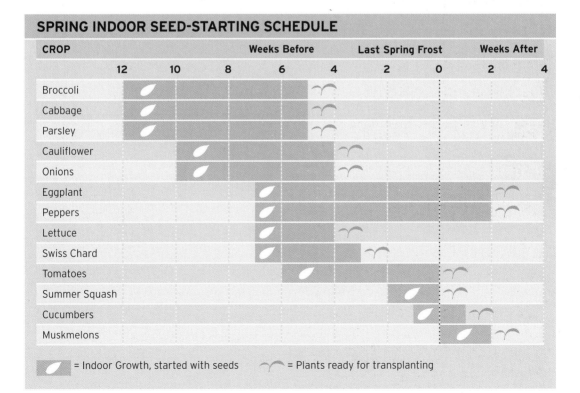

CROP	Weeks Before					Last Spring Frost			Weeks After	
	12	10	8	6	4	2	0	2	4	
Broccoli										
Cabbage										
Parsley										
Cauliflower										
Onions										
Eggplant										
Peppers										
Lettuce										
Swiss Chard										
Tomatoes										
Summer Squash										
Cucumbers										
Muskmelons										

= Indoor Growth, started with seeds   = Plants ready for transplanting

OUTDOOR PLANTING SCHEDULE FOR SPRING AND SUMMER CROPS

CROP	Weeks Before				Last Spring Frost			Weeks After					
	8	6	4	2	0	2	4	6	8	10	12	14	16

VERY EARLY SPRING (4-6 weeks before last spring frost)

Crop	Start	Harvest
Broccoli	transplant, 4 wks before	~4 wks after
Cabbage	transplant, 4 wks before	~4 wks after
Parsley	transplant, 4 wks before	~2 wks after (growth to 16)
Peas	seed, 6 wks before	~6 wks after
Spinach	seed, 6 wks before	~2 wks after
Cauliflower	transplant, 3 wks before	~4 wks after
Lettuce (Leaf)	transplant, 3 wks before	~0
Lettuce (Leaf)	seed, 3 wks before	~3 wks after
Onions	transplant, 3 wks before	~11 wks after

EARLY SPRING (2-4 weeks before last spring frost)

Crop	Start	Harvest
Beets	seed, 2 wks before	~4 wks after
Carrots	seed, 2 wks before	~7 wks after
Radishes	seed, 2 wks before	~1 wk after
Swiss Chard	transplant, 2 wks before	~1 wk after (growth to 16)
Swiss Chard	seed, 2 wks before	~4 wks after (growth to 16)

SPRING (on last frost day)

Crop	Start	Harvest
Beans (bush)	seed, 0	~8 wks after
Beans (Pole)	seed, 0	~8 wks after (growth to 16)
Corn	seed, 0	~8 wks after
Squash (summer)	transplant, 0	~6 wks after (growth to 16)
Squash (summer)	seed, 0	~8 wks after (growth to 16)
Tomatoes	transplant, 0	~11 wks after (growth to 16)

LATE SPRING (after last spring frost)

Crop	Start	Harvest
Cucumbers	transplant, 1 wk after	~8 wks after
Cucumbers	seed, 1 wk after	~11 wks after
Eggplant	transplant, 2 wks after	~12 wks after
Muskmelons	transplant, 2 wks after	~12 wks after
Muskmelons	seed, 2 wks after	~16 wks after
Peppers	transplant, 2 wks after	~11 wks after
Squash (winter)	seed, 2 wks after	~16 wks after

= Growth Period, started with seeds   = Growth Period, started with transplants

= Harvest Period

PLANTING SCHEDULE FOR CONTINUOUS HARVEST CROPS

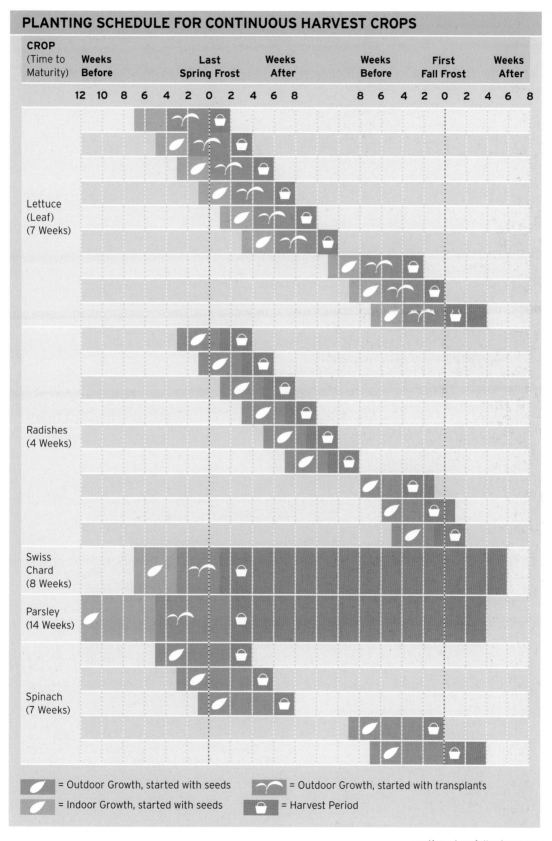

= Outdoor Growth, started with seeds

= Outdoor Growth, started with transplants

= Indoor Growth, started with seeds

= Harvest Period

continued on following page

PLANTING SCHEDULE FOR CONTINUOUS HARVEST CROPS

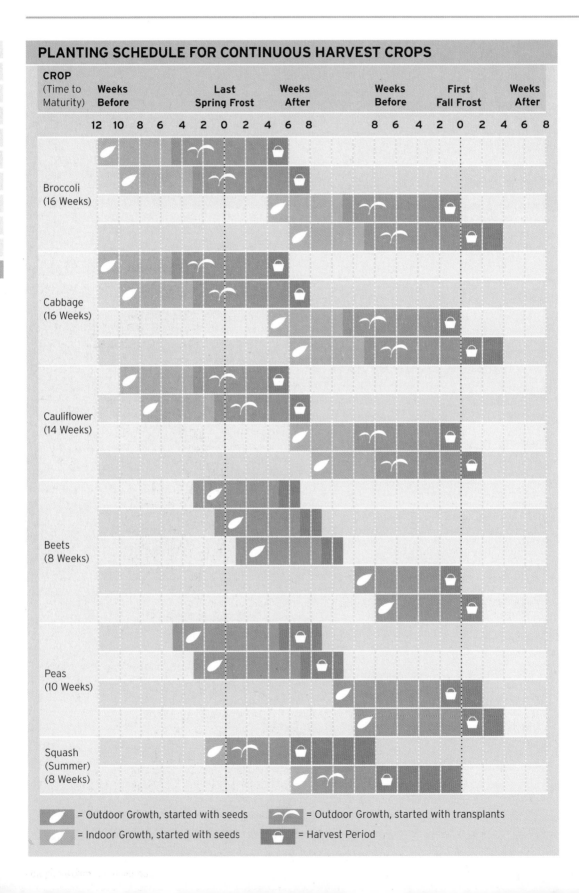

= Outdoor Growth, started with seeds

= Indoor Growth, started with seeds

= Outdoor Growth, started with transplants

= Harvest Period

PLANTING SCHEDULE FOR CONTINUOUS HARVEST CROPS

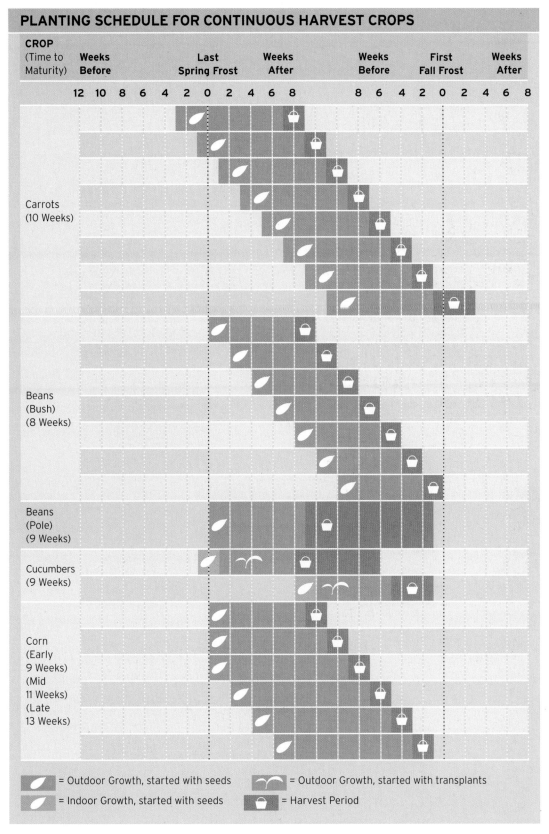

= Outdoor Growth, started with seeds

= Outdoor Growth, started with transplants

= Indoor Growth, started with seeds

= Harvest Period

continued on following page

PLANTING SCHEDULE FOR CONTINUOUS HARVEST CROPS

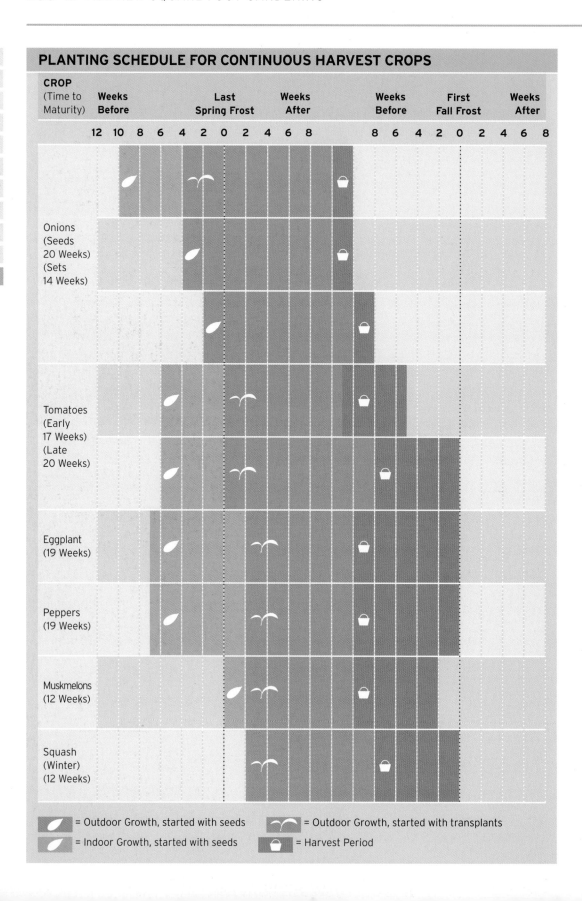

CROP (Time to Maturity)	Weeks Before			Last Spring Frost		Weeks After			Weeks Before		First Fall Frost		Weeks After	

Onions (Seeds 20 Weeks) (Sets 14 Weeks)

Tomatoes (Early 17 Weeks) (Late 20 Weeks)

Eggplant (19 Weeks)

Peppers (19 Weeks)

Muskmelons (12 Weeks)

Squash (Winter) (12 Weeks)

= Outdoor Growth, started with seeds

= Outdoor Growth, started with transplants

= Indoor Growth, started with seeds

= Harvest Period

PLANTING SCHEDULE FOR CONTINUOUS HARVEST CROPS

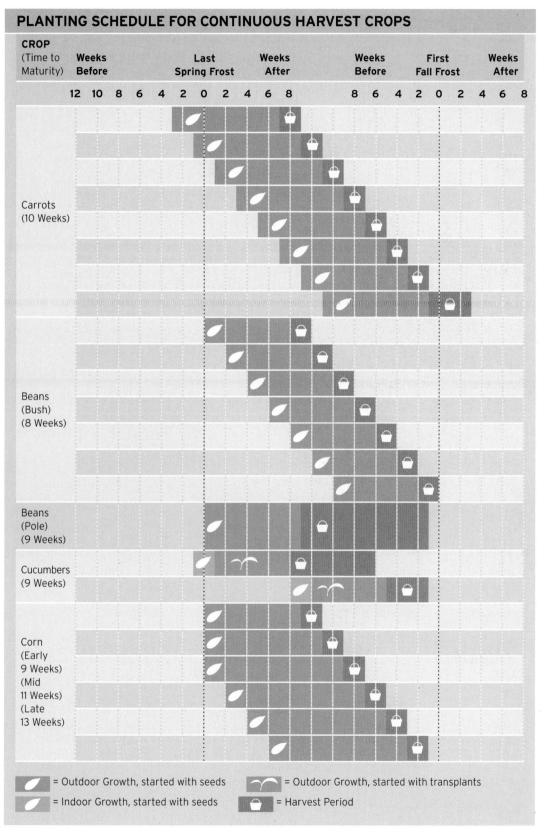

CROP (Time to Maturity)	Weeks Before						Last Spring Frost	Weeks After				Weeks Before			First Fall Frost		Weeks After		
	12	10	8	6	4	2	0	2	4	6	8	8	6	4	2	0	2	4	6	8

Carrots (10 Weeks)

Beans (Bush) (8 Weeks)

Beans (Pole) (9 Weeks)

Cucumbers (9 Weeks)

Corn (Early 9 Weeks) (Mid 11 Weeks) (Late 13 Weeks)

= Outdoor Growth, started with seeds

= Outdoor Growth, started with transplants

= Indoor Growth, started with seeds

= Harvest Period

continued on following page

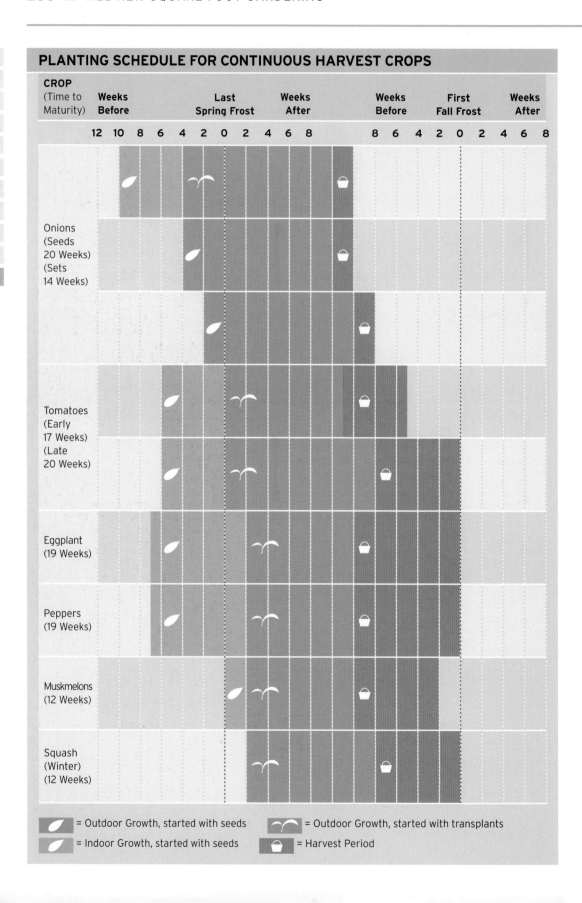

PLANTING SCHEDULE FOR CONTINUOUS HARVEST CROPS

CROP (Time to Maturity)	Weeks Before				Last Spring Frost			Weeks After					Weeks Before			First Fall Frost			Weeks After		
	12	10	8	6	4	2	0	2	4	6	8		8	6	4	2	0	2	4	6	8

Onions (Seeds 20 Weeks) (Sets 14 Weeks)

Tomatoes (Early 17 Weeks) (Late 20 Weeks)

Eggplant (19 Weeks)

Peppers (19 Weeks)

Muskmelons (12 Weeks)

Squash (Winter) (12 Weeks)

= Outdoor Growth, started with seeds

= Outdoor Growth, started with transplants

= Indoor Growth, started with seeds

= Harvest Period

PLANTING SCHEDULE FOR FALL CROPS

CROP	Weeks to Maturity	Weeks Before							First Fall Frost		Weeks After		
		16	14	12	10	8	6	4	2	0	2	4	6
Broccoli	16	Indoor (seeds)				Outdoor (transplants)				Harvest			
Cabbage	16	Indoor (seeds)	Indoor (seeds)			Outdoor (transplants)				Harvest			
Cauliflower	14		Indoor (seeds)			Outdoor (transplants)				Harvest			
Carrots	11			Outdoor (seeds)						Harvest			
Peas	10			Outdoor (seeds)						Harvest			
Beets	8					Outdoor (seeds)				Harvest			
Lettuce	7						Outdoor (seeds)	Outdoor (transplants)		Harvest			
Spinach	7						Outdoor (seeds)			Harvest			
Radishes	4							Outdoor (seeds)		Harvest			

Legend:
- = Outdoor Growth, started with seeds
- = Outdoor Growth, started with transplants
- = Indoor Growth, started with seeds
- = Harvest Period

CROPS FOR A FALL HARVEST

SUMMER CROPS STILL GROWING (harvest continues until first frost)	NEW OUTDOOR PLANTINGS IN MIDSUMMER (5–10 weeks before first fall frost)	NEW OUTDOOR PLANTINGS IN LATE SUMMER (0–5 weeks before first fall frost)
Beans	Broccoli (transplanting)	Lettuce (transplanting)
Swiss Chard	Cabbage (transplanting)	Radishes (seeds)
Corn	Cauliflower (transplanting)	
Cucumber	Beets (seeds)	
Eggplant	Carrots (seeds)	
Peppers	Lettuce (seeds)	
Muskmelon	Spinach (seeds)	
Winter Squash	Peas (seeds)	
Tomatoes		

Legend:
- = Indoor Growth, started with seeds
- = Plants ready for transplanting

Index

Meet Mel Bartholomew

Mel Bartholomew's path to arguably the most influential backyard gardener was an untraditional one. A civil engineer by profession and frustrated gardener by weekend, Bartholomew was convinced unmanageable single-row gardening was a waste of energy and output. After his research yielded responses such as "but that's the way we've always done it," Bartholomew condensed the unmanageable single-row space to 4 × 4 feet, amended the soil, and bingo . . . he developed a gardening system that yields 100 percent of the harvest in 20 percent of the space.

Bartholomew's Square Foot Method quickly gained popularity and strength, ultimately converting more than one million gardeners worldwide. *Square Foot Gardening*, the highest-rated PBS gardening show to date, launched in 1981 and ran weekly for five years, followed later by a weekly Square Foot Show on the Discovery Network. In 1986 the creation of the Square Foot Gardening Foundation and the "A Square Yard in the School Yard Program" brought the technique to an estimated three thousand schools nationwide.

As fan mail and testimonials from thousands of gardeners across the country arrived, Bartholomew realized that his Square Foot Method was relevant on a global scale. Converted into Square Meter Gardening, Bartholomew seized an opportunity to bring the dietary benefits of his revolutionary system to millions of malnourished Third World citizens. His global humanitarian effort, orchestrated through the Square Meter International Training Centers in Lehigh, Utah, and Homestead, Florida, trained international humanitarian organizations and leaders in the Square Meter Method. Since its launch, Bartholomew's global outreach initiative has spread from Africa to Asia to South America and is recognized as a resounding success by nonprofit human interest groups.

And there are no signs of slowing down. Bartholomew's global outreach continues throughout the world while closer to home, attention has shifted to increasing the Square Foot presence in the California school system. Bartholomew is determined to continue and strengthen the well established Square Foot programs and institutions across the nation and the globe.

Bartholomew operates his nonprofit Square Foot Gardening Foundation in Eden, Utah.

Mel Bartholomew